Jaguar Books on Latin Am... Y0-BUB-521

Series Editors

WILLIAM H. BEEZLEY, Professor of History,
    University of Arizona
COLIN M. MACLACHLAN, Distinguished Professor of History,
    Tulane University

Volumes Published

John E. Kicza, ed., *The Indian in Latin American History: Resistance, Resilience, and Acculturation* (1993; rev. ed., 2000). Cloth ISBN 0-8420-2822-6 Paper ISBN 0-8420-2823-4

Susan E. Place, ed., *Tropical Rainforests: Latin American Nature and Society in Transition* (1993). Cloth ISBN 0-8420-2423-9 Paper ISBN 0-8420-2427-1

Paul W. Drake, ed., *Money Doctors, Foreign Debts, and Economic Reforms in Latin America from the 1890s to the Present* (1994). Cloth ISBN 0-8420-2434-4 Paper ISBN 0-8420-2435-2

John A. Britton, ed., *Molding the Hearts and Minds: Education, Communications, and Social Change in Latin America* (1994). Cloth ISBN 0-8420-2489-1 Paper ISBN 0-8420-2490-5

David J. Weber and Jane M. Rausch, eds., *Where Cultures Meet: Frontiers in Latin American History* (1994). Cloth ISBN 0-8420-2477-8 Paper ISBN 0-8420-2478-6

Gertrude M. Yeager, ed., *Confronting Change, Challenging Tradition: Women in Latin American History* (1994). Cloth ISBN 0-8420-2479-4 Paper ISBN 0-8420-2480-8

Linda Alexander Rodríguez, ed., *Rank and Privilege: The Military and Society in Latin America* (1994). Cloth ISBN 0-8420-2432-8 Paper ISBN 0-8420-2433-6

Darién J. Davis, ed., *Slavery and Beyond: The African Impact on Latin America and the Caribbean* (1995). Cloth ISBN 0-8420-2484-0 Paper ISBN 0-8420-2485-9

Gilbert M. Joseph and Mark D. Szuchman, eds., *I Saw a City Invincible: Urban Portraits of Latin America* (1996). Cloth ISBN 0-8420-2495-6 Paper ISBN 0-8420-2496-4

Roderic Ai Camp, ed., *Democracy in Latin America: Patterns and Cycles* (1996). Cloth ISBN 0-8420-2512-X   Paper ISBN 0-8420-2513-8

Oscar J. Martínez, ed., *U.S.-Mexico Borderlands: Historical and Contemporary Perspectives* (1996). Cloth ISBN 0-8420-2446-8 Paper ISBN 0-8420-2447-6

William O. Walker III, ed., *Drugs in the Western Hemisphere: An Odyssey of Cultures in Conflict* (1996). Cloth ISBN 0-8420-2422-0 Paper ISBN 0-8420-2426-3

Richard R. Cole, ed., *Communication in Latin America: Journalism, Mass Media, and Society* (1996). Cloth ISBN 0-8420-2558-8 Paper ISBN 0-8420-2559-6

David G. Gutiérrez, ed., *Between Two Worlds: Mexican Immigrants in the United States* (1996). Cloth ISBN 0-8420-2473-5 Paper ISBN 0-8420-2474-3

Lynne Phillips, ed., *The Third Wave of Modernization in Latin America: Cultural Perspectives on Neoliberalism* (1998). Cloth ISBN 0-8420-2606-1   Paper ISBN 0-8420-2608-8

Daniel Castro, ed., *Revolution and Revolutionaries: Guerrilla Movements in Latin America* (1999). Cloth ISBN 0-8420-2625-8 Paper ISBN 0-8420-2626-6

Virginia Garrard-Burnett, ed., *On Earth as It Is in Heaven: Religion in Modern Latin America* (2000). Cloth ISBN 0-8420-2584-7 Paper ISBN 0-8420-2585-5

Carlos A. Aguirre and Robert Buffington, eds., *Reconstructing Criminality in Latin America* (2000). Cloth ISBN 0-8420-2620-7 Paper ISBN 0-8420-2621-5

Christon I. Archer, ed., *The Wars of Independence in Spanish America* (2000). Cloth ISBN 0-8420-2468-9   Paper ISBN 0-8420-2469-7

John F. Schwaller, ed., *The Church in Colonial Latin America* (2000). Cloth ISBN 0-8420-2703-3   Paper ISBN 0-8420-2704-1

On Earth
as It Is in Heaven

On Earth
as It Is in Heaven
Religion in Modern Latin America

Virginia Garrard-Burnett
Editor

Jaguar Books on Latin America
Number 18

A Scholarly Resources Inc. Imprint
Wilmington, Delaware

© 2000 by Scholarly Resources Inc.
All rights reserved
First published 2000
Printed and bound in the United States of America

Scholarly Resources Inc.
104 Greenhill Avenue
Wilmington, DE 19805-1897
www.scholarly.com

Library of Congress Cataloging-in-Publication Data

On earth as it is in heaven : religion in modern Latin America / Virginia Garrard-Burnett, editor.
    p.   cm. — (Jaguar books on Latin America ; no. 18)
    Includes bibliographical references.
    ISBN 0-8420-2584-7 (hardcover : alk. paper)
    ISBN 0-8420-2585-5 (pbk. : alk. paper)
    1. Latin America—Church history—19th century. 2. Religious pluralism—Latin America—History—19th century. 3. Latin America—Religion—19th century. 4. Latin America—Church history—20th century. 5. Religious pluralism—Latin America—History—20th century. 6. Latin America—Religion—20th century. I. Garrard-Burnett, Virginia, 1957–   . II. Series.
    BR600.06   1999
    278'.08—dc21   99-32335
                                          CIP

∞ The paper used in this publication meets the minimum requirements of the American National Standard for permanence of paper for printed library materials, Z39.48, 1984.

In loving memory of my father,

the Rev. James W. Garrard,

who taught me that inquiry

and belief can go together.

About the Editor

Virginia Garrard-Burnett is Senior Lecturer at the University of Texas, Austin, in the Institute of Latin American Studies and the Department of History. She earned an M.A. in Latin American Studies and a Ph.D. in history from Tulane University. Garrard-Burnett is the author of *Protestantism in Guatemala: Living in the New Jerusalem* (1998) and has written numerous articles on Protestantism in Latin America. She is the coeditor with David Stoll of *Rethinking Protestantism in Latin America* (1993).

Acknowledgments

My thanks for this volume go to many people, especially the editors of this series, Colin MacLachlan and William Beezley, who have offered encouragement and trenchant advice throughout this project. I would also like to offer special thanks to Scholarly Resources's Richard Hopper, whose patience with my work habits has been a continuing source of comfort. And I am especially grateful to Linda Pote Musumeci, whose patience and encouragement renewed my enthusiasm for this project.

A special note of gratitude is owed to Douglass Sullivan-Gonzales and Lindsay Hale, who, with perhaps unmerited confidence in my editing skills, granted me permission to include work in this volume that has not yet been published outside of their dissertations. And finally, a word of thanks goes to the students in my undergraduate honors course and graduate seminar on religion and society in Latin America at the University of Texas. Their reactions, experiences, and insights have taught me much over the past few years, and it was with them in mind that I put this book together.

Contents

VIRGINIA GARRARD-BURNETT, Introduction, **xiii**

I   Liberalism, Catholicism, and the Church-State Conflict
1   DOUGLASS CREED SULLIVAN-GONZALES, The Carrera Years:
    Conservative Politics and the Church in Guatemala, **3**
2   JAN RUS, Whose Caste War? Indians, Ladinos, and Mexico's
    Chiapas "Caste War" of 1869, **23**

II   Popular Religion and "Folk Catholicism"
3   ALLISON GARDY, Emerging from the Shadows: A Visit to an Old
    Jewish Community in Mexico, **63**
4   DUNCAN EARLE, The Metaphor of the Day in Quiché,
    Guatemala: Notes on the Nature of Everyday Life, **71**
5   LINDSAY HALE, *Pretos Velhos* in Brazil: The Old Black Slaves of the
    Umbanda Religion, **107**

**III The Catholic Church in Transition: Liberation
      Theology and Beyond**
6   SCOTT MAINWARING, Brazil: The Catholic Church and the Popular
    Movement in Nova Iguaçu, 1974–1985, **135**
7   PHILIP WILLIAMS, The Limits of Religious Influence: The
    Progressive Church in Nicaragua, **167**

IV   Protestantism and Religious Pluralism
8   SHELDON ANNIS, The Production of Christians: Catholics and
    Protestants in a Guatemalan Town, **189**
9   R. ANDREW CHESNUT, Born Again in Brazil: Spiritual Ecstasy and
    Mutual Aid, **219**

Suggested Readings, **235**
Suggested Films, **251**

Introduction

Virginia Garrard-Burnett

No region of the world may be so strongly identified with Roman Catholicism as Latin America. Even in the waning days of the twentieth
century, hundreds of thousands of Latin Americans crush together to catch
a glimpse of the Pope, while heads of state bend to kiss his ring—or, as in
the case of Nicaragua's former president, Violeta Chamorro, to give him
a peck on the cheek. In ordinary times, the commonplace elements of
every day—a cross placed in memoriam by the side of the road, a statue
to the Virgin in a busy marketplace, a scapular that peeks through the
shirt of a businessman, the place names that commemorate a pantheon of
saints, both well-known and obscure—all serve as constant reminders that
Latin America is, at least by tradition and culture, a very Catholic land.

Yet the face of religion is changing in Latin America, and it is the
purpose of this volume to examine the region's religious diversity. Religious change is evidenced by new landmarks that now appear on the social and geographic landscape of the region. Concrete-block Protestant
churches in rural *municipios* blare hymns and sermons from scratchy sound
systems while earnest young men in white shirts ride their bicycles through
urban slums, offering a different message of salvation.[1] The current presi-
dents of Peru and Argentina, though now claiming Catholic membership,
were born to Buddhist and Islamic immigrants, respectively. At the same
time, the hidden religions that have their roots in pre-Hispanic America
or Africa gain new adherents and credibility as modern Latin Americans
search for spiritual ties that link them to who they once were. Catholicism, too, is enjoying a renewed popularity: for the first time in more
than a century, the enrollment at Catholic seminaries is steadily rising,
and a new charismatic expression of Catholicism known as *Renovación* is
drawing people back to the *capillas*.[2]

All this flies in the face of the general paradigms of the sociology of
religion, the social science that measures just how religion, as a social
system, works in a society. In the tradition of this discipline, religion's
place becomes more circumscribed as a society becomes more advanced,
and the role of religion becomes strictly limited to the spiritual sphere.

Within this understanding, as a society becomes more "modern" it becomes less religious—that is to say, more secular.[3] By any measure, Latin America has become inarguably more "modern" in the twentieth century, based on such standard measurements as urbanization, economic diversification, and dramatic improvements in communications and transportation as well as by more controversial markers such as the decrease in cultural diversity and transition from subsistence economies to dependent capitalism. The changes that have occurred over the course of the twentieth century are so dramatic, and so simultaneously creative and destructive, that they rank with those brought by contact and conquest in the sixteenth century. But modernization has not brought secularization to Latin America. Instead, it has produced a fertile environment where a broad spectrum of religious expressions and sensibilities can flourish.

What *is* new in Latin America is religious pluralism and the breakdown of the official monopoly long held by the Roman Catholic Church. There is no question that Catholicism was at the center of the Spanish conquest of the Americas. The stereotype of conquest in the name of "God, Gold, and Glory" is based in truth, but the role played by Catholicism and Catholic identity (as opposed to an individual Spaniard's personal beliefs and pious practice) is much more complex than this basic equation suggests. Certainly, the Catholic Church was as powerful a political player as existed anywhere in Europe in the fifteenth and sixteenth centuries, and this fact accounts in part for why the rationale for conquest and the rules for its conduct were cast in terms that melded religious and imperial motives quite seamlessly. For example, the legal basis for Spain's and Portugal's exploration in the New World, the papal bull *Inter Caetera*, which gave Spain in 1493 the right to explore new lands found west of a meridian passing one hundred leagues west of the Azores and Cape Verde Islands, was mandated by the Pope, not some secular potentate. But no other European power questioned its legal authority until the Reformation (which began in 1517) rendered papal edicts moot in Protestant Northern Europe. By the same token, this same treaty had within it an inherent contract: the "Catholic kings" of the Iberian Peninsula could claim the lands of the New World for their own, but they also had the obligation to convert those who lived in those lands to the True Faith. It is little wonder, then, that the early Spanish explorers grounded their first outposts in these strange new lands with names such as "Vera Cruz" (True Cross) and "Santa Fe" (Holy Faith).

To cynical modern eyes, it is difficult to reconcile the zealous Christian rhetoric of the conquistadors with the more peaceable sensibilities that we now associate with an ideal ethic of "Christian behavior." But for Spaniards in the sixteenth century, Christianity and, specifically, Catholicism was a militant faith so fully interwoven with what we now consider to be secular issues such as identity and citizenship that it was impossible to untangle the different strands. Columbus's first voyage in 1492 left Spain just five months after the North African Moors abandoned their last Iberian outpost, the southern port city of Granada. The Spanish liberation of Granada signaled the end of the seven-hundred-year occupation of the peninsula by Muslim North Africans. The war (known as the Reconquista) to evict the Moors lasted more than two hundred years, during which time the Spaniards identified themselves first as Christians fighting the infidels, and only secondarily as allegiants of the various Iberian kingdoms. It was the Moors' final eviction in 1492 that precipitated Spain's entry as a major player into the world arena, symbolized by three portentous events: Columbus's famous first voyage of discovery; the order for the eviction of Spain's large Jewish population, the Sephardim; and the publication of the first dictionary of the Castilian language, presented to Queen Isabella as "a companion to empire."[4]

Since many of the first Spaniards in the New World were themselves veterans of the Reconquista, it is not surprising that they would bring with them the crusader's mentality and methods. The Reconquista gave Spaniards a perspective on civil hierarchy in which religion was a deciding factor. Like all Europeans at the time, Spaniards in the early sixteenth century identified the known world of the West less by secular geopolitical definitions than by terms of "Christendom." For Spaniards, the world was divided into the dichotomy that Argentinean scholar and statesman Domingo Faustino Sarmiento would much later designate as "civilization and barbarism."[5] The definition of who comprised the category of "civilized"—the *gente decente* (decent people)—invoked a much wider range of criteria than we, from our vantage point, might suspect: it measured the "civility" of a people by the color of their skin as well as by their class, general conduct, material achievements, art, eating habits, mode of dress, and, of course, religion. Thus, while the Aztec cities might be quite "civilized" in Spanish eyes (Bernal Díaz del Castillo, the chronicler, recalled that the first sight of the magnificent Aztec city of Tenochtitlán so astonished Hernán Cortés's soldiers that they thought they were dreaming), the Aztecs' religious beliefs and, especially, their bloody rituals relegated them to the category of barbarians, deserving of conquest but also in mortal need of exculpation.[6]

Given this context, we may probably take at face value Bernal Díaz's repeated accounts of Cortés, Mexico's conqueror, being restrained by his own friars from expunging Aztec deities peremptorily and erecting crosses and statues to the Virgin Mary in their place. For the Spanish conquerors, loyalty to the holy Catholic faith might have little to do with personal morality and ethics, but it had everything to do with political fealty and personal identity. Moreover, the Catholic worldview also gave a precise answer to the larger question of where one fit into the immutable hierarchy of humanity.[7]

The secular and sacred aspect of Catholic identity applied not only to Spanish military men but also to the Spanish friars who came to the New World. The personal vision and the behavior of these friars varied significantly— ranging from the famous examples of the Franciscan, Diego de Landa, bishop of Yucatán, who burned the ancient sacred books of the Maya and had Indian "heretics" executed, to Dominican friar Bartolomé de Las Casas, whose fiery and insistent demands on behalf of the indigenous population justly earned him the title, "Defender of the Indians." But no Spaniards, either clergy or lay, were troubled by concerns of cultural relativism. By peaceful persuasion or by force, they believed that it was their destiny and duty to show the Indians the single path, narrow but glorious, to eternal salvation.[8]

The process of conversion, which Robert Ricard called the "spiritual conquest" of the Americas, was both ambitious and ultimately ambivalent.[9] Through some coercion and a significant amount of innovation on the part of the friars—methods to attract Indians to the faith sometimes included dances or plays, ballads, and songs, translated into the language of the listeners—Indians under Spanish control, with some notable exceptions, converted readily, if only nominally, to Christianity. While Catholic orthodoxy permeated the spiritual lives of many converts as time went on, for others the "conversion" was entirely superficial. Some hung on tenaciously to their own beliefs while occulting them beneath a Catholic veneer. Others superimposed Christian doctrine onto a traditional context, producing a body of belief that they considered to be Catholic but that bore little resemblance to orthodox European faith or ritual. This latter process, which is generally (if erroneously, as some have argued) referred to in the scholarly literature as "religious syncretism," continues to be a factor within Catholicism in most areas of Latin America where the indigenous population remains large today.[10]

The fusion of religious ideas and imagery also became common in Latin America among slaves, who were brought to the New World from Africa beginning in the late sixteenth century and in large numbers in the seventeenth, eighteenth, and well into the nineteenth centuries. For Africans, the process of conversion, mirroring their circumstances, was even less voluntary than it was for Indians. On the other hand, Portuguese slaveholders in Brazil and Spaniards in the Caribbean and coastal zones, where slavery was practiced on a grand scale, generally did not feel an obligation to go much beyond a perfunctory conversion of their charges.

Among slave owners, Christianity seemed to offer a means of controlling slaves and mitigating the chances of rebellion, while African religions represented both idolatry and a potentially dangerous source of slave empowerment. Given these conditions, some slaves nonetheless managed to hold onto their own religions and hide them from the masters. This they did by lending the Catholic saints the qualities of their own *orishas* (deities) and by obscuring the meaning of certain religious practices, such as drumming, into what appeared to be harmless entertainment. With the passage of time, African beliefs began to coexist comfortably with Christian ones, thus producing religious systems such as Brazil's Umbanda and Cuba's Santería that are neither fully African nor fully Christian and that are unique to the regions where they originated.[11]

The reach of the Church in colonial Spanish and, to a somewhat lesser extent, Portuguese America (where the Church was neither as rich nor as powerful) stretched beyond the conquest of hearts and spirits. As an institution, the Catholic Church was the single most influential political and economic player in the colonial world, with a presence and authority that often exceeded that of the Crown. At one level, the Church and Crown shared power in both practice and parity, as evidenced by an unusual arrangement known as the *patronato real*, which allowed the Crown (rather than Rome) to "maintain the Church and propagate the faith," including the establishment and construction of all churches and monasteries and the collection of the tithe.[12] By a more ordinary measure, however, the Church was more of an actual presence in the remote regions of the New World than the colonial governments, located back in the distant capitals of Mexico City, Lima, Buenos Aires, or Quito, could ever hope to be. Even in areas so isolated that a priest might pass through only once every few years to sanctify marriages, baptize babies, and pray for the souls of the dead, a community might typically maintain a chapel and observe the major celebrations and obligations of the Christian year—thus vesting its members with a measure of loyalty to the Church, but not necessarily to the Crown or, later, to the state.

The Church was also the most pervasive economic institution in colonial Spanish America and Brazil at a time when few other international financial organizations existed to serve the region. It acquired vast funds through bequests, tithes, fees paid for sacraments, dowries of girls who entered convents, rentals on Church-owned properties, and the interest paid on loans which the Church allowed itself to make so long as the rates were not usurious.[13] From medieval times until around the beginning of the nineteenth century, a vocation in the Church was avidly sought by good families with second sons who could not inherit their fathers' land, or with daughters who wanted to become nuns either out of true religious

zeal or a desire to avoid the only alternative open to them, that of marriage and motherhood. Such wealthy, pious families gave generous sums
to the Church, which could and did keep these monies in trust.

In addition, wealthy families also bequeathed buildings and land to
the Church, which it held in permanent *mortmain* (literally, "dead hand")—
meaning that once owned by the Church, such property could not be bought
or sold but only rented. By the end of the eighteenth century, the Church
was the single largest landowner in all of Latin America. It was the actual
owner of many properties rented by *criollos* (Spaniards born in the Americas); it was also the primary financial institution from which most criollos borrowed money to buy land or invest in other ventures.[14]

The Church put much of its money into education, over which it had
virtually sole control in Latin America until the late nineteenth century.
With the exception of a few Crown colleges, the Church (most often the
Jesuits) founded and operated all the schools in Spanish America up
through the university level; as a result, every educated person in Latin
America during the colonial period was the product of a Catholic education. The Church, moreover, was also the keeper of public morals and
intellectual hegemony. The Spanish Inquisition, established by Queen
Isabella in 1478, monitored the influx into the region of dangerous or
subversive thought (such as Lutheran tracts, or books written by the theo-
rists of the Enlightenment) and guarded religious and political conformity.[15] So conflated were these last two ideas that it was entirely appropriate
for a religious court to try political crimes—as evidenced in at least one
episode in which English pirates, caught marauding off the Atlantic coast
of Central America, were tried and executed by the Inquisition not for
their crimes of piracy, but for being Protestants.[16]

It is hardly surprising, then, that when independence came to Latin
America in the first decades of the nineteenth century, the Catholic Church
found itself at the center of controversy. Here, two significant issues were
at stake. The first was the type and form that the new nations should take:
republic, kingdom, confederacy, or autocracy? And second, what role, if
any, should the Church take in the construction of nationhood? The fault
lines of the controversy fell between two sets of national elites, the Liberals and the Conservatives. The Liberals were the modernists, seeking to
create nations out of Spain's old colonies that were modeled after those
industrializing, capital-rich states of the North Atlantic. Having imbibed
the ideas of the Enlightenment, the Liberals sought theoretical democracy and genuine free trade, ideological equality (at least in regard to
their own standing abroad), and rapid "progress" measured by road construction and capital investment. The Conservatives preferred a more
gradual approach to nation building and economic development; for them,

the Spanish colonial tradition provided the template for patriarchal social, economic, and political development.

For both, the Catholic Church was a potent symbol and powerful power broker. To the Liberals, the Church represented what was most backward and medieval about the Spanish colonial model; worse still, it was the only early "national" institution that could compete with the emerging state for the hearts and minds of the populace. To the Conservatives, on the other hand, the Church symbolized the very best of the colonial legacy. For them, it raised a moral and political bulwark against what Conservatives saw as the calumnies of Liberalism. But more than that, in return for their support, the Church also offered the Conservatives a system of symbols and images, already heavy with valence for the general population, on which could be hung the trappings of secular nationhood. Such was the case, for example, with the Virgin of Guadalupe, who was co-opted from strictly Catholic significance into the symbol of Mexican nationalism; or the Sacred Heart of Jesus, which became the focus of Ecuadorian national identity under Conservatives in the nineteenth century.[17]

The elite discourse between the emerging Liberal state and the Catholic Church, that emblematic institution of conservatism, also had a profound impact on local populations, although not necessarily in the ways that Liberal policymakers anticipated. This was particularly true in areas of Latin America where the indigenous population was large and the colonial influence of the Church had been relatively strong, such as in the Maya areas in southern Mexico or the western highlands of Guatemala. In these regions, the Maya considered the Church to be an ally against the kinds of Liberal innovations that brought ladino lowlanders onto traditional indigenous lands and pushed Indians into wage peonage on their new agricultural estates. This is not to say that Indians necessarily found champions in the local clergy, whom they often considered to be greedy and rapacious, or in the orthodox doctrines of Catholicism, with which they were often unfamiliar or even dismissive. But we can say that the indigenous populations recognized that the Church shared a common enmity toward the *kaxlán* (outsiders) who represented a way of life hostile to their own interests.[18]

When Liberals regained control of most areas of Latin America in the second half of the nineteenth century, their agendas of "Order and Progress" carried a powerful anti-Catholic subtext. As Liberal anticlerical measures brought more stress to the institutional Roman Catholic Church, it slowly began to recede on the social landscape of Latin America. The official Church's decline was particularly evident in two zones located far from state and ecclesiastical authorities, where the Church's institutional resources had always been stretched thin even in more sanguine times. These were the densely populated but nearly inaccessible indigenous areas, and the distant frontier regions, far from the metropolis, of the emerging states.[19]

While the Church as an institution began to vanish from the distant countryside as the nineteenth century progressed, Catholicism did not. To the contrary, a type of popular Catholicism as practiced and interpreted by an enthusiastic local laity quickly emerged to supplement and eventually replace orthodox Catholicism in many indigenous regions and on the far frontier, where it developed and thrived without Church sanction or benefit of clergy. The manifestations of popular religion in these areas were not merely reactions to the reduced presence of the Church, but instead represented local adaptations of vital elements of the faith, with or without the blessing of the official Church. In some areas, this unlicensed "folk Catholicism" typically grafted elements of local spirituality, legend, and shamanism onto orthodox dogma, resulting in a fusion of indigenous and Catholic beliefs that were specific and resonant to a given community. Elsewhere, traditional beliefs that years of Christian contact had never fully snuffed out gained a more public forum again. Much later, in the 1940s, the Church sent missionaries to Latin America to weed out syncretic practices and reintroduce Catholic orthodoxy to communities where "folk Catholicism" remained the dominant system of belief. There, the priests met with antagonism and occasionally mortal violence from villagers who vigorously protested, "¡Pero ya *somos* católicos!" (But we already *are* Catholics!). [20]

The formal, institutional Roman Church had not, of course, disappeared in the Liberal reforms of the late nineteenth century. During the decades prior to World War II, however, the institutional Church took it for granted that Latin America was an unassailable Catholic bastion, despite the hostility of many of the secular governments. This was true inasmuch as people almost universally in Latin America considered themselves to be Catholic, if only nominally so. On the other hand, by midcentury, new kinds of ideologies—mostly political—had, for many, begun to flame the passions that had once been kindled by active Catholic religiosity.

The Church at large had commenced much earlier to address the threat to its spiritual hegemony in a papal encyclical issued by Pope Leo XIII, popularly known as the "Working Man's Pope." In 1891, Leo introduced the pivotal document, "*Rerum Novarum*: On the Condition of Labor," which, while maintaining the Church's long-held stance on the sanctity of private property, also advanced the position that social morality and the principles of justice and charity should regulate the relationship between capital and labor.[21] Although this encyclical resulted in important new currents in Catholic social thought and praxis, most notably the Catholic

Action movement, "Rerum Novarum" nonetheless had a much greater effect in Europe than in Latin America, at least in the first half of the twentieth century.

In the post-World War II period, however, this changed dramatically. The spread of communism throughout Eastern Europe and then to Cuba served notice that no land could be considered inexorably Catholic, not even in Latin America. It was in the immediate wake of the 1959 Cuban Revolution that the Church took stock of the fact that it needed to establish a broad new paradigm to combat a variety of forces that threatened its ancient base of influence over the faithful in all parts of the Catholic world. Many of these hostile forces were those associated with the "modern" world: communism, secularism, and urbanization and other demographic changes that pulled people away from traditional life-styles and worldviews. In addition, by the early 1960s other forces, such as Protestantism and other types of religious pluralism, also presented an ever-greater challenge to Catholic spiritual hegemony.

With this in mind, in October 1962, Pope John XXIII convened the Second Vatican Council (Vatican II). Its object was to "open the Church" and, essentially, to reclaim Catholicism's moral and temporal authority by reasserting its relevance to the modern world. Between 1962 and 1965 the Council issued sixteen major documents that set the course for the most dramatic change in universal Catholicism to take place since the Counter-Reformation in the sixteenth century. The most important of these changes included a dramatically increased role for the laity; an emphasis on Bible reading and reflection over formulaic ritual; increased accessibility to the sacraments through liturgical revision and the abandonment of the Latin Mass for modern vernacular languages; a conciliatory attitude to ecumenism, including a definition of Protestants as "separated brethren"; and a renewed emphasis of the Church's role in the problems of the secular world.[22]

It is this last change that caught the interest and enthusiasm of many clergy in Latin America, who believed that Vatican II signaled a new commitment in the Church's obligation to the poor. In 1968 the bishops of Latin America convened the Second General Conference (CELEM) in Medellín, Colombia, where they called for a specific application of Vatican II to the region. In particular, the convening bishops articulated the Church's "preferential option for the poor" and called for biblically based *concientição* or *concientización* in Spanish (consciousness-raising) to help the poor take control of their lives in the secular world. This rearticulated action-based faith became known as Liberation Theology, after a Peruvian priest named Gustavo Gutiérrez who had published an influential book by that title in 1971.[23] Liberation Theology had a galvanizing effect throughout Latin America, bringing thousands of the faithful to an informed understanding of their beliefs and to social action for the first time.

Within a decade, however, the Church had begun to move in a different direction. In 1979 the Latin America bishops met again, this time in Puebla, Mexico, where they issued documents that suggested a subtle but definitive official distancing from Liberation Theology. The reasons for this retreat were varied but largely pragmatic. First, and most important, was the Church's sense of responsibility for the literally thousands of clergy and lay Catholics who had become politicized through *concientización* and who had died or "disappeared" because of their activism. (Indeed, it was only a few months after the Puebla meeting that El Salvador's Archbishop Oscar Romero was assassinated by a death squad while celebrating Mass.) Second, the year 1979 marked the election of John Paul II, a conservative pope whose experience as a Catholic in Communist Poland made him leery of Church associations with revolutionary popular movements. Undergirding these concerns was the bishops' perception that Liberation Theology had become a divisive issue within the Catholic Church's structure, pitting radical against conservative and rich against poor, as well as threatening to wrench apart the very body of the Church itself.[24] Yet even as the official Church moved away from Liberation Theology, the poor did not readily relinquish their option, and the movement remained quite strong at the grass-roots level.

After the assassination of Archbishop Romero in March 1980, the Salvadoran Church officially adopted a policy known as *acompañamiento*, which implied that it would accompany the poor and oppressed in their struggle but would not place itself on the front lines. In Nicaragua, Christian activists played an important role in the Sandinista victory in 1979, but relations between the official Church and the revolutionary government quickly deteriorated, and divided the Nicaraguan Church. Such considerations and pressure from the Vatican encouraged the Latin American bishops to distance themselves from Liberation Theology. In 1994, CELEM convened once again, this time in Santo Domingo, where it issued yet another series of pastoral letters that further removed the formal Church from the precepts of Liberation Theology. Nevertheless, it continues to remain a force in Catholic lives throughout much of Latin America today.

By this point, however, it was not only Liberation Theology that undermined the Church's religious hegemony. In the last decades of the twentieth century, Latin Americans began to convert to Protestantism in large numbers; indeed, by 1990, several countries, including Brazil and Guatemala, numbered Protestants at nearly one-third of their total populations. The reasons for this shift to a type of Christian discipline that is historically alien to the region stemmed from a variety of factors. Some of the most important included the dislocations caused by urban migration, economic transition, and civil war; the well-funded efforts of missionaries and Protestant evangelists from the United States; and the desire of middle-class Latin Americans to emulate the prosperity of North Americans by adopting their religion.

The majority of growth took place in a proliferation of tiny congregations, usually Pentecostal, which owed neither allegiance nor affiliation to any international denomination, and which offered a body of belief and worship that is particular to the place and the makeup of the members. When viewed from the vantage points of these churches, the expansion of Protestantism is part of a long historical process of the adaptation and contextualization of religion in Latin America that began with the Conquest and continues into the present day.

From the conventions of the sociology of religion, Latin America defies the canon. As the region has become more modern, and as it has been, in the words of Sheldon Annis (one of the authors in this volume), "bombarded by twentieth century forces," religion has become more important, not less so. It is true that Catholicism has lost its exclusive claim on Latin America—a claim that was always based more in principle than in fact, given the many heterodoxies of popular belief. But as religious pluralism has become a way of life, the competition for hearts and minds has also forced Catholicism to become more vital. As Latin America enters the next millennium, it offers us a place to test new paradigms about the role that faith and belief play in people's lives and culture.

Notes

1. See David Martin, *Tongues of Fire: The Explosion of Protestantism in Latin America* (Oxford: Basil Blackwell, 1990); David Stoll, *Is Latin America Turning Protestant?* (Berkeley: University of California Press, 1990); Virginia Garrard-Burnett and David Stoll, eds., *Rethinking Protestantism in Latin America* (Philadelphia: Temple University Press, 1993); and Edward Cleary and Hannah Stewart-Gambino, eds., *Power, Politics, and Pentecostals in Latin America* (Boulder: Westview Press, 1997).

2. See Edward L. Cleary and Hannah Stewart-Gambino, eds., *Conflict and Competition: The Latin American Church in a Changing Environment* (Boulder: Lynne Rienner, 1992).

3. See David Martin, *A General Theory of Secularization* (Oxford: Basil Blackwell, 1978).

4. Kirkpatrick Sale, *The Conquest of Paradise: Christopher Columbus and the Columbian Legacy* (New York: Plume, 1990), 18.

5. Domingo Faustino Sarmiento, *Facundo: Civilización y barbarie* (Barcelona: Clásicos Universales Planeta, 1986 [1845]).

6. Bernal Díaz del Castillo, *The Conquest of New Spain*, translated by J. M. Cohn (London: Penguin Books, 1963).

7. See Sabine MacCormack, *Religion in the Andes: Vision and Imagination in Early Colonial Peru* (Princeton: Princeton University Press, 1991); and Lewis Hanke, *Aristotle and the American Indians: A Study of Race Prejudice in the Modern World* (Bloomington: Indiana University Press, 1970).

8. See Inga Clendinnen, *Ambivalent Conquests: Maya and Spaniard in Yucatán, 1517–1570* (New York: Cambridge University Press, 1987); and Lewis Hanke, *The Spanish Struggle for Justice in the Conquest of America* (New York: Little, Brown & Co., 1949).

9. Robert Ricard, *The Spiritual Conquest of Mexico: An Essay on the Apostolate and the Evangelizing Methods of the Mendicant Orders in New Spain, 1523–1572* (Berkeley: University of California Press, 1966).

10. See Irene Silverblatt, *Moon, Sun, and Witches: Gender Ideologies and Class in Inca and Colonial Peru* (Princeton: Princeton University Press, 1987).

11. See George Eaton Simpson, *Black Religions in the New World* (New York: Columbia University Press, 1978).

12. See Nancy M. Farriss, *Crown and Clergy in Colonial Mexico, 1759–1821: The Crisis of Ecclesiastical Privilege* (London: Athlone Press, 1968); and Charles Gibson, *Spain in America* (Stanford: Stanford University Press, 1964).

13. See David A. Brading, *Church and State in Bourbon Mexico: The Diocese of Michoacán* (Cambridge: Cambridge University Press, 1994).

14. See Richard E. Greenleaf, ed., *The Roman Catholic Church in Colonial Latin America* (New York: Alfred A. Knopf, 1971).

15. See Richard E. Greenleaf, *The Mexican Inquisition in the Sixteenth Century* (Albuquerque: University of New Mexico Press, 1969).

16. Ernesto Chinchilla Aguilar, *La Inquisición en Guatemala* (Guatemala: Ministerio de Educación Pública, 1953), 67, 69.

17. See Jacques Lafaye, *Quetzalcoatl and Guadalupe: The Formation of Mexican National Consciousness, 1531–1813* (Chicago: University of Chicago Press, 1976); and Guillermo Barreto,*¿Santo o demónio? Cronología de la 'vida y milagros' de García Moreno* (Quito: Editorial Mundo Nuevo, 1970).

18. Robert Wasserstrom, *Class and Society in Central Chiapas* (Berkeley: University of California Press, 1983).

19. See, for example, Marta Weigle, *Brothers of Light, Brothers of Blood: The Penitentes of the Southwest* (Santa Fe: Ancient City Press, 1976).

20. For examples of the impact of Catholic Action in Guatemala, where traditionalist belief was quite strong in the *altiplano* in the 1940s, see Kay Warren, *The Symbolism of Subordination: Indian Identity in a Guatemalan Town* (Austin: University of Texas Press, 1978); Ricardo Falla, *Quiché rebelde: Estudio de un movimiento de conversión religiosa, rebelde a las creencias tradicionales en San Antonio Ilotenango, Quiché, 1948–1970* (Guatemala City: Editorial Universitaria de Guatemala, 1978); and John Watanabe, *Maya Saints and Souls in a Changing World* (Austin: University of Texas Press, 1992).

21. Robert C. Broderick, ed., *The Catholic Encyclopedia* (Nashville: Thomas Nelson, 1987), 523.

22. See Broderick, *The Catholic Encyclopedia*, 596–97. See also Penny Lernoux, *Cry of the People: The Struggle for Human Rights in Latin America—The Catholic Church in Conflict with U.S. Policy* (London: Penguin Books, 1980); and Philip

Berryman, *The Religious Roots of Rebellion: Christians in Central American Revolutions* (Maryknoll, NY: Orbis Books, 1984).

23. Gustavo Gutiérrez, *Teología de la liberación: Perspectivas* (Lima: CEP, 1971), published in English as *A Theology of Liberation*, translated and edited by Caridad Inda and John Eagleson (Maryknoll, NY: Orbis Books, 1973).

24. See Paul E. Sigmund, *Liberation Theology at the Crossroads: Democracy or Revolution?* (New York: Oxford University Press, 1990).

I

Liberalism, Catholicism, and the Church-State Conflict

1

The Carrera Years: Conservative Politics and the Church in Guatemala

Douglass Creed Sullivan-Gonzales

The fissure that divided politics all over Latin America from the time of Independence to the end of the nineteenth century was solidly grounded in Church issues. The Liberals, or modernists, sought rapid change in the name of "progress," while the Conservatives moved at a more moderate pace toward nationhood and economic development. For both, the Catholic Church was the most iconic symbol of the legacy of the colonial heritage.

The following section deals with Liberal and Conservative approaches to the Catholic Church. In the period covered by Sullivan-Gonzales's article, Liberal policies in the United Provinces of Central America, of which Guatemala was a part until the confederacy dissolved in 1838, had taken a heavy toll on Church wealth and authority. Guatemala's Conservative head of state, Rafael Carrera, attempted to redefine the greatly weakened Church's place in society. A caudillo who ruled Guatemala from 1839 until his death in 1865, Carrera took power during an uprising known as the War of La Montaña, which toppled the regime of the Liberal governor, Mariano Gálvez. Carrera's regime was marked by Conservative policies and cordial relations with the Catholic Church in dramatic contrast to the Liberal and anticlerical administration that had preceded it.

It is important to bear in mind that the Liberal-Conservative division was part of an elite discourse, for members of both parties alike came out of the small sector of society that François Chevalier famously referred

Text excerpted from "Piety, Power, and Politics: The Role of Religion in the Formation of the Guatemalan Nation-State" (Ph.D. diss., University of Texas, 1994), 37–42, 44–54, 56–58, 60–61, 63, 66–70, 72–80 (graphs omitted). © 1994 by Douglass Creed Sullivan-Gonzales. Reprinted by permission of Douglass Creed Sullivan-Gonzales. This work was later published as *Piety, Power, and Politics: The Role of Religion in the Formation of the Guatemalan Nation-State, 1821–1871* (Pittsburgh: University of Pittsburgh Press, 1998).

to as *"hombres ricos y poderosos" (rich and powerful men).** Although Carrera himself was actually a* mestizo *(a person of mixed European and Indian heritage) from the provinces, he was absorbed into the ruling class when he assumed power. Thus the Church-state struggle played out at a national level and only slowly percolated down to the masses.*

Douglass Sullivan-Gonzales is assistant professor in the Department of History at the University of Mississippi. He has published a number of articles on Church-state relations in Latin America in the nineteenth century.

In December 1840, Rafael Carrera wrote an open letter to the Vicar General, Antonio Larrazábal, which questioned the Church's lethargy and inability to fill the vacant parishes that now dotted the Guatemalan landscape. Part of the Carrera movement's unquestioned esprit de corps had been based on the commitment to vindicate a repressed Church; now, less than a year into his administration, the needs of many of his constituents still went unfilled. Not only did the lack of ministers perturb the caudillo but the sheer incompetence of those remaining also pushed his manic temperament to the edge. Carrera's frustration led to suspicion of Larrazábal's intent. Striking hard, Carrera charged that "it certainly seems to me that you have arranged for many towns to be priestless, possibly with the goal of returning the people to their primitive state of idolatry and barbarism."[1] Indeed, parish after parish had written the Vicar General requesting a minister for the village church.[2]

Why the slow response? After a decade of repression the Catholic Church had begun to rebuild its institution, reinviting the entry of regular orders and looking to strengthen the authority of aged secular priests. Almost two decades would elapse before the state-sponsored tithe would be fully operating throughout the country. Could the Church rebuild itself and regain its colonial prestige? Examining the results of the Church's attempts to recapture its power base during the Carrera years demonstrates the drastic decline of beneficed appointments, the simultaneous rise of the interim priests, and the rekindled colonial struggle between secular and regular clergy. Finally, the regional economic base of the Church can be explored through an examination of the *diezmo* (tithe) and the *cuartas* (yearly parish contributions to the general operating expenses of the Guatemalan Archdiocese).

Earlier research concerning the revival of the Catholic Church during Carrera's military rule has focused on two key events: the easing of state restrictions on secular priests and regular orders and the reinstate-

*François Chevalier, *Land and Society in Colonial Mexico* (Berkeley: University of California Press, 1963), 148.

ment of the state-sponsored tithe. Up to now, statistics on the number of clerics serving parishes during the Carrera years have been derived from a single document published by Vicar General Larrazábal, as he entrusted the Guatemalan Church's authority to the new Archbishop, Francisco de Paula García Peláez, in 1844.[3] Larrazábal's *Memoria* provides a point of reference in our analysis of the Church's decline and recuperation from 1829 through 1868, but additional statistical reports prepared by the Guatemalan Church itself enable us to reconstruct in much more detail the decline and return of the religious institution.

No greater issue touched the hearts of the everyday faithful within the emerging Republic than the availability of competent priests to administer the holy rites of the church. Marriage, baptism, penance, Communion, and funeral rites required the presence of ordained clergy. Yet these basic religious duties provoked greater questions: Who should appoint the clergy? And who should designate the appropriate parish for a particular priest? The power of appointment of bishops and priests in Latin America had been entrusted to the Crown ever since the Conquest through its patronage of the Church. The sixteenth-century Hapsburg monarchy of Spain went to great lengths to ensure its control over these crucial religious workers in the growing empire. With the advent of reformist Spanish Bourbons in the mideighteenth century, the Crown slowly cut its links to the religious leaders and preferred to develop its military and administrative might as an effective means of control. Nonetheless, the Bourbon rulers never relinquished patronage rights over clerical appointments. With the collapse of the Spanish Empire and the successful revolts in the Spanish American colonies, the emerging national governments were quick to assume these rights, thus instituting decades of power struggles between the state and the Church. John Lloyd Mecham's unsurpassed analysis of this contest in Latin America details how Central America fared no better than other nations in the region.[4]

The Central American Federation that emerged after the collapse of Agustín de Iturbide's Mexican empire assumed national patronage over the Catholic Church, much to the dismay of Rome. El Salvador's renegade assembly voted to recognize its own diocesan bishop in the early 1820s, thus severing ties with the mother church in Guatemala, and it eventually won recognition for this act from Rome by the late 1830s.[5] The memorable conflict of the Central American Church with Liberal forces in 1829 over such issues as the right of patronage resulted in an exiled Archbishop, the closure of regular orders, and, more significantly for our immediate analysis, the constant shuffling of beneficed interim priests. To compensate, Catholic leaders began to depend on interim appointments—which did not require state sanction—in order to soften the political blows suffered from the Liberal exercise of patronage. The Church would never recover from this strategic decision. The nuances of this political wrestling match cannot be overlooked if we are to understand the shifts in power between Church and political leaders. State approval of parish appointments became a political chess game: the Church's influence among the popular sector was too great and too mistrusted to be left in the Church's hands alone. Political leaders moved quickly to assume patronage in order to control clerical appointments in troubled areas.[6]

Secular clergy took possession of parishes in two ways. The most coveted was the beneficed parish (*cura propio*), a permanent appointment, theoretically for a lifetime, removable only by Rome's command.[7] These permanent appointments came after a *concurso*, a competition among the qualified aspirants. Potential candidates would submit their résumés noting how many years they had pastored, whether they spoke an indigenous language common to the parish, and why they sensed a calling to this particular parish.[8] After a nominating board appointed by the Archbishop made its recommendations, regal and ecclesiastical authorities would usually confirm the decisions of the board. With the emergence of nation-states, continued state affirmation of clerical appointments came to be seen as a threat to the Church. Through such a practice the state could easily place clerics sympathetic to its political cause in permanent appointments and thus ensure a certain political continuity. The 1829 crisis with the Liberal Guatemalan state brought to a boil the simmering conflicts of power.

On the eve of the 1829 Church-state débacle, 74 percent of Guatemala's parishes were filled by permanent appointments. An 1828 *concurso* had filled thirty-seven churches with beneficed parish priests.[9] Almost forty years later, in 1868, only 8 percent of the parishes would have permanent priests while 92 percent were merely interim appointments. Table 1 presents a detailed picture of the forty years of change within the Catholic Church from 1829 through 1868 affecting the total number of clergy, both regular and secular, serving parishes, and the number of permanent and interim appointments to parish churches.

These statistics reflect just an 11 percent drop in the number of priests serving Guatemala's churches from 1829 through 1844, hardly a radical change in the makeup of the Church. But these numbers in no way demonstrate the despair that gripped Vicar General Larrazábal when he wrote despondently in 1841 to exiled Archbishop Ramón Casaus y Torres that "our situation is pitiful: many parishes abandoned and from every part of the country we receive requests for someone to come and care for their spiritual needs."[10] The Church's perception was of great loss. More significantly, the total number of clergymen does not shed light on the dramatic drop in beneficed appointments from 1829 (74%) to 1844 (31%). What had happened, and why?

Table 1. Clergy Serving Parishes in Guatemala, 1829–1868

Year	Beneficed Clergy		Interim Clergy		Total Number of Priests Serving Parishes
1829	81	73.64%	29	26.36%	110
1831	63	56.76%	48	43.24%	111
1844	30	30.61%	68	69.39%	98
1852	14	14.43%	83	85.57%	97
1868	9	8.41%	98	91.59%	107

Source: "Lista de 136 curatos que se administran en propiedad," Guatemala, January 1829, AHAG 1829.32, Box T1 93; "Lista de 1831," Guatemala, 1831, AGCA B Leg 1112 Exp 24886; Antonio Larrazábal, *Memoria*; "Catálogo General," Guatemala, 1852, AHAG 1852.40.9; and "Lista de las parróquias," Guatemala, 1868, AHAG, 1868.175, Box T4 79. The 1829 and 1831 rosters were chosen because they precede and follow Morazán's measures regarding the Church. The 1844, 1852, and 1868 lists are the only official ones encountered in the Guatemalan Catholic archives.

Liberal political success and the resulting measures against the Church were largely responsible for the dramatic change, but administrative decisions made by clerical leaders reinforced a worsening situation. With his military and political base assured in 1829, Francisco Morazán [president of the United Provinces of Central America, 1826–1834, 1834–1838] quickly asserted patronage rights over the Church by shuffling clergy who opposed him to less desirable parishes and favoring those who had supported him. He sent most clergy to parishes other than their permanent appointments "in the interest of public order";[11] and within two years, almost half the parishes were being served by interim appointees. By 1844 they occupied over two-thirds of Guatemala's parish churches.

What was the net result of these measures? The general attractiveness of being a priest was tarnished and, ultimately, job security was threatened. From 1829 to 1841 only seven men were ordained, yet over the same period thirty-five priests who had been serving parishes in 1831 had died.[12] At this rate, the Church was facing complete ruin. This quantitative contrast with the colonial Church could not be more notable: no less than 105 candidates had applied for the beneficed parish in Asunción Mita in 1756.[13] Now no beneficed parishes [which receive revenue from an endowment] were being distributed.

Church leaders, especially newly appointed Archbishop Francisco García Peláez, made the tough and strategic decision to avoid appointing priests to permanent livings in order to limit the potential political harm suffered at the hands of the volatile and ever-changing governments. In a confidential letter to the papal representative in Mexico in 1852, García Peláez confessed his political decision that had left the Church with only fourteen beneficed parishes. First of all, García Peláez admitted his "well-founded fear that the civil government would attempt to use the right of patronage" for beneficed appointments.[14] The Archbishop defined the issue at hand: the very liberty of the Church would be compromised if the civil government controlled the placing of beneficed priests.[15] Second, after a decade of rule by Carrera's forces, including three years of civil war from 1848 to 1851, García Peláez still had misgivings about the current government's stability. Even though one *concurso* was held in 1861 to place nine priests in beneficed parishes, the number of permanent appointments plummeted.[16] By 1868 only these nine appointments survived.

The Archbishop's final reason for limiting the number of beneficed parishes was even more eye-opening than the others. He stated that "the lack of ideal subjects for beneficed parishes" inhibited his willingness to create them. First, he lamented that many members of the current clergy serving in Guatemala were or had been members of the regular orders. Second, many were foreigners, immigrants from other dioceses.[17] Both comments reveal historic continuities and discontinuities.

The age-long struggle between regular and secular clergy so well analyzed by Adriaan C. van Oss had not abated. Distrust and competition at both the highest and lowest levels of clergy continued to undermine a weakened institution. The Archbishop was not alone in his myopic vision of the Church's interest in this intra-institutional conflict. Both regular and secular clergy often appealed to their separate roots when confronted with political decisions in the heat of battle.[18]

The regular orders—Franciscans, Dominicans, and Mercedarians—had been the first to reach the conquered territories, but during the eighteenth century their missions were increasingly incorporated into the growing dioceses administered by secular bishops and priests. This change occurred with much resentment on the part of the regular orders as well as the populace. Van Oss mentions that troops were even required to escort one priest into San Pedro Soloma in order to "separate" the Mercedarian priest from the parish.[19] The regular orders were specifically targeted by Liberal forces in the late 1820s since their role in fomenting opposition to Liberal factions was notorious. All orders save one were closed during the purge of 1829.[20] Table 2 gives us an indication of the numerical strength of those regulars serving parishes over the four decades. The regular orders certainly suffered under Liberal political measures, but by the early 1840s they had made a definite comeback. García

Peláez's remark to the papal representative in 1852 grew out of the fact that almost one-third of his clergy had ties to the regular orders.

Table 2. Regular and Secular Clergy Serving Parishes in Guatemala, 1829–1868

Year	Regular Clergy		Secular Clergy		Total
1829	23	20.91%	87	79.09%	110
1831*	20	18.02%	91	81.98%	111
1844	29	29.59%	69	70.41%	98
1852	29	29.90%	68	70.10%	97
1868	29	27.10%	78	72.90%	107

Source: See Table 1.

*For the purpose of measuring continuity, the 1831 and subsequent figures include as regulars those members of the orders who had initiated secularization procedures or who had completed the process in order to comply with the governmental ban on religious orders. In 1831, legally, there were no members of the regular orders ministering in Guatemala. After the Carrera insurrection, the majority of these ex-regulars returned to their orders.

A study of the Franciscan friar José Antonio Murga reflects many of the tensions that simmered below the surface in regular-secular relations. Like many others, Murga had left his order to stay in Guatemala after 1829 as a secularized priest and serve a parish in the eastern Mita district. Conflict with the secular Church first surfaced in 1834 when the beneficed parish priest, Miguel Vicente Merino, claimed that he was not receiving the percentage of income to which he was entitled once Murga had been put in charge of the parish.[21] Although Merino was not actively in charge of his parish, he still was entitled to a portion of his benifice's income. Murga pleaded that poverty forced him to renege on his obligations, and a protracted debate over who owed whom only terminated when Murga fled to El Salvador because of rising political and social conflict in the Mita area in the late 1830s.[22]

Murga further provoked Church leaders when in El Salvador he simply appropriated two parishes and their incomes, serving as parish minister without proper authorization. He defended his flouting of ecclesiastical authority by saying that the Supreme Chief (Morazán) ordered him to be a parish minister to this municipality in El Salvador and "to work with the patriots for peace and the conservation of order" because the people of Atiquizaya had been in contact with the rebels (Carrera). At that time, Murga identified himself as a sixty-six-year-old Liberal.[23] In Murga's mind, even though he had left the cloister of his Franciscan order and sought secularization, he remained in essence a friar. Therefore, he did not need any document from the secular, ecclesiastical authorities in order to preach. "The Prelate knows very well," Murga retorted to Larrazábal, "that the priests of the Regular orders never ask the Curia for a license to say Mass."[24] Larrazábal challenged Murga's technical argument but extended him a written license just to avoid further problems.[25] Murga then complicated his situation by being caught in concubinage; and, through Morazán's intervention, he sought restoration to his position after penance.[26]

By 1840, Murga was without a parish, probably due to his unsavory relationships. Somehow, this elderly Liberal (and soon to be Conservative) managed to get into the spotlight one more time. In a very terse letter dated June 1840, Rafael Carrera aggressively informed Church officials that the municipality of Atiquizaya had approached him and requested the return of Murga to its parish. Carrera reproached Larrazábal's indifference, saying that he "not only does not give them what they wish but mistreats them by refusing to heed their wishes, forcing them to come to me while I have no authority to give them what they wish." And then Carrera went to the heart of the matter: "These are not the first who come complaining against [Larrazábal]; repeatedly, many others have come from other villages and have left without any consolation. Because of this scandalous conduct in a public person, I have contacted the Supreme Government to remedy the situation. If these people become disgusted against those who govern them, it will produce unwanted difficulties."[27]

In a biting reply, quite different from the tame response that he would pen later on, Larrazábal commented that he was annoyed at the charges and queries into why he had separated Murga, that "miserable monk," from the parish. And to rub salt into the wound, Larrazábal reminded Carrera that Morazán had also requested that Murga be reinstated after Murga was caught in a compromising relationship with a woman. Morazán, Larrazábal sarcastically noted, had also urged him to action as "a measure of pacification of the state."[28] Such divisive battles certainly heightened the secular hierarchy's mistrust of the regulars while encouraging the regular orders' penchant for autonomy.

Besides García Peláez's hostility toward priests linked to regular orders, he expressed a reluctance to admit priests from other dioceses to permanent parishes. Such a stance challenged the theological notion of the organic unity of the Catholic Church and reflected a growing nationalist sentiment within Guatemala. Yet the entry of foreign priests into Guatemala had come at the request of Larrazábal, García Peláez's forerunner, and had been continued by García Peláez himself. Beset by solicitations from numerous parishes and pressured by the popular caudillo, Larrazábal had turned for help to exiled priests from Mexico and Europe "as the last resort in order to avoid complete ruin of his congregation."[29] Nevertheless, priests from other dioceses were viewed first as foreigners and only then as members of the same religious corpus. Table 3 gives us a look at the nationality and percentage of "foreign" clergy serving in Guatemala from 1829 through 1868.

Table 3. Foreign Clergy Serving Parishes in Guatemala, 1829–1868

Origin	1829	1831	1844	1852	1868
El Salvador	2	2	n/a	2	0
Honduras	1	1	n/a	2	0
Nicaragua	2	1	n/a	0	0
Costa Rica	2	1	n/a	0	2
Mexico	1	1	n/a	0	4
Cuba	0	0	n/a	1	0
South America	0	0	n/a	1	0
Spain	2	2	n/a	12	12
Italy	0	0	n/a	1	1
France	0	0	n/a	0	1
Total	13 [sic]	10 [sic]	17 [sic]	19	20
Percentage	11.8%	9.0%	17.3%	19.6%	18.7%
Excluding Central Americans					
Total	6	5	n/a	15	18
Percentage	5.4%	4.5%	n/a	15.5%	16.8%

Source: See Table 1.

It shows a dramatic change in the makeup of Guatemala's parish clergy over the four decades. First of all, foreign clergy nearly doubled their proportion from a meager 9 percent in 1831 at the high point of Liberal policies directed against the Church to nearly 20 percent in 1852. García Peláez's antiforeign stance doubtless also grew out of this significant change. More important, the 1829 and 1831 data show that the majority of these clergy were from neighboring dioceses of Central America and Mexico, while in 1852 and 1868, Europe, and especially Spain, accounted for two-thirds of the foreign clergy. This historic change contrasted with the colonial Church when in 1770 the episcopacy reported that 95 percent of the diocese's priests were natives of the diocese.[30] Archbishop García Peláez's reservations highlighted a certain discontent with this growing presence of European clergy and, certainly, the dormant and historic colonial tensions between the Creole and Spaniard. He was not disposed to give these foreigners the privileges of a beneficed parish.

If not beneficed parishes, then what option remained for the Guatemalan clerical authority? Interim appointments, or *encargados*, became the option, not by default but by design. As García Peláez wrote to the papal representative, the Church could nominate interim appointments without any intervention from government authorities. If the civil authorities have any problem with an interim parish priest, they "do not take matters into their own hands but work through Church channels."[31] For all practical purposes the Church hierarchy had little influence on civil decisions affecting beneficed parishes but was the critical channel through which the government worked when it wanted to challenge an interim appointment. Yet what seemed to be a triumph for the Church in a test of wills with the state would eventually become a Pyrrhic victory.

Guatemalan parish records provide an insight into the degree to which churches enjoyed relative stability or were rocked by chaotic change from the time of Independence to the late 1850s. Two separate mandates from Archbishop García Peláez, in 1849 and in 1862, called on parish priests to submit a roster of all those who had served their parish from 1820 through 1849 and from 1837 through 1862.[32] Each parish submitted a list of those clergy who had pastored there, listing the priest's arrival and departure date. Partial and complete listings submitted by a hundred parishes netted over 1,500 entries for the period ranging from 1819 through 1862. This information made it possible to calculate the median stay of priests in each parish and to test two hypotheses: the Catholic Church in the Spanish highlands suffered severely under Morazán yet recovered significantly during Carrera's rule; and the shift from beneficed to interim appointments during this forty-year period diminished long-term parish assignments.

An analysis of parish tenure during this forty-year period reveals two dominant patterns in time served by parish priests. Table 4 breaks down the parish assignments into groups by the number of years served to show the overall picture of tenure. These figures tell us that almost 33 percent of parish priests served between one and five years, while 38 percent served less than six months. Nearly 62 percent stayed less than one year, while only 11 percent served more than five years during this forty-year period. Taken by themselves, these figures present a bleak picture of the Catholic Church. If they are broken down by regions and by time, a different picture emerges.

In order to get a sense of the dynamics of this period, I have broken it down into four decades to mirror the changing relations between Church and state. The first one, 1819–1828, includes the final years of the colonial administration and the first uncertain years of Independence; the second one, 1829–1838, embraces Morazán's policies against the Church and the culmination of the Carrera insurrection; the third one, 1839–1848, encompasses the first decade of Carrera's rule and ends with his self-exile in the face of Guatemala's erupting civil war; and the fourth and final period, 1849–1858, comprises Carrera's return, the consolidation of his regime, and his strategic alliance with Church clerics.

Table 4. 1,445 Parish Assignments and Tenure in Guatemala, 1819–1858

Years Served	Number of Parish Assignments	Percentage	Cumulative Percentage
20	15	1.04%	1.04%
10<20	39	2.70%	3.74%
05<10	110	7.61%	11.35%
01<05	471	32.60%	43.94%
1/2<01	255	17.65%	61.59%
000<1/2	555	38.41%	100.00%

Source: Francisco García Peláez to Clergy, Guatemala, 1849, AHAG Box T4 89; Francisco García Peláez to Clergy, Guatemala, 1862, AHAG 1862.305, Box T3 78; and Francisco García Peláez to Clergy, Guatemala, 1862, AHAG 1863.29.

The geographical grouping of the observations significantly affected the results. Parishes were clustered into administrative divisions, or vicariates, that closely mirrored the evolving departmental structure of Guatemala. Thirteen vicariates comprised the Archdiocese in 1844; and by 1868, seventeen. Yet these divisions by themselves revealed no meaningful pattern of change in Guatemala during these formative years. But if we follow the linguistic divide between Spanish and Indian communities, suggested by Murdo Macleod, the results are significantly different. Spanish speakers dominated in Guatemala City, Sacatepéquez, Jalapa, Santa Rosa, and Chiquimula, whereas indigenous peoples prevailed in the western mountainous areas of Huehuetenango, San Marcos, Totonicapán, Quiché, Quezaltenango, Sololá, Chimaltenango and in the central highland area of present-day Alta and Baja Verapaz.

Averaging the number of turnovers in all the parishes by decades sheds light on the stability of the Guatemalan Catholic Church. With Morazán's explicit policies to sever the Church from its constituency by expelling most of the regular orders and shuffling priests from parish to parish, the figures should show an increase in the number of turnovers in the Guatemalan parishes. Table 5 indeed shows an increase from the first to the second decade. Two decades later, the average number of turnovers declined and approached those of the first decade. Thus, during the Carrera period, parishes were experiencing fewer turnovers compared to the 1830s.

Table 5. Average Number of Turnovers in Guatemala's Parishes, 1819–1858

	1819–1828	1829–1838	1839–1848	1849–1858
Average	4.53	6.2	5.31	5.08

Source: See Table 4. The most significant data absent from this analysis come from the General Vicariate, the seat of the Church's operation, and include all those churches within and surrounding Guatemala City.

As viewed in Table 6, the Spanish highlands underwent the most marked shift in turnovers, averaging a very low 2.80 turnovers per parish in the 1820s, and more than doubling in the 1830s and 1840s. Not until the 1850s did the Spanish highland churches begin to stabilize. Parishes in the Indian highlands mirrored to a lesser degree the same shifts from the 1820s to the 1850s. Though less drastic than the Spanish highlands, parishes in the Indian highlands changed hands more often in the 1830s but returned to 1820 levels by the third decade. Churches in the lowlands did the opposite: there were fewer changes in the 1830s than in the 1820s. Table 7, which averages the number of turnovers in the Spanish and Indian highlands together, demonstrates the inverse relationship between the highlands and the lowlands, Evidently, the lowland parishes, home to miserable climatic conditions, became more coveted during Morazán's 1829 repression and the 1837 insurrection. Not until the Carrera years did the highland parishes stabilize.

Table 6. Average Number of Turnovers in Guatemala's Parishes by Three Geographical Regions, 1819–1858

Region	1819–1828	1829–1838	1839–1848	1849–1858
Spanish highlands	2.80	6.14	6.09	4.73
Lowlands	6.80	5.64	6.62	6.62
Indian highlands	4.63	6.39	4.56	4.80

Source: See Table 4.

Table 7. Average Number of Turnovers in Guatemala's Parishes by Two Geographical Regions, 1819–1858

Region	1819–1828	1829–1838	1839–1848	1849–1858
Spanish highlands; Indian highlands	4.08	6.32	5.06	4.77
Lowlands	6.08	5.64	6.62	6.62

Source: See Table 4.

Table 8 analyzes the median stay of parish priests in Guatemala and confirms the conclusion that churches suffered under Morazán's policies and benefited during the Carrera years. Taken together, the median stay of a parish priest in Guatemala was 1 year and 4 months during the 1820s, but, beginning with Morazán's rise to power in 1829, parish priests stayed at their parish just a little over 6 months. During the next two decades, parish tenure increased from 8 months in the 1840s to 11 months in the 1850s.

Table 8. Median Stay of Parish Priests in Guatemala, 1819–1858 (in years)

	1819–1828	*1829–1838*	*1839–1848*	*1849–1858*
Median	1.33	0.58	0.67	0.92

Source: See Table 4.

Analyzing regional variations of the median stays of parish priests sheds light on significant differences. Table 9 demonstrates that the Spanish highlands endured the severest change from 2.33 years in the 1820s to only 6 months in the 1830s, while the Indian highlands dropped from 1.42 years in the 1820s to just less than 7 months in the 1830s. Parish tenure in the lowlands declined relatively little, yet the median parish stay more than doubled in the Spanish highlands from the 1830s to the 1850s, from 6 months to 1 year. Parish tenure increased significantly in the Indian highlands from the 1830s to the 1850s, while the lowlands experienced a continued decline to the 1840s to recover only somewhat in the 1850s.

Table 9. Median Stay of Parish Priests per Geographical Region in Guatemala, 1819–1858 (in years)

Region	*1819–1828*	*1829–1838*	*1839–1848*	*1849–1858*
Spanish highlands	2.33	0.50	0.58	1.00
Lowlands	0.87	0.79	0.50	0.67
Indian highlands	1.42	0.58	0.75	1.08

Source: See Table 4.

Thus, both hypotheses are confirmed. The Catholic Church suffered severely under Morazán's anticlerical policies. Church leaders moved frequently and were not able to develop long-term relations with parishioners. The institutional Church, especially those parishes in the Spanish highlands, rebounded during the Carrera years but never matched the stability of the 1820s.

What was the net effect of short-term interim appointments for the Catholic Church? Archbishop Pedro Cortés y Larraz, during his pastoral visits of the 1770s, had worried about the effect of priests, especially coadjutors, who had no benefice to root them into communities. Priests moved from one parish to another as they pecked their way up the ecclesiastical order. He disparagingly called them "mercenaries" as they wandered to and fro throughout the Guatemalan countryside.[33] Van Oss noted that most nonbeneficed priests changed posts frequently in their search for better coadjutorships or for ways to strengthen their chance at a beneficed parish.[34] By the 1840s, a combination of war, disease, economic attrition, and Church politics had produced institutional chaos within the ranks of the Catholic Church. What effect did these multiple changes have upon popular support?

Numerous letters from parishioners demonstrate that the faithful were unhappy with the interim arrangements and preferred a beneficed appointment. The townspeople of Don García requested a proprietary priest in 1858 because they were tired of sharing their priest with Santa Lucía Cotzumalguapa. The distance between the two towns made it impossible for the priest to attend both regularly.[35] The municipality of Cuajiniquilapa wrote the Archbishop requesting a priest at least for Lent and Easter, while the mayor of Sacualpa said that the people were demoralized without a pastor.[36] The parishioners of Petapa asked for a priest for the coming festival days in 1862, while the faithful in Tejutla begged the Archbishop not to transfer their priest in 1856.[37] Indigenous parishioners in San Pedro Carchá, in Verapaz, wrote the Archbishop in 1858 thanking him for sending a priest who spoke their language, and implored him never to remove him.

Archbishop García Peláez thanked them for their support but stated frankly that "as with the other interim appointments your priest will be with you [only] as long as the circumstances warrant it."[38] Faced with shortages of priests and bound by his conviction not to appoint beneficed clergy for the time being, he transferred priests from one parish to another in the hopes of sustaining some symbolic presence of the Church in nearly abandoned communities. Although he checked government influence in spiritual matters, the Archbishop had restricted the long-term impact of his religious subordinates among the faithful.

In the aftermath of the civil war, Carrera sought to push for the reestablishment of a priestly presence among the strife-torn areas of eastern Guatemala. Many religious and political officials expressed the popularly held belief that the lack of ministers in eastern Guatemala created the opportunity for anarchy and lawlessness. Commenting on the causes of the civil war that wracked Guatemala from 1848 through 1851, Cuajiniquilapa's corregidor, Justo Milla, concluded that " the instability of public functionaries, principally the parish priests, brought about the last uprising of the *montañeses*."[39] Carrera believed that competent ministers in the troubled areas would resolve the tensions, and he maintained regular contact with the Archbishop and selected clerics in his efforts to pacify the eastern mountains. With such institutional and military support, clerics were able to return to the eastern Spanish highlands and settle for longer periods of time. As reflected in Table 9, the median stay of clerics doubled in the 1850s from its 1830s low.[40]

In what way did the economic strength of parishes affect the parish priests' mobility? An analysis of the *cuartas episcopales*, or Bishop's fourth, gives us an idea of the financial strength of Guatemala's parishes. The episcopacy had determined the standard income of each parish, and it counted on 2 percent of yearly parish revenue to be sent to the General Vicar's office and 3 percent to the seminary. Parish priests were expected to pay these amounts, and they had to receive a special dispensation if they could not. Data are only available for the period 1832–1853. Examining the receipts of the *cuartas episcopales* for this period, as shown in Table 10, gives a sense of the regional economic strength of the Guatemalan parishes during extremely chaotic years.

Table 10 demonstrates that both the Spanish highlands and lowlands suffered overall losses when comparing the 1830s with the 1840s but showed slight gains during the third period. The Indian highland parishes endured a moderate loss between the first and second periods and then regained a substantial portion in the third one. A portion of this table is certainly explicable by historic events: the late 1830s and late 1840s civil wars terrorized the Spanish highlands, and the surrounding economy suffered dearly. Yet the Indian highlands, which suffered similar instability, provided a more constant bulwark against the changing economic tides.

Table 10. Average Annual Receipts of *Cuartas* by Geographical Regions, 1832–1853

	Spanish Highlands (in pesos)	Index	Lowlands (in pesos)	Index	Indian Highlands (in pesos)	Index
1832–1838	491.90	100.00	595.00	100.00	1518.10	100.00
1839–1848	290.50	59.06	291.90	49.06	1146.60	75.53
1849–1853	317.40	64.53	309.00	51.93	1230.40	81.05

Source: See "Cuartas Episcopales," unnumbered cardboard box now in center aisles of AHAG. Since reliable population statistics do not exist for the period, the three results can only be compared by the shift within each region, and not between regions.

Since the available data on the *cuartas episcopales* are not complete beyond 1853, a look at the tithe records (*diezmo*), restored in 1841 and fully operational by the late 1840s, allows us to get a sense of regional income for the 1850s.[41] The Spanish highlands dominated in absolute terms from 1848 through 1859 (except for 1854), while the Indian highlands and lowlands were almost even from 1855 and onward. Historically, indigenous peoples were exempt from the *diezmo*, and among them only those who had purchased land previously taxed were called on to give their portion. The 1854 peak in the Indian highlands most likely represents cochineal income from the vicariate of Chimaltenango, located on the border with the Spanish highlands. With the channeling of cochineal income through a specific government office in 1855, receipts from the Indian highlands returned to normal levels. There was also an overall increase in the Spanish highlands despite a setback during the cholera years of 1837–38, thus suggesting that the basis of the Guatemalan economy was expanding in the Spanish highlands and lowlands. In addition, the Guatemalan economy in the 1850s confirms in part the reasonable decrease in parish turnover in the Spanish highlands from 1849 through 1858.

In a pastoral visit to the vicariate of Chimaltenango in 1861, Honduran Bishop Juan Félix de Jesús Zepeda y Zepeda wrote to Archbishop García Peláez about the ruin of so many parish houses in the region. Two basic problems gave rise to this situation, according to the Bishop. A beneficed priest was committed to a parish on a long-term basis and would have a reason to take care of his property. An interim priest lacked the influence, power, and respect among his constituents to motivate the community to care for its church's property. The Bishop was deeply troubled by the absence of a profound love between the interim priest and his congregation, one that he had seen bind the *cura propio* with his parishioners and made him the "true father of his family."[42] From his perspective, the Bishop noted that the parishioners resisted the interim priest by refusing to comply with the mandates of the Church. Moreover, the Bishop yearned for the triumph of the past and, overcome with nostalgia, reflected on the earlier triumph of the regular orders. Members of the regular orders had been pious, had spoken the languages of the indigenous peoples, and had not been tempted by personal ownership of property. With a certain brashness, he pointed to the rise of the secular clergy as the cause of this situation as well as their attempt to minister to a flock singularly when the work required many. The Bishop lamented the postcolonial revolutions, the audacity of some people in making the Indians equal to other classes, and the demoralized and impoverished towns that had once secured a certain level of civilization and prosperity. "Three centuries of work have been lost for the most part."[43]

Church leaders, beset by an aging clergy and unable to find recruits willing to take the risks of a job that provided minimum and uncertain benefits, scrambled to meet both the demands of a temperamental military leader and the sincere cries of a despairing flock. The call for assistance from foreign clergy and the move to interim appointments so that churches might have a Mass every now and then was certainly a short-term solution to the critical long-term problems. By the mid-1850s, Archbishop García Peláez had begun to control the situation: the chaos of the 1830s and early 1840s had abated, appointments to parishes were more stable though still not permanent, and the Church had started to recover economically. But, faced with an uncertain political future, he had chosen a way that guaranteed the Church hierarchy's control over appointments. In doing so, he had unwittingly limited the long-term effectiveness of his religious institution.

Notes

1. Rafael Carrera, *Rafael Carrera Teniente General y General en Jefe del Ejército del Estado de Guatemala, a sus conciudadanos* (Guatemala: Imprenta del Ejército, December 12, 1840), Archivo Histórico Arquidiocesano "Francisco de Paula García Peláez" (hereafter AHAG) Box T4 58.
2. For example, see references to such letters in Rafael Carrera to Antonio Larrazábal, Guatemala, June 9, 1840, AHAG no. 19, Box T4 62; and Rafael Carrera to Antonio Larrazábal, Guatemala, June 13, 1842, Archivo General de Centro America (hereafter AGCA) B 83.2 Exp 25172 Leg 1114.
3. Antonio Larrazábal, *Memoria documentada, que al Illmo. Sr. Arzobispo Coadjutor de esta Santa Iglesia, Dr. Francisco García Peláez* (Guatemala: Imprenta del Ejército, 1844), no. 4–5; Mary Holleran, *Church and State in Guatemala* (New York: Columbia University Press, 1949), 235–36; Adriaan C. van Oss, *Catholic Colonialism: A Parish History of Guatemala, 1524–1821* (New York: Cambridge University Press, 1986), 187; R. Bendaña, "Guatemala," in Enrique Dussell, *Historia general de la iglesia en América Latina*, vol. 6 (Salamanca: Ediciones Sigueme, 1985), 250; Luis Diez de Arriba, *Historia de la Iglesia Católica en Guatemala*, vol. 2 (Guatemala: Tipografía Nacional, 1989), 65. Bendaña's analysis of Larrazábal's *Memoria* asserted that, in 1805, 453 priests served the Archdiocese of Guatemala while only 186 were left in 1844; and Van Oss reported 453 in 1805 and 119 in 1872. Actually, these authors assume, mistakenly, the same unit of analysis. By 1844, El Salvador's Church is independent of Guatemala's. The unit of analysis in 1805 is all of Central America—that is, the Archdiocese of Guatemala. By the mid-1850s, Nicaragua, El Salvador, and Costa Rica have independent dioceses. Moreover, by "priests" are we referring to all ordained ministers within the territory, or just those actively serving a parish or bureaucratic position in the capital? To solve this statistical dilemma, we shall refer only to priests serving parishes in what came to be the Republic of Guatemala. This category will exclude those in the bureaucracy and the cloistered regular orders.
4. John Lloyd Mecham, *Church and State in Latin America: A History of Politico-Ecclesiastical Relations* (Chapel Hill: University of North Carolina Press, 1934).
5. Agustín Estrada Monroy, *Datos para la historia de la iglesia en Guatemala*, vol. 2 (Guatemala: Tipografía Nacional, 1975), 426ff.
6. Van Oss, *Catholic Colonialism*, 186–87; Monroy, *Datos*, vol. 2, 521ff.
7. Van Oss, *Catholic Colonialism*, 59–60.
8. For example, see D. T. Batres to Secretary General, Guatemala, July 8, 1831, AGCA B 83.13 Exp 24945 Leg 1113.

9. Ibid.

10. Antonio Larrazábal to Ramón Casaus y Torres, Guatemala, April 29, 1841, AHAG no. 60, Box T3 56.

11. Francisco Morazán to José Antonio Alcayaga, Guatemala, April 22, 1829, AHAG 1829.63, Box T1 93.

12. See Antonio Larrazábal to Rafael Carrera, Guatemala [1841], AHAG 1849.260, Box T2 97; and Antonio Larrazábal, *Memoria*, No. 3. The first document states that only 7 were ordained from 1829 through 1841, while the second document lists the priests who had died from July 1829 through February 1844. If we include interim priests, the number who had died reaches 41. They mostly died of old age: in 1829 the average age of a beneficed priest was forty-five, and he had served as a priest for an average of twelve years. The eldest was ninety years old, while the youngest was twenty-seven. At least 5 priests died in the Carrera insurrection, but no record indicates how many died during the 1837 cholera epidemic. See "Lista de los 136 curatos," AHAG 1829.32, Box T1 93. The pattern set during the Liberal period continued under the Conservatives: from 1844 to 1854, 84 priests died, while only 47 were ordained. Clearly, the Church had slowed but not stopped the process of diminishing its personnel by the late 1840s and early 1850s. See Francisco García Peláez to Leandro Navor, Guatemala, September 12, 1854, AHAG no. 557, Box 66 T7.

13. Van Oss, *Catholic Colonialism*, 174–75.

14. Francisco García Peláez, "Catálogo General [for Apostolic Delegate, Luis Clementi]," Guatemala, 1852, AHAG 1852.40.35, Box T2 105.

15. Francisco García Peláez to Luis Clementi, Guatemala, July 24, 1852, AHAG 1852.202, Box T2 107.

16. Francisco García Peláez, "Concurso 1861," Guatemala, April 22, 1861, AHAG 1861.175.1, Box T3 84.

17. Ibid.

18. Van Oss, *Colonial Catholicism*, 126–52.

19. Ibid., 140.

20. Monroy, *Datos*, vol. 2, 527; and see Shannon Hernandez, "Charity, the State, and Social Order in Nineteenth-Century Guatemala, 1778–1881," M.A. thesis, University of Texas at Austin, 1992.

21. Miguel Vicente Merino to Vicar General, Mita, [1834], AHAG 1834.83.7, Box T 87.

22. José Antonio Murga to Diego Batres, Mita, March 13, 1834, AHAG 1834.1, Box T 87; Murga to Batres, Mita, August 8, 1835, AHAG 1834.83.38, Box T 87.

23. José Antonio Murga to Diego Batres, Atiquizaya, El Salvador, November 13, 1838, AHAG 1834.83.106–107, Box T 87.

24. José Antonio Murga to Antonio Larrazábal, Atiquizaya, El Salvador, December 8, 1838, AHAG 1834.83.113, Box T 87.

25. Antonio Larrazábal to Promotor Fiscal, Guatemala, 18 December 1838, AHAG 1834.83.121, Box T 87.

26. Antonio Larrazábal to Minister of Justice and Ecclesiastical Matters, Guatemala, July 14, 1840, AGCA B 83.2 Exp 25172 Leg 1114.

27. Rafael Carrera to Ministro de Relaciones del Supremo Gobierno, July 9, 1840, AGCA B 83.14 Exp 82514 Leg 3594.

28. Antonio Larrazábal to Senior Minister of Government, Justice, and Religious Issues, Guatemala, July 13, 1840, AGCA B 83.2 Exp 25172 Leg 1114.

29. Antonio Larrazábal to Ramón Casaus y Torres, Guatemala, April 29, 1841, AHAG no. 60, Box T3 56.

30. Van Oss, *Catholic Colonialism*, 160.

31. Francisco García Peláez to Luis Clementi, Guatemala, July 24, 1852, AHAG 1852.202, Box T2 107.

32. Francisco García Peláez to Clergy, Guatemala, 1849, AHAG Box T4 89; García Peláez to Clergy, Guatemala, 1862, AHAG 1862.305, Box T3 78; García Peláez to Clergy, Guatemala, 1862, AHAG 1863.29. To compile the data base for analysis, we created a roster for each parish based on these three sources that spanned the period from 1819 through 1862. It was possible to correct some mistakes where the two records overlapped, but otherwise it was not possible to verify the record of each parish. We have thus taken at face value those records submitted by the parish priests. Since each priest was responsible for a certain financial quota to the Archbishop's office depending on the time and parish he served, there was a certain financial incentive not to exaggerate his stay in a parish. My special gratitude goes to José Chaclan, archivist at the AHAG and historian for Guatemala's University of San Carlos, for his unyielding energy and painstaking interest in compiling this information. Without his assistance, it would have been an impossible task.

33. Pedro Cortés y Larraz, *Descripción geográfico-moral de la diocesis de Goathemala*, vol. 1 (Guatemala: Tipografía Nacional, 1958), 43.

34. Van Oss, *Catholic Colonialism*, 173.

35. Jacinto Soto to Francisco García Peláez, Don García, September 1858, AHAG 1856.82.31, Box T2 117.

36. Municipality of Cuajiniquilapa to Francisco García Peláez, Cuajiniquilapa, April 24, 1854, AHAG 1854.86, Box 66 T7; Alcalde to García Peláez, Sacualpa, September 16, 1847, AHAG 1854.92, Box 66 T7.

37. Municipality to Francisco García Peláez, Petapa, 1862, AHAG 1855.113, Box T2 114; Municipality to García Peláez, Tejutla, October 1856, AHAG 1856.341, Box T2 118.

38. Angel Sierra to Francisco García Peláez, San Pedro Carchá, July 22, 1858, AHAG 1858.220, Box T3 97; García Peláez to Sierra, Guatemala, July 26, 1858, ibid.

39. Justo Milla to Francisco García Peláez, Cuajiniquilapa, [October 1853], AHAG 1853.81, Box 66 T7.

40. For example, see Francisco García Peláez to Rafael Carrera, Guatemala, September 17, 1847, AHAG 1847.3.8, Box T2 92.

41. *Libro 2. de ingresos de la renta decimal, con arreglo a el acuerdo de el Mui Ilustre y Venerable Cabildo de esta Sta. Iglesia Metropolitana, de veinte y siete de julio de mil ochocientos quarenta y siete se formo* (Guatemala: Tipografía Nacional, 1848–1859), AHAG Box T5 137. See also *Resolución modificando el cobro del diezmo: Memoria sobre el destino de sus productos; y sobre la situación de esta Santa Iglesia Metropolitana, y manifiesto del venerable cabildo de la misma, y del Sr. Vicario Capitular Gobernador, publicando estos documentos* (Guatemala: Imprenta del Ejército Acargo de F. Tellez, 1841).

42. Sr. Juan Obispo de Arendal to Francisco García Peláez, Chimaltenango, March 22, 1861, AHAG 1860.33.1, Box 62 T6.

43. Ibid.

2

Whose Caste War? Indians, Ladinos, and Mexico's Chiapas "Caste War" of 1869

Jan Rus

The Caste War of Chiapas has been written about by a variety of historians and ethnographers. In the traditional interpretation, served up by Mexican historians of the late nineteenth century, the Caste War is precisely that: a deadly ethnic rivalry between Indians and non-Indian ladinos, which points up the Indians' low measure on the yardstick of "civilization and barbarism" and their need to be redeemed through modernity. In more recent ethnohistories, the Caste War is described as a "revitalization movement," a religious manifestation of social and political discontent that emerges within a population oppressed and marginalized from society at large. Such movements, usually based on local prophecy and tradition, promise to believers vindication in this world and salvation in the next. Rus suggests here that a more accurate reading of the Caste War is one where politics, race, and religion converge in such a way as to make it impossible to differentiate each element, and misleading to try.

Jan Rus is director of the Native Language Program, INAREMAC, in San Cristóbal de las Casas, Chiapas, Mexico. He is the author of numerous articles on nineteenth-century Chiapan history and is the coauthor of Trabajo en las fincas *(San Cristóbal de las Casas: Taller Tzotzil, INAREMAC, 1990).*

From *Spaniards and Indians in Southeastern Mesoamerica: Essays on the History of Ethnic Relations*, ed. Murdo J. MacLeod and Robert Wasserstrom (Lincoln: University of Nebraska Press, 1983), 127–29, 131–52, 154–68 (maps and tables omitted). © 1983 by the University of Nebraska Press. Reprinted by permission of the University of Nebraska Press.

Between 1868 and 1870, the people of Chamula and several related Tzotzil-speaking communities of the Chiapas highlands rose in a savage and cruel war of extermination against their "ladino" neighbors. Mobilized by an unscrupulous leader who fooled them into believing he could talk to a set of crude clay "saints," they first withdrew to the forest, where they built a temple to their new religion. Here the leader, in order to increase his power, had a young boy crucified on Good Friday, 1868, as an Indian "Christ."

Conscientious ladino authorities, horrified by such barbarity, strove for more than a year to make the Indians see the error of their ways and return to civilization. Unfortunately, all of their efforts were finally in vain: joined by a mysterious ladino outcast who trained them in military maneuvers, the Indian hordes swept out of the mountains in June 1869, pillaging and slaughtering all not of their own race. Their first victims were the very priests and schoolteachers who had gone among them to enlighten them. In short order, they also massacred the families of small ladino farmers who had dared to take up vacant lands on the borders of their territories. Finally, they attacked the nearby capital of San Cristóbal itself, retreating only when driven back by ladino reinforcements spontaneously rallied from throughout the state. Although soundly beaten in every subsequent engagement, such were their fanaticism and cunning that it was still to be almost a year before the state militia was able to run the last of their renegade bands to earth.

Introduction

This version of the "Caste War of 1869," essentially that handed down to us by nineteenth-century ladino journalists and historians,[1] is still invoked today in the highlands of Chiapas to prove the precariousness of civilization's hold on the Indians and to demonstrate the danger of allowing even the slightest autonomous activity in their communities. Although anthropologists and others have worked it over in recent years,[2] often with the stated purpose of telling the Indians' side of the story, none seems to have questioned either its specific details or the overall impression it creates that the energy for the "Caste War" was drawn entirely from the Indians' own peculiar religious transformation of their hatred for ladinos. What makes this unfortunate is that almost none of the story appears to be true.

Originally, the purpose of this work was to review the history of Indian-ladino relations in the decades leading up to the "Caste War" in an attempt to develop a more satisfying picture, perhaps even an explanation, of the Indians' behavior. What it hoped to establish was that the Chamulas did indeed have objective reasons to rebel and that the "Caste

War," far from being a sudden explosion, was actually the culmination of years of unrest. It also hoped to show that it was not sufficient to attribute the rebellion simply to religious hysteria—that calling it a "revitalization movement" not only obscured the fact that a vigorous tradition of native Christianity existed before and after 1869, but begged all of the interesting questions about why the Indians should have risen at this particular moment in this particular way.

What in fact emerged from this review, however, was something quite different. As it now stands, what took place in Chiapas in the late 1860s was not a "caste war" at all, at least not to the Indians. Instead, the provocation and violence were almost entirely on the side of the ladinos; the Indians, far from having been the perpetrators of massacres, were the victims!

Obviously, such a sharp reversal of the "traditional" history calls for substantiation. In attempting to provide it, the present work departs from earlier treatments in two ways. First, given what seem to be misrepresentations in the classic sources—many of them written long after the facts— it attempts to build strictly from primary materials: diaries, official reports, and the recently discovered correspondence of the parish priests in the "rebel" communities. Second, and more important, it attempts to locate the "Caste War" in an overall history of Chiapas's development from independence in the 1820s through the first establishment of a national Mexican state in the late 1860s.

Seen in this larger context, the attacks on the Indians in 1869–70 appear to have been little more than the final act of a drama that began when Chiapas's ladinos began competing among themselves for control of the state's land and labor following independence. Through the decades, this competition led both to increasingly bitter confrontations within ladino society itself and to the progressive impoverishment of the state's Indians—a fact on which the liberal, lowland-based ladino faction attempted to capitalize in the mid-1860s by turning the Indians against its conservative rivals and their allies in the church. Realizing only afterward that the Indians' receptivity to this politicization jeopardized their own control of them as much as the conservatives', the liberals then joined the conservatives in the punitive expeditions that came to be known as the "Caste War."

Unfortunately, the Indians have been victimized twice by these events: once by the violence itself, and a second time by the myth that they, not the ladinos, were to blame. In a final section, then, the work will attempt to trace the course of this myth during the last century, looking both at the interests it has served and the elaborations and distortions it has collected as it has gone along. Perhaps in this way it can restore some balance to discussions of the nature and possibilities of Chiapas's native societies, both of which have long been skewed by the memory of the "Caste War."

The Competition for Chiapas, 1821–1855

To Chiapas's ladino elite, the end of the colony in 1821 marked the beginning of a protracted, and increasingly violent, struggle for local power. Although stable political parties did not form until much later, two broad class and regional tendencies were apparent from the beginning: on one side the "conservatives" of San Cristóbal and the highlands; on the other, the "liberals" of Tuxtla, Chiapa, and the lowlands.[3]

San Cristóbal was the traditional capital of Chiapas and the seat of its diocese. Its elite were civil and religious bureaucrats and the owners of large estates: men who lived on the rents and taxes of the large surrounding Indian population. Following independence, such people saw themselves as the natural heirs of the power and privilege that had belonged to the colonial church and crown. Accordingly, they campaigned for a government of continuity after 1821—a centralized, paternalistic regime that would not only preserve the status quo but deliver it into their hands.

The lowlands, on the other hand, were already by the 1820s becoming host to a vigorous commercial agriculture. Their natural leaders were ranchers and merchants: men who, as they became successful, became hungry for more land and, especially, more Indian laborers. Under the centralist government favored by San Cristóbal, however, access to such resources would be controlled by a self-interested administration of highlanders. Hoping, then, for the local autonomy that would at least permit them to reorganize and develop their own region, such men opted after 1821 for a liberal, federal form of government.

Conflict between these two factions, whatever the appearances, was never so much over ideals or future models of society as over division of the spoils left by the colony. Chief of these was land—particularly, at first, Indian land. This was followed closely by labor and, what was essentially the same thing, tax revenues. Office-holding being the one proven route to a share of these, opportunities for "public service" were avidly sought by ambitious men on both sides—so avidly, in fact, that the continual *pronunciamientos* and revolts gave Chiapas more than twenty-five governors before 1850.[4] Meanwhile, through all of this instability, the one constant was a steady decline in the position of the Indians.

Of greatest consequence to native peoples was the loss of their lands. At the close of the colonial period, a great deal of Chiapas's territory was tied up in *terrenos baldíos*, or "vacant lands"—vast expanses that had been held in trust by the crown as a buffer around the Indian communities. Although these lands were technically part of the Indian townships, the Indians themselves were legally excluded from them, being limited instead to the *ejidos* laid out around their churches. However, they were also off limits to ladinos. Arguing after independence that to leave such an immense resource unexploited would unnecessarily retard the state's development, successive governments between 1826 and 1844, liberal and conservative alike, progressively simplified the process by which private citizens could "denounce," or claim, them. As a result, by 1850 virtually all the state's Indian communities had been stripped of their "excess" lands.[5]

The effects of this landgrab cannot be overemphasized. Lowland communities, invaded during the 1830s and 1840s by aggressive farmers who actually intended to use their lands, found themselves driven out of their townships altogether during this period. Their communal ties broken, many melted into the deculturated lower classes of nearby ladino towns and "assimilated." In the highlands, on the other hand, where denser populations, less fertile soils, and a more torpid economic tradition prevented the kind of development that would have dissolved communities, the land-grabbers instead folded whole townships—always with the exception of a small central ejido—into great feudal estates. Of the twenty-five intact Tzotzil and Tzeltal townships that existed at independence, all suffered this fate to one degree or another.[6] Such, for example, was the case of Chamula.

Although attempts had been made to expropriate its terrenos baldíos as early as the 1830s, it was not until 1846 that the Larraínzar family succeeded in "denouncing" the three-quarters of Chamula's land—476 *caballerías* (47,600 acres) out of a total of 636—not protected by its ejido. This tract, together with those in two adjacent townships expropriated at the same time, formed the estate of "Nuevo Edén," containing a total of some 874 caballerías.[7] Although it had not been strictly legal for Chamulas to be living in these lands before their denunciation, population pressures had in fact forced many to take up residence there as early as the mid-eighteenth century.[8] Faced after denunciation with the choice of moving off or remaining as serfs, most of these clandestine settlers stayed, becoming laborers on sugar and tobacco plantings belonging to the Larraínzars in lower elevations. It can be calculated that by the early 1850s a minimum of 740 families were in this situation, each adult male of whom furnished three days of labor per month to keep his plot—a total of 26,640 man-days of unpaid labor a year for lands where their ancestors had lived without fee for generations.[9]

Although certainly one of the more spectacular depredations of its kind, "Nuevo Edén" was hardly unique. On the contrary, highland ladinos of more modest means and ambition also took advantage of the new laws, with the result that by 1850 practically every township in the region had acquired a permanent settlement of ladino "farmers" and "merchants." Through land denunciations, usurious loan practices, and sales of alcohol and overpriced commodities, such "homesteaders" were able in the barely twenty-five years from 1826 to the 1850s to transform more than a quarter of Chiapas's Indians from "free" villagers into permanently—and legally—obligated peons and laborers.[10]

This, in turn, partially accounts for the fate of native labor after independence: much of it simply went to those who got the land. The question, however, is more complicated than that. Although direct competition for land between liberals and conservatives was muted, at least at first, by the fact that there were terrenos baldíos in both highlands and lowlands, competition for control of native labor and taxes was not so easily dampened. On the one hand, the overwhelming majority of Indian workers lived in the highlands; on the other, the expansion of commercial agriculture in the lowlands made that region the one with the greater demand for laborers. Unfortunately, highland conservatives were loath to turn over control of "their" Indians to meet this demand, with the result that competition for Indian labor early became one of the great sources of interregional conflict.

In the years immediately after independence, Chiapas's conservative government had granted day-to-day control of Indian affairs throughout the state to the church. Through its parish priests it was thus empowered, as it had been under the colony, to register vital statistics, provide census (and thus tax) rolls, oversee the collection of native taxes, and defend the Indians' persons and property. In exchange, the government agreed to permit the church to collect its traditional emoluments, authorizing the use of civil force if necessary.[11]

The problem with this arrangement, from the liberals' point of view, was that it virtually cut them off from access to highland workers. First, it made the highland clergy, ever protective of its own interest in stationary, paying parishioners, gatekeepers of Indian labor.[12] Second, in a state where the head tax frequently accounted for more than 90 percent of the government's revenues, and where a disproportionate share of the heads belonged to highland Indians, it gave that same clergy a virtual veto over the state budget.[13] Accordingly, when the liberals came to power in 1830 one of their first acts was to secularize administration of the Indians, naming officials to handle all civil affairs in the native communities.[14]

For a decade and a half, that was where matters remained. In 1844, however, the conservatives' last major alteration of the state's agrarian laws—the one that permitted them to denounce even those terrenos baldíos already occupied by permanent Indian settlers—suddenly threatened the liberals' access to labor all over again. With denunciation of lands like those of Chamula, highland conservatives suddenly acquired almost exclusive control of the labor of entire communities. In response, liberal governments of the late 1840s, in an effort to "liberate" the Indian workers they needed, outlawed serfdom and even tried retroactively to enlarge the Indians' ejidos and force the return of lands to fill them.[15] Unfortunately, such efforts had little effect: before they could be enforced, Mexico was overtaken by yet another political crisis and the conservatives regained control of the state government.

While ladinos thus maneuvered among themselves for a better grip on the state's land and labor, the effect of the changes of these first decades on the Indians was little short of devastating. The condition of Chamula by the early 1850s is again perhaps typical of the highland Tzotzils and Tzeltals in general: by 1855, the community was providing the equivalent of twenty thousand man-days of labor a year to the government as its head tax.[16] At the same time, the value of the taxes, provisions, and personal service it rendered annually to its priests and their superiors—all of which continued to be required by law—came to another seventeen thousand man-days, a figure that does not even include the cost of the actual religious celebrations themselves.[17] Add to these exactions the labor on "Nuevo Edén" and the stipend the community was forced to pay both its secretary and schoolteacher, and the men of Chamula, numbering at most three thousand in the mid-1850s, were providing almost a month of labor per man per year to their various overlords, an almost intolerable burden for a people already on the lower edge of subsistence.[18]

In spite of the harshness of this regimen, however, the Indians of the central highlands seem to have been remarkably restrained and orderly in their protests during this period. Surviving records of the years 1840–1859 tell of communities occasionally refusing to pay their priests what were considered unfair charges (eleven cases); of native leaders disputing the authority of secretaries and other petty officials (two cases); and of community members disagreeing with ladino settlers over land boundaries and wages (four cases).[19] What is perhaps most interesting about these cases, however, is that they are known at all only because they were eventually resolved by the superior civil and ecclesiastical authorities to whom the Indians themselves appealed. Essentially the Indians continued to respect—or at least obey—the laws and procedures to which they had been subject under the colony even while ladinos trampled them in their headlong race to enrich themselves.

Indeed, given their relative positions, it is ironic that the insecure, unstable element of Chiapas society during the first thirty years after independence was not the Indian one but the ladino. In addition to political factionalism, ladinos were also tortured by the conviction that a race war with the Indians was both imminent and inevitable, a fear that seems to have become particularly pronounced from the mid-1840s on—not coincidentally the period of greatest escalation in exploitation. Thus, for instance, a leitmotif of the bishop's letters to the parish priests in the 1840s became his questioning about the Indians' physical and moral condition, their particular vices, and, especially, the degree of their acceptance of the status quo.[20] Thus again the widespread panic that ensued in 1848 when news of the Caste War of Yucatán was quickly followed by rumors that Tzeltal Indians from several *municipios* were meeting in secret, perhaps to plan a caste war right in Chiapas. Although no ladino was attacked, even verbally, in this 1848 "uprising," such was the hysteria that fifty Indian "ringleaders" were arrested and sent to San Cristóbal, and many settlers fled their new lands to return permanently to civilization.[21]

Breakdown and Civil War, 1855–1864

By the mid-1850s, fear of the Indians, so prominent just a few years before, was being pushed aside as ladinos became ever more preoccupied with developments in their own society. The political and economic squabbles of the 1830s and 1840s had by this time hardened into bitter regional factionalism. Conservatives, in retaliation for what they considered unreasonable attacks on their interests in the serfdom and ejido laws of the late 1840s, had tried in the early 1850s to wreck the agricultural economy of the lowlands by prohibiting the export of cattle and threatening to rescind titles to former terrenos baldíos.[22] Lowlanders, in turn, having no recourse locally, were driven by such measures to identify ever more closely with the national liberal opposition, adopting even its anticlericalism as it became clear in the middle of the decade that San Cristóbal's ecclesiastical hierarchy had thrown itself behind the conservatives.[23] The result was a dizzying escalation of hostility between highlands and lowlands, liberals and conservatives. Any resolution short of war seemed increasingly unlikely.

The explosion finally came with the national liberals' overthrow of the government in Mexico City in 1855. In an effort to break once and for all the "colonial institutions" they blamed for Mexico's distress, the resulting liberal government embarked almost immediately on a series of reforms designed to submit them to "popular," "democratic" rule. Foremost of their targets was the church, and within months they had not only undermined the authority of religious courts but nationalized church lands and abolished the civil enforcement of religious taxes. Ecclesiastics, of course, condemned these measures, and national conservatives, thus provided with the excuse they needed, pronounced against the government. The resulting War of Reform raged in central Mexico through 1860, finally ending with the liberals' reentry into Mexico City in January 1861.[24] Even then the fighting did not end. Die-hard conservatives, unwilling to accept the liberals' triumph, now looked outside of Mexico for aid to continue their resistance. They soon found it in England, Spain, and France, which, using unpaid debts as an excuse, invaded Mexico on the conservatives' behalf in late 1861. Although England and Spain soon withdrew, the French remained until mid-1867, trying, in league with Mexican conservatives, to impose a European, Catholic monarchy.[25]

Events in Chiapas during this period closely paralleled those in central Mexico, the principal distinction being that Chiapas's wars were fought not by national armies, but entirely by bands representing the state's own sharply-defined regional factions. Thus, for instance, the War of Reform in the state began with the adherence in July 1856 of one Juan Ortega to the anti-Reform pronouncements that had emanated from central Mexico a few months earlier. In a matter of weeks, other highland dissidents had joined him, and by the fall of 1856 they were carrying on a running guerrilla war with the state's constitutional liberal authorities. Indeed, so hostile did they make the atmosphere in the highlands that in October the liberals withdrew from the region, taking the state capital to Chiapa until its safety in San Cristóbal could be guaranteed. Ortega's revolt continued until late 1860, when, with the defeat of the national conservative forces, further resistance became pointless. Peace reestablished, the state capital was returned to the highlands in February 1861.[26]

The record of this first war's effect on the Tzotzils is fragmentary and contradictory. On the one hand, they seem to have welcomed the liberals' rise in 1855 because many of the leading conservative politicians—among them the owners of "Nuevo Edén"—sold their lands back to the native communities (the only ones who would buy them) and fled the state.[27] On the other, led by their priests, they also apparently provided bearers and supplies to the conservative rebels during those periods when they were operating in their territories.[28] Wherever their sympathies actually lay, however—and the fact is they had little reason to favor either side—the war itself seems to have benefited the Indians: no head tax was collected from 1856 to 1861; commerce was interrupted, thus relieving them of the burdens of long-distance cargo-bearing and mule-skinning; and religious taxes, although they were paid through 1858, were suspended after mid-1858 because many of the priests who had collaborated most actively with the conservatives fled when the balance in the highlands began to tip in favor of the liberals.[29] As a result, the years 1856–1861 were probably among the Indians' best since 1821.

Unfortunately, such relatively good times were not to last. With the resumption of liberal control over the highlands in 1861, the "benign neglect" of the late 1850s suddenly came to an end. New secretaries were appointed, and through them the liberals set out to rebuild the state treasury by reviving the head tax. However, in 1862, before this effort could bear fruit, the need for troops to send against the French came to overshadow all other concerns. Chiapas was ordered by the federal government to provide and maintain a battalion of a thousand men in the central Mexican campaigns, and conscription for this purpose fell especially hard on the poor. Chamula, for instance, was required to supply a hundred soldiers—a demand that caused the pueblo to be virtually deserted during the first half of 1862 as families fled into the forest to avoid the draft.[30] Eventually, of course, the government would get its soldiers anyway, but no one was about to "volunteer" by making himself conspicuous.

Meanwhile, highland conservatives, alarmed by the liberals' inroads into "their" Indians, and encouraged by news of interventionist triumphs in central Mexico to try to counteract them, began trying to reestablish themselves in the native communities in mid-1862. The reception of the priests who were their emissaries was, however, at best wary. On the one hand, the Indians recognized their control of native religion, and thus their indispensability as religious practitioners. On the other, they also knew that the return of the priests meant the resumption of religious taxes— taxes their liberal secretaries had been assuring them for a year were no longer legal. Something of the resulting ambivalence comes through in the July 1862 report of Chamula's new priest, Manuel María Suárez, on his first interview with the community's leaders: "I exhorted them to comply with their ancient obligations and duties to the Church, to which they replied that it was only a shortage of grain that had prevented them from doing so in recent years, but that, their harvest completed, they will again begin to pay."[31] In fact, this supposed "shortage of grain" was probably an evasion: during the same period, the Indians of other communities, prompted by their secretaries, refused outright to pay the church. In Cancuc, for instance, officials informed their new priest in early 1863 that not only were they not obligated to pay him but that neither did they intend to give him anything to eat unless he could buy it![32] In Chamula, however, such flat rejection was apparently still not possible in 1862. Indeed, parish records for 1860–1863 indicate that all religious taxes due in those years were eventually—though retroactively—paid.[33]

This retroactive payment is probably explained by the sudden reversal of liberal-conservative fortunes in the highlands in late 1862 and early

1863. During the second half of 1862, liberal setbacks in the war against the French led Chiapas's conservatives to feel ever more confident in their efforts to regain control of at least their own region. Local liberals, on the other hand, their mastery of the situation fading, again withdrew their capital to the lowlands, this time to Tuxtla, on January 1, 1863. For a few months, competition between the two parties for control of the Indians was closely contested, but then, in April, Ortega again pronounced, and within a month attacked and took San Cristóbal. Although soon driven out on this first attempt, he returned in August at the head of a force of six hundred men and this time succeeded in investing the city. In spite of a bombardment that, in the process of defeating the small liberal garrison, destroyed the city hall and much of the center, he and his troops were enthusiastically received by the church and the local elite, all of whom quickly pledged loyalty to the "Intervention" and new "Mexican Empire."[34]

Through the fall of 1863, Ortega and his allies organized the highlands and raised an army to subdue those parts of the state that chose to remain "in a state of rebellion" against the empire. Finally, in late October, leading a force of some twelve hundred men—two hundred of them Chamulas "recruited" by their parish priest—the *imperialistas* set off to attack [the town of] Chiapa.[35] Despite superior numbers and the element of surprise, however, they were beaten back by the local liberal militia, suffering grievous—mostly Indian—casualties in the process. Within ten more weeks, liberal forces had besieged San Cristóbal, and after an eleven-day fight that left the center of the city in ruins, the Ortegistas were driven back into the hills.[36]

If anything, the material demands placed on the Indians by the brief imperial government were even harder than had been those of the liberal regime of 1861–62. Whereas the liberals had asked contributions and then levies of men, the conservatives took not only soldiers—and more of them than the liberals—but also forced labor crews, for the building of extensive fortifications in San Cristóbal.[37] In addition, the Indians were also forced to pay religious taxes, the priests making free use of imperial forces to support their authority.[38]

Even harder on the Indians than the material exactions to which they were subject between 1861 and 1864 were the conflicting political pressures. As much as each party wanted for itself the Indians' numbers and taxes, it seems to have wanted at least as much to deny those resources to its opponents. This explains the efforts of secretaries and priests alike to turn the Indians against their opposites. Not surprisingly, however, these efforts were profoundly traumatic for the Indian communities themselves. Whereas traditionally such communities had maintained strong chains of command firmly attuned to the dominant ladino authorities, now they were being forced to choose among competing authorities, none of whom could offer much certainty even of their own tenure. As a result, no matter what choice the Indians made, the other side was bound to disapprove, and, perhaps, retaliate. This explains the caution of Chamula's officials when, with a liberal secretary still in the community, they demurred at the priest's first requests for payment in 1862. It also explains their eventual contributions to both sides, each during its respective period of dominance.

Under such contradictory pressures, it should not be surprising that discipline within communities, sustained even through the most exploitive days of the 1840s and early 1850s, was beginning to break down. In Chamula, for example, there were disturbances in September 1862 and again in January 1863—"half the community turning against the other half," with twenty-three killed in a single day during the first.[39] Given the ladinos' hypersensitivity to inter-ethnic violence just a few years before, however, what was even more striking was that now, through their own efforts to politicize the native communities, they themselves were unraveling the social controls that had formerly made such violence almost unthinkable. On September 22, 1863, for instance, in the midst of his efforts to mobilize Chamula for the empire, the parish priest was briefly threatened by disgruntled community members who actually killed three of his Indian companions. Far from reflecting on his own activities, however—on the implications of preparing Chamula soldiers for a war against the liberal state government—he thought only of avenging himself on his assailants: "Although I miraculously escaped with my life, I beg the ecclesiastical government for permission to testify against the perpetrators before the imperial authorities, advising you in advance that Señor Ortega has promised me they will be shot. I thus ask dispensation so as to incur no irregularity for this effusion of blood."[40]

Politicization of the Indians, 1864–1867

With the final defeat and expulsion of Ortega in early 1864, the liberals were for the first time undisputed masters of Chiapas. San Cristóbal, its army dispersed, its public buildings destroyed, and many of its leaders in exile in Guatemala and central Mexico, was not only beaten politically but ruined economically as well. Gone were most of its prewar sources of income: serfs, church estates, and possession of the state capital. In decline, as more and more Indians came to understand the meaning of the recent wars and reforms, was income from religious taxes. As a result, commerce in the city also suffered, and many merchants and artisans, unable to make a living in the highlands, migrated to the lowlands and coast between 1864 and 1870.[41]

Unfortunately, the conservatives' loss was not entirely the liberals' gain. For one thing, the war with the French continued in central Mexico for three more years—years during which, the national economy being disrupted, there was almost no demand for Chiapas's agricultural exports. This, in turn, retarded the lowlanders' efforts to assert control of the highland labor force that should have been their "prize" for winning the wars: having no market for their products, they had little incentive to organize migrant workers to produce them.[42]

There being no other outlet for liberal energies after Ortega's defeat, the lowlanders soon took to quarreling among themselves for control of the state's government and armies. Finally, in December 1864, with a complete breakdown of public order a real threat, Porfirio Díaz, commander of the liberal forces in central Mexico, declared that a state of war existed in Chiapas and appointed Pantaleón Domínguez its military governor.[43] Domínguez belonged to no local faction: his following consisted entirely of members of the Chiapas battalion he had commanded against the French in 1862. Instead of placing him above petty squabbles, however, this status seems to have made him a special target for the wrath of local liberals, many of whom now united to denounce his "usurpation" of the state's "democratic traditions"! As a result, between 1864 and 1867 he had to contend not only with conservative guerrillas in outlying districts but with two pronunciamientos by fellow liberals and the indignity of a brief arrest at the hands of mutinous subordinates. In spite of these trials, however, when the imperialists were finally driven from Mexico in 1867, Domínguez succeeded in having himself chosen Chiapas's constitutional governor.[44]

Among the few things on which liberals could agree during the first part of Domínguez's tenure was the necessity of punishing San Cristóbal and the conservatives for their "treason" of 1863–64. Many, for example, thought that the ex-imperialistas, already deprived of their rights to vote and hold office, should also be forced to pay reparations for the costs of the war.[45] Given San Cristóbal's impoverishment, however, and the lowlanders' own lack of unity, such payments were never collected. Instead, Domínguez settled on more bureaucratic, passive means of revenge: public expenditures in the highlands were virtually suspended, lowlanders were appointed to all civil offices, and efforts were made to block access to arms and ammunition. As for replacing the church and conservatives as gatekeepers of Indian labor, here the government's distraction was perhaps most obvious, its measures most half-hearted. Some efforts were made through the secretaries to inform the Indians of their new rights under the reforms and to discourage them from paying religious taxes.[46] In addition, the head tax, already in abeyance since mid-1862, was suspended, ostensibly as an offering for the Indians' loyalty, although in fact there were no officials in the highlands capable of collecting it.[47]

Considering the relative leniency of these measures (lenient when compared to what the more radical lowlanders would have liked to demand), it is perhaps ironic that the national government's attempts after mid-1867 to heal the nation's wounds and reconcile former enemies should actually have had the opposite effect in Chiapas, aggravating liberal-conservative antagonisms rather than soothing them. First, in the late summer of 1867 the national government decreed that former *imperialistas* were to be amnestied. Their civil rights restored, they would thus be eligible to participate fully in the elections planned for later in the fall.[48] Then, in November, it was announced that all state capitals displaced by the war should be returned to their original elites.[49] Taken together, what these "conciliatory gestures" meant in the case of Chiapas was that just as normal economic activity was about to resume, just as the lowlands were again going to need highland labor, the highlanders were to be restored to full control over that labor.

Domínguez's reaction was swift. In an attempt to "obey without complying," he moved the capital not to San Cristóbal but "part way"—from Tuxtla to Chiapa—vowing that there it would stay "until funds permitted the organization of sufficient forces to give it security" in the highlands.[50] At the same time, to make sure the church and conservatives would never again threaten that security or block access to highland labor, he embarked on an all-out campaign to break their hold on the Indians.

To some extent, the persuasion of the secretaries between 1864 and 1867 had already begun to loosen this hold: reports from various communities during this period indicate that the movement against paying church taxes was slowly but steadily gaining momentum. Beginning in late 1867, however, liberal attacks were aimed not just at the church's financial arrangements in its Indian parishes but at its very grip on native religion itself. The assault began with the reiteration of earlier guarantees of religious tolerance and immunity from the forced collection of religious payments. Then, in November, a decree was issued abolishing the offices of *mayordomo* and *alférez*—religious *cargos* that were at once the pinnacle of native religious participation and the means by which parish priests collected funds from their Indian congregations.[51] Acting through the secretaries, the government went so far as to encourage the Indians to abandon the churches altogether if necessary to avoid such service—to practice Catholicism without the priests and their temples![52]

The success of these initiatives seems to have taken even the liberals by surprise. For more than three centuries Indian religious observance—the core of native communal life—had been controlled by a non-Indian clergy. By the mid-1860s, however, the conduct of this clergy, as of ladinos generally, had become so exploitive, so destructive, that given the chance to free themselves of any part of it the Indians leapt to take it. From throughout the highlands letters flooded into the ecclesiastical government from late 1867 through early 1869 telling of communities spurning the priests' services and worshiping on their own. If any priest dared complain, or even question the new laws, the communities, backed by their secretaries, immediately carried the case to the liberal government in Chiapa and had him reprimanded. Such repudiation of the clergy was reported from Zinacantán, Oxchuc, Huistán, Tenejapa, Chalchiguitán, Pantelhó, Chenalhó, Mitontic, and Chamula during this period—this in addition to Cancuc, which had made a similar choice several years earlier.[53]

The course of native religion after these breaks varied from community to community, apparently depending as much on the character of the priests as on the nature of the communities themselves. In Oxchuc and Huistán, for instance, where the priest was weak, community members continued to frequent their parish churches, simply ignoring the impotent father's nagging requests for money.[54] In Tenejapa, where the priest—Manuel Suárez, late of Chamula—was more interested in his own standard of living than in religion, parishioners also continued to worship in the church, while the priest occupied himself with complaining to his superiors about his declining income and requesting permission to make it up by peddling the church's ornaments, in particular a "chalice of very ancient manufacture that nobody will miss because it is kept in a locked chest anyway."[55] In Zinacantán, on the other hand, where the priest was more conscientious, the Indians partially withdrew from the church, celebrating many of their services away from the pueblo rather than face constant scoldings. Meetings at the shrine in the hamlet of Atz'am, for example, became important during this period.[56] Finally, in Chamula and its annexes (Mitontic, Chenalhó, San Andrés, Magdalenas, Santa Marta, and Chalchiguitán), the vicar and his assistants, rather than accept the new conditions of the mid-1860s and moderate their demands, had actually tried between 1865 and 1868 to reimpose the taxes and controls of the early 1850s. In response, many of the Indians under their charge, when given the chance, withdrew from their churches and pueblos altogether, establishing an independent religious and marketing center of their own. It was this withdrawal, and ladino reactions to it, that finally led to the violence of 1869.

The Separatist Movement, 1867–1869

Against the trend in the highlands as a whole, religious income from the vicarate of Chamula actually rose after 1865, for a while even rivaling that of the pre-reform period. In part, this was due to the piety—and uncertainty—of the Indians themselves: given doubts about who would finally emerge in control of the highlands, they seem, at least for the time being, to have been willing to accept a return to the status quo ante. Equally important, however, was the rigor of their new vicar after mid-1865, Miguel Martínez. In a period when the rest of the highland clergy seems to have been in retreat, Martínez was almost uniquely zealous in his efforts to restore the Indian parishes to their former profitability. According to later allegations, he extracted funds improperly from the native *cofradías*, withheld religious services from those too poor to pay for them, and even flogged native officials who failed to meet their tax quotas.[57] In the uncertain period from 1865 through 1867 such excesses were apparently possible; after the anticlerical decrees of late 1867 they most certainly were not.

The first sign of unrest came in late 1867 with news that people from a large area of the townships of Chamula, Mitontic, and Chenalhó had begun gathering to venerate a set of magical "talking stones" discovered near the hamlet of Tzajalhemel by a Chamula woman, Agustina Gómez Checheb.[58] So important had this phenomenon become by the end of the year that Pedro Díaz Cuzcat, a fiscal from Chamula, journeyed to Tzajalhemel to investigate. After a brief inspection, he announced that he too, like Checheb, could "talk" to the stones, and almost as quickly declared that they represented the saints and had asked that a shrine be built for them on the place of their appearances. By the end of January 1868, the crowds at Tzajalhemel had become larger than ever, attracted now not only by the stones but by the regular sermons of their priest, Cuzcat.[59]

It is significant that Cuzcat was a *fiscal*. According to an 1855 document describing Chamula's religious structure for future priests, the fiscales were the principal brokers between the church and the local community: in addition to acting as translators for the priests, they also kept all parish records, taught catechism to the young, and even led religious services themselves in the priests' absence.[60] For this they were paid a small stipend, and often served for a decade or more at a time.[61] They were, in fact, the closest thing to a native clergy. Not only, then, did Cuzcat undoubtedly know of the government's decrees with respect to Indians and the church when he set out for Tzajalhemel, but he also had the religious authority necessary to attract others to the new cult he intended to found.

So quickly did worship at the shrine grow after Cuzcat's arrival that, by mid-February 1868, Father Martínez himself was forced to visit Tzajalhemel to try to put a stop to it. What he found there was a small native house, a box-altar with candles and incense burning on it, and a small clay "saint" that worshipers tried at first to hide from him. Perhaps mindful of the government's decrees, his reaction on this first occasion was relatively mild: after lecturing those present about the perils of idolatry, he ordered them to disperse and, apparently convinced they would, returned forthwith to Chamula.[62]

In fact, however, the next two months proved to be one of the new religion's periods of fastest growth. Having been mistreated by ladinos of all parties, especially during the preceding civil wars, many Indians seemed to find in the isolated shrine a kind of sanctuary, a place where they could not only pray in peace but could meet and trade with their neighbors without fear of ladino interference. By March, Indians from throughout the vicarate of Chamula and from such nearby Tzeltal communities as Tenejapa had begun to attend regularly, making Tzajalhemel not only an important religious center but one of the highland's busiest marketing centers as well.[63]

All of this, of course, had profound effects on the ladinos. As attendance at Tzajalhemel increased, religious income and commerce in the surrounding ladino towns necessarily decreased. To the lowlanders, this was a great triumph. Since their reason for attacking the church in the first place had been to strike at the power of the highland conservatives, these economic side-effects were an unexpected bonus. To the highlanders, on the other hand, the new developments appeared in a much more ominous light. If it continued, the growing Indian boycott could only mean one thing: utter ruin. Their anxiety became particularly acute in the weeks following Easter (April 12), 1868, when for the first time in memory Indians were almost completely absent from the ceremonies—and businesses—of San Cristóbal.[64] Crying that the long-feared "caste war" was finally upon them, the city's ladinos organized themselves into self-defense companies and sent out urgent pleas for aid to the rest of the highlands.[65]

Finally, on May 3—the Día de Santa Cruz, another important Indian celebration that San Cristóbal passed without native commerce—the new conservative *jefe político* of the highlands struck. Accompanied by a force of twenty-five men, he raided Tzajalhemel, seized Checheb and the "saints," and ordered the Indians to go home. Much to the highlanders' consternation, however, the liberal state government—seeing in this raid proof that its anti-conservative policies were working—promptly ordered Checheb released and the Indians' freedom of worship respected. In attacking the separatists directly, the conservatives had inadvertently strengthened them.[66]

Their hands thus tied politically, the highlanders tried a new tack. On May 27 they sent a commission of three priests to reason with the Indians, to try to talk them back into paying religion. Finding the masses gathered at Tzajalhemel "sincere" in their beliefs—that is, still Catholic—but nevertheless "deluded," the members of this commission blessed a cross for them to worship and warned them in the direst terms of the dangers of praying before unconsecrated (that is, "unfranchised") images. Convinced that their superior theology had won the day, they returned triumphant to San Cristóbal that same afternoon.[67]

Whether due to this commission's persuasiveness or something else, activity at the shrine did in fact decline during the next two months, a normal crowd attending the fiesta of Chamula's patron saint, San Juan, on June 24. In August, however, before the feast of Santa Rosa, Tzajalhemel became busier than ever. Emboldened by the continued, tacit support of the state government, the Indians enlarged their temple, purchased a bell and trumpets, chose sacristans and acolytes to care for the building and altar, and named a mayordomo of Santa Rosa to organize the festivities.[68] Indeed, they showed every intention of making ceremonies in Tzajalhemel as full of pomp and satisfaction as those in the traditional pueblos themselves.

After Santa Rosa, life in Tzajalhemel settled into a routine closely modeled on that of the older pueblos in other ways as well. By this time, Cuzcat had begun to assume more and more of the duties of the parish priests with whom he had formerly had such close contact. On Sundays, he donned a robe and preached at dawn and vespers—services announced by the sacristans with a touch of the bell. On other days, there were petitions to hear, sacraments to dispense, and always the cult of the saints to tend.[69] In addition, there were small daily markets to supervise, and larger, regional gatherings on Sundays and feast days. Although imitation may be the sincerest form of flattery, highland ladinos were far from pleased. Aside from the few alcohol sellers and itinerant peddlers who had begun to frequent the new pueblo, Tzajalhemel remained for most anathema.[70]

Finally, on December 2, 1868, they could stand it no longer: concerned more with their own economic survival than with legal niceties, San Cristóbal's leaders dispatched a force of fifty men to put an end to the separatist movement once and for all. Although the Indians tried briefly to resist this invasion and defend their shrine, the ladinos fired into their midst and easily set them to flight. Checheb and several others were arrested, the images and implements were impounded, and the shrine itself was stripped of its decorations. Although Cuzcat escaped, he too was captured as he passed through Ixtapa on his way to beg the state government for relief. He was sent on to Chiapa in irons, and it was to be almost two months before he could prove his innocence of any wrongdoing—at which point the governor, instead of releasing him unconditionally, merely returned him to San Cristóbal, where he was promptly rearrested by the conservatives on February 8, 1869.[71]

The "Caste War," 1869–70

In order to understand what happened next, it becomes necessary to review developments in ladino society itself during late 1868 and early 1869. In the highlands, on the one hand, the local economy, already weak at the end of 1867, had if anything declined even further during 1868. Although the Indian boycotts and accompanying strife had hurt the region economically, they also seem to have shaken it out of the political lethargy that had afflicted it since 1864. The decisive suppression of the Tzajalhemel movement was one sign of this change; another was the founding, in early 1869, of a weekly newspaper, *La Brújula*, to press the case for restoring San Cristóbal to its former political and economic position. Through its pages, the city's leading ex-imperialists now demanded not only return of the state capital but arms and munitions for a highland militia and public funds to repair buildings damaged and destroyed in 1863–64. Undaunted by their own history of pronunciamientos and insurgence, they also indulged in the most extravagant polemics about the state government's "disrespect" of federal law and authority in denying them these things.[72]

In the lowlands, on the other hand, the situation was just the reverse: economically the region had begun to recover during 1868, but politically it was more divided than at any time since the mid-1860s. According to many, the government had taxed the region unfairly (perhaps because it was the only one capable of paying) and yet had failed to provide such basic services as repair of the roads and ports now needed for continued economic growth. Even more damning, it had failed to extend positive control over the Indian communities of the highlands, and with the revival of lowland agriculture the "negative control" represented by Indian separatism now threatened lowland interests almost as much as highland ones.[73]

Realizing that unless he could consolidate his power quickly he would soon lose it, Domínguez set out in late 1868 to quiet the complaints of the state's two dominant regions while at the same time tightening his grip on its administrative apparatus. He began in December by quietly acceding to the suppression of the Tzajalhemel movement. Then, in early 1869, he announced his intention to begin enforcing the state tax code, particularly

the head tax, counting on it not only to provide the funds for needed public services but also to win the support of local officials throughout the
state who were to be granted 8 percent of what they collected in commissions. The new taxes were to be paid quarterly, the first installment coming due May 30—and, to make them more compelling, the collectors were
authorized to jail indefinitely the ayuntamiento of any township that failed
to cooperate.[74]

Unfortunately, Domínguez, his attention fixed on ladino society, does
not seem to have given much thought to the effect his decrees might have
on the Indians. From December 1868 through mid-April 1869 there had
been no activity in Tzajalhemel, and apparently he assumed that the
Chamulas and their neighbors would continue to accept meekly whatever
new conditions were imposed on them. The assumption, however, was
wrong—tragically so. When the new secretaries and schoolteachers began detaining people in their pueblos in April and early May to charge
them the first quarter's head tax, the Indians, led this time by dissident
members of their own *ayuntamientos*, simply returned to their refuge in
the forest. Again commerce with non-Indians fell off, again church attendance declined, again ladinos throughout the vicarate of Chamula complained to the regional authorities in San Cristóbal.[75]

Events moved rapidly toward a showdown. By mid-May, feeling in
San Cristóbal was running strongly in favor of another raid—one that
promised to be even more violent, more of a "lesson," than that of the
preceding December. Before such an attack could take place, however,
Ignacio Fernández de Galindo, a liberal teacher from Central Mexico who
had lived in San Cristóbal since early 1868, and who on several occasions
had defended the Indians' rights in public debates, slipped out of the city
on May 26 with his wife and a student, Benigno Trejo, to warn the Indians of their danger.[76]

What happened next is largely a matter of conjecture. Those who
would see the separation of 1869 as a simple continuation of that of 1868—
and both as the result of a conspiracy between Galindo and Cuzcat—claim
that Galindo convinced the Indians he was a divinely-ordained successor
to Cuzcat and then organized them into an army to make war on his own
race. According to his own later testimony, on the other hand, he merely
informed the Indians of their rights and offered to help them turn aside
raids on their villages—and that only with the intention of preventing
bloodshed.[77]

Whichever of these explanations is the more correct, the one that was
believed in San Cristóbal in 1869 was the former. Under its influence, the
Indians' withdrawal was by early June being seen not as just another an-
noying boycott but as the concentration of forces for an all-out attack on

whites. Finally, in what appears to have been a last attempt to talk the Indians into submission (and perhaps simultaneously to survey their forces), Father Martínez and the secretaries of Chamula, Mitontic, and Chenalhó arranged to meet in Tzajalhemel the morning of June 13. As it happened, Martínez and his escort from Chamula—the secretary-teacher, the secretary's brother, and Martínez's own Indian servant—arrived early for this appointment. Finding only a few Indians at the shrine, they nevertheless went ahead and tried to persuade them to abandon their "rebellion" and go home. The Indians, for their part, are reported to have received these representatives respectfully, even asking the priest's blessing before he left. Unfortunately, they were so respectful that they turned over the shrine's new religious objects when he asked for them. With that the die was cast: before Martínez and his companions could return to Chamula, they were overtaken by a body of Indians who, learning what had happened in Tzajalhemel, had pursued them, determined to retrieve their possessions. In the ensuing struggle, Martínez and the ladinos with him were killed. The "Caste War" was on.[78]

Ladino blood having been spilt, panic swept the highlands. In the city, the self-defense companies, certain an Indian attack was imminent, prepared for the siege. In the outlying villages and hamlets, those who had no immediate escape route gathered at a few of the larger hamlets and prepared to fight. Perhaps the Indians saw in these gatherings potential acts of aggression; perhaps, one set of killings having been committed, some among them felt they no longer had anything to lose. In any case, on June 15 and 16, in what were arguably the only Indian-initiated actions of the entire "war," men from the southern end of the vicarate of Chamula attacked and killed the ladinos sheltered in "Natividad," near San Andrés, and "La Merced," near Santa Marta.[79] At about the same time, the people of Chalchiguitán assassinated their schoolteacher and his family and their priest as they fled toward Simojovel, and the Chamulas dispatched five ladino peddlers on the road to San Cristóbal.[80] Even at its height, however, the violence does not appear to have been indiscriminate: eleven cattle-buyers from Chicoasén seized near Tzajalhemel on June 13 were released unharmed a day later, and ten ladinos and their children resident in Chenalhó during the entire "Caste War" emerged unscathed in mid-July.[81] Apparently most of the Indians' rage was directed at those with whom they had old scores to settle or who had in some way threatened them.

Finally, on June 17, Galindo, in what was evidently an attempt to redirect the Indians' energy, led several thousand of them to San Cristóbal to secure the release of Cuzcat. Despite the terror this "siege" seems to have caused San Cristóbal's already edgy citizens, the Indians' behavior was not what might have been expected of an attacking army: not only did they come under a white flag, but they came at dusk, when fighting would be difficult. What Galindo offered in their behalf was a trade: Cuzcat, Checheb, and the others in exchange for himself, his wife, and Trejo as good-faith hostages.[82]

Explaining this apparent capitulation has always called for the greatest ingenuity on the part of those who would see the events of 1869 as a premeditated "caste war": why would Galindo, "general" of a "force" typically described as overwhelmingly superior, have delivered himself voluntarily into the hands of his "enemies"? The answers have ranged from cowardice to stupidity to the belief that the Indians would soon attack to free him.[83] In fact, however, none of the suggested solutions makes as much sense as that he simply thought he had done no wrong; that in acting as an intermediary between the Indians—inflamed by recent tax measures and the unjust imprisonment of a popular leader—and the ladinos—fearful of a race war—he was actually defusing the situation and performing a service to both. Indeed, after the exchange had been consummated, he not only showed no fear of his fellow ladinos but actually "headed for his house as though nothing had happened"![84] San Cristóbal's leaders, however, were not so complaisant: no sooner had the Indians withdrawn than they invalidated the agreement, claiming it had been made under duress, and arrested Galindo, his wife, and the student.[85]

From June 17 to 21, the Indians celebrated Cuzcat's release in Tzajalhemel. Expecting reprisals at any moment, however, they left some six hundred of their number camped above the roads leading from San Cristóbal as sentries—sentries whose digging sticks and machetes would be of but little use if a ladino attack did come. Nevertheless, this continued Indian presence played right into the hands of *La Brújula*'s editors, who now wrote that there could "no longer be any doubt that the Indians were sworn enemies of the whites," that their most fervent desire was to "ravish and kill San Cristóbal's tender wives and sisters, to mutilate the corpses of its children." The only solution, they wrote, was a "war to the death between barbarism and civilization," a war in which—and here was the key—Chiapas's ladinos would for the first time in decades recognize their essential unity.[86]

In spite of the passion of this appeal, however, San Cristóbal's situation at first aroused little sympathy in the lowlands. Indeed, as late as June 18 news of Father Martínez's death was carried in the official newspaper under the restrained heading "Scandals."[87] On the morning of June 20, however—more than a month after the crisis had begun, and a week after the first killings—Domínguez suddenly activated the lowland militia and set off to relieve San Cristóbal. What had happened? First, news of the continuing "siege" of San Cristóbal after June 18 does seem to have aroused many in the lowlands, who now feared that the Indians were escaping any ladino control. Second, and perhaps even more important, there had been elections for local office throughout the lowlands on June 11. When the results were announced the evening of June 19, Domínguez's party had been resoundingly defeated, and, since the elections had been widely regarded as a vote of confidence, a pronouncement against the governor was expected momentarily. By mobilizing the forces that would have carried out such a coup, Domínguez neatly sidestepped his own ouster.[88]

From the moment Domínguez and his three hundred heavily-armed troops marched into San Cristóbal in the mid-afternoon of June 21, the Indians' fate was sealed. Within minutes they had attacked those camped north and west of the city—people who in almost a week had taken no hostile action—leaving more than three hundred of them dead by nightfall. Forty-three ladinos also died in this "glorious battle," most of them apparently local men who turned out to watch the sport and got in the way of their own artillery.[89]

After this first engagement, Domínguez and his new conservative allies looked to their own affairs in San Cristóbal. Fear of the Indians now lifted, San Cristóbal tried Galindo and company on the twenty-third, the "defense" attorneys being the very ex-imperialists who had fanned the flames of the "Caste War" during May and early June. Naturally Galindo could not win, and he and Trejo were executed June 26.[90] Domínguez, meanwhile, his government penniless, his expulsion from office delayed only by the "Caste War," occupied himself with composing urgent appeals to local authorities around the state for volunteers and contributions to the cause of "civilization versus barbarism." Within a week, these requests brought him more than two thousand pesos and seven hundred men, more than enough to preserve his government and provide for the coming military campaign.[91]

Finally, on June 30, their ranks swelled to over a thousand men, the ladino forces set out for the definitive attack on Chamula. According to *La Brújula*, they arrived in that pueblo to find the Indians "arrayed in a truly advantageous position atop a hill," a circumstance that forced them to fight "a valiant hand-to-hand battle to gain the higher ground." In spite of these difficulties, however, and in spite of the fact that the Indians outnumbered them three to one, the government forces somehow prevailed, killing more than three hundred Indians while suffering only eleven minor injuries of their own![92] Indeed, in light of the very numbers, a more realistic account of this "battle" is probably that offered by one of the lowland soldiers present, Pedro José Montesinos:

> When we first spied the Chamulas, hundreds of them were scattered in disordered groups on the hillsides, and before we were within rifle distance all, women and children as well as men, knelt on their bare knees to beg forgiveness. In spite of the humble position they took to show submission, however, the government forces continued to advance, and they, undoubtedly hoping they would be granted the mercy they begged with tears of sorrow, remained on their knees. At a little less than 200 meters, the soldiers opened fire on their compact masses—and despite the carnage done to them by the bullets, despite their cries for mercy, continued firing for some time.
>
> When the government forces finally reached the Chamulas, their thirst for the blood of that poor, abject race still not slaked, there were suddenly such strident yells that even knowing nothing of what they said one knew their meaning: with those shouts they threw themselves against the government forces with an almost inhuman valor. These poor men, unable to secure the clemency they implored with tears and prostration, charged with a barbaric bravery.[93]

Following this triumph of "civilization over barbarism," Domínguez repeated a call he had first made several days earlier for the "rebellious communities" to present themselves and surrender. Almost immediately, what was left of the ayuntamientos of Chamula and Mitontic sent word through the teacher of Zinacantán that they wished to make peace. Their suit was accepted on July 4.[94] Meanwhile, on July 3 a squadron of soldiers had been sent to reconnoiter Tzajalhemel. Although they found the site deserted, they also found a note, written on official paper, nailed to the door of the shrine. It was a plea from Cuzcat to Governor Domínguez that he be forgiven, that he was innocent of any part in a plan to attack ladinos. Considering that he had been in jail for the half-year before June 17, this claim is not hard to believe. The soldiers burned the temple and returned to San Cristóbal.[95]

Ladino leaders now turned to a discussion of what to do next. The highlanders, having suffered for a year and a half the Indians' boycott of their churches and businesses, wanted revenge and argued for further military action. In addition, they proposed that armed garrisons of highland soldiers be stationed in all Indian communities, whether they had rebelled or not.[96] Clearly, they intended to use the "Caste War" to strengthen their hold at least on the highlands.

Domínguez, however, chose a course more in keeping with the long-term interests of the lowlands—and himself. First, he placed at the head of each of the pacified communities a native functionary loyal to the state government, enjoining them to prove their loyalty by leading their constituents in the pursuit of the remaining "rebels." Then he ordered the bulk of the state militia—lowlanders unlikely to bow to highland interests—to remain in San Cristóbal to lead this pursuit while he himself returned to Chiapa with the core of professional soldiers to "preserve order" (and thus strengthen his own hand) in the lowlands.[97]

Meanwhile, survivors of the attacks of June 21 and 30 had by this time fled back into the forests north and east of their communities. On July 7, the militia remaining in San Cristóbal had word that one of the "mobs" of these refugees was camped in the hamlet of Yolonchén, near San Andrés. Immediately a force of 360 men was dispatched to deal with it, engaging the Indians—men, women and children—in a fight that left 200 of them dead as against four ladinos.[98] Following this raid, on July 16 an army of 610 infantry, 30 cavalry, and one crew of artillery left San Cristóbal to begin the tour of the Indian townships prescribed by Domínguez. Through July 26, when they returned to the city, they tramped through all the communities as far north as Chalchiguitán—650 ladinos foraging on Indian lands, routing from their homes hundreds of terrified natives who, thus deprived of their livelihoods, were forced to join the refugees from the south in pilfering the stores and butchering the cattle of the abandoned ladino farms that lay in their path. Perversely, the soldiers' descriptions of these ruined farms were then published in *La Brújula* as further evidence of the destruction being wreaked on the state by the "Indian hordes."[99]

Perhaps most sadly, Indians themselves participated in all these persecutions. Irregular militiamen from Mitontic and Chenalhó took part in the July 16 expedition, and when a second one left San Cristóbal on August 7 it took with it several hundred men from Chamula itself. In their eagerness to prove themselves, these "loyal" Indians were even more ruthless than their ladino masters at hunting down and killing their fellows. Indeed, after mid-September primary responsibility for restoring order was left in their hands, the only direct ladino participants being a squadron of sixty infantry and fourteen cavalry stationed in San Andrés.[100]

Through the fall, there continued to be occasional "contacts" with the "rebels"—from their descriptions, cases in which individual refugees, or at most small family groups, were run down by the soldiers and their native allies and killed. Then, on November 13, the government forces finally caught up with one last camp of exhausted fugitives north of San Andrés. Rather than waste munitions on them, the ladinos sent in 250 Indian lance-bearers, an action that produced the following glowing report from Cresencio Rosas, the expedition's commander: "After an impetuous attack that yielded sixty rebel dead, we retrieved lances, axes, machetes and knives from the field, and took many families prisoner. I send my congratulations to the government and the entire white race for this great triumph of the defenders of humanity against barbarism."[101]

Following this battle, pacification of the central highlands itself was finally judged complete. Some resistance did continue just to the north among bands of highland Indians who had taken advantage of the confusion to flee the haciendas where they had been held as laborers. However, on April 18, 1870, and again on July 27, volunteers from Simojovel attacked the camps of these people, killing thirty-two on the first occasion and thirty-six on the second.[102] With that, the great "Caste War" was finished.

The Myth of the "Caste War," 1871–1981

After 1869, the lowlanders finally had what they sought for decades: effective control of the highland Indians. Although the church resumed its activities in the native communities as soon as they were secured, it never regained the power it had had before the 1860s. Highland conservatives, on the other hand, did recover some authority over the Indians, though nothing like what they had previously enjoyed: in 1872, the state capital was returned to San Cristóbal, and through resumption of their roles as merchants and civil servants the Cristobalenses were able to indebt the Indians, and so dispose of their labor. This was an arrangement apparently acceptable to the lowlanders through the 1870s and 1880s. Assured of access to Indian labor, they seemed for the time being to have been willing to leave to highlanders the tasks of organizing and administering that labor at its source.

Meanwhile, there was very little mention of the "Caste War" in ladino society after 1871. When it was introduced, as for instance in Flavio Paniagua's 1876 geography of the state, it was treated as simply one of many interesting facts about the Chamulas and their neighbors, people who were otherwise credited with being very "industrious and hardworking."[103] The repression having been successful, and ladino society itself being prosperous and harmonious for the first time in half a century, no one had any particular interest in reopening the wounds of the 1860s.

Among the Indians, on the other hand, the violence of 1869–70 was not so easily forgotten. Whether they had participated in the "resistance" that preceded it or not, the fighting had affected them all, and all now had to come to grips with it. At least in the larger communities, however, the explanations that have survived have virtually all been anti-Cuzcat—and ultimately anti-Indian. The reasons for this are not hard to find. First, the new leaders imposed on these communities in 1869 continued for several years to use the "Caste War" to justify their rule. In Chamula, for instance, opponents of the ayuntamiento were still in late 1870 being executed on the grounds that they had led, or tried to revive, the "Caste War."[104] Not surprisingly, this had a chilling effect on those who might otherwise have spoken in favor of Cuzcat and Tzajalhemel. Then too, many who had participated in the withdrawals of 1868–69 emigrated from the highlands during the repression and immediately after, some as refugees who never returned, others as forced exiles to Gulf and Pacific coast plantations, and still others as refugees from the too "loyal" ayuntamiento.[105] This removed from the community many who could have passed on a favorable view of the Indians' movement. Unfortunately, those who remained, in order to survive, accepted—and propagated as "ethnohistory"— a version of the events of 1868–1870 not so different from that of the most conservative of highland ladinos: Cuzcat and his followers became religious fanatics bent on killing ladinos, and the persecution and repression that followed became justified measures of ladino self-defense.[106]

In the late 1880s, after almost twenty years of neglect, San Cristóbal's elite suddenly rediscovered the "Caste War," two books on the subject being published within a few months of each other in 1888–89, and articles and flyers appearing regularly for the next several years.[107] What had happened was that the lowlanders, with the approval of the national government, had begun to talk about moving the state capital, permanently, from San Cristóbal to Tuxtla. The coffee and fruit plantations of Chiapas's southern Pacific coast—up to three hundred miles from San Cristóbal—had begun to boom by this time, and the cattle, cane, and cotton of the central lowlands were also flourishing. There had even begun to be talk of connecting Chiapas to the rest of Mexico by rail. Tuxtla, closer to the center of these developments, was already the state's commercial capital, and the liberals who controlled the state government saw no reason why it should not be the political capital as well.

Against these arguments, all the Cristobalenses could offer were their city's supposedly "aristocratic" traditions and its position at the center of the state's Indian population. The first being a point hardly likely to influence the liberal politicians who would decide between the two cities, they concentrated on the second. What they now claimed was that the peace and prosperity of the highlands, and with them of the entire state, depended on the capital's remaining where it could best "impose respect on the numerous Indian pueblos" of the central plateau. The last time the capital had been removed, they argued, the Indians had taken advantage of its remoteness to stage a rebellion that had threatened the very existence of the state's whites. Who knew what might happen if it were moved again?[108]

With time and the demands of politics, this retelling of the story of the "Caste War" had acquired some interesting new twists. Not wishing to blame the violence on the very liberals they hoped to sway, the high-landers now made Galindo not a liberal from central Mexico but an ex-iled imperialist who had hoped to destroy Chiapas's "decent liberal society." Indeed, according to one, he had even had the Indians address him as "monsieur"! (Considering that Flavio Paniagua and Vicente Pineda, the authors of the two books, were themselves ex-imperialists and life-long opponents of liberalism, this was a particularly cynical distortion.) Second, the Indians' religion—actually a tame, if native, variant of Catho-licism—was made as outlandish as possible to emphasize the savagery into which the natives would sink if not closely supervised. Thus the in-vention of the crucifixion of an Indian boy on Good Friday, 1868, an event not mentioned in even the most virulently racist newspaper stories of 1868–1871—stories that otherwise exulted in exaggerating the Indi-ans' cruelty and inhumanity. Finally, the actual battles of the "Caste War" itself were magnified until it seemed that the Indians had actually been on the point of overrunning San Cristóbal and slaughtering its inhabit-ants. In this new telling, the encampments on the edge of the city between June 17 and 21 became a bloody siege; the "battles" of June 21 and 30 became closely fought confrontations from which the ladino soldiers had been lucky to escape with their lives; and the persecution of July-November 1869 became a merciless guerrilla war in which Indian fanat-ics managed to hold off the entire state militia.[109]

But for all the effort that went into this elaborate justification for keeping the capital in San Cristóbal, in 1892 the federal government au-thorized its transfer to Tuxtla anyway. If the highland revisionists did not accomplish their first purpose, however, they did permanently blacken the reputation of the Indians. Ironically, when the state government de-cided a few years later to bypass San Cristóbal and manage the highland workforce itself, it fell back on the conservatives' own argument that the Indians needed to feel a strong, direct authority to remain peaceful. Us-ing this as an excuse, in 1896 the lowlanders removed all the communi-ties north of San Cristóbal from the city's control and placed them under administrators dependent on Tuxtla itself.[110] To further insure the preser-vation of peace—and the enforcement of labor contracts—lowland troops were stationed in all the major communities and native government, such as it was, was truncated.

This was the situation when Frederick Starr, in 1901, became the first American anthropologist to visit Chiapas. One of the many bits of infor-mation he collected to accompany his accounts of the Indians' brutal ex-ploitation at the hands of the state's ladinos was Paniagua's and Pineda's account of the "Caste War," complete with crucifixion.[111] The horror of this story, providing as it did "objective" proof of the Indians' low level of civilization, was by this time an accepted justification of the system of debt and plantation labor to which they were being subjected.

And so it has continued to be through the almost eighty years since. Unfortunately, modern anthropologists, collecting tales of the "Caste War" from native informants, and then looking to the "classic" sources to check their accuracy, have only compounded the problem: essentially, the Indians' stories, products of the post-"Caste War" repression, seem to confirm the racist accounts of the nineteenth-century conservatives. Indeed, by this time many of the Indian stories may be little more than native retellings of those accounts that have filtered back into the communities through the priests, schoolteachers, and others. So seductive has been the "window on the native soul" offered by these stories that scholars, instead of remaining skeptical, have simply repeated them, lending the imprimatur of their science to what may only be a myth.

Lately, still another genre has been added to writings about the "Caste War," that of the romantic radicals who see in the events of 1868–1870 a glorious popular revolution—proof positive that the Chamulas and their neighbors have risen violently, en masse, in the past, and could perhaps do so again. That they were supposedly led by a ladino vanguard only enhances the attraction of the story for exponents of this school.[112]

In fact, however, the Indian movement of 1867–1869, when it *was* their movement, appears to have been a peaceful one. What they sought was to be left alone to farm their fields, conduct their markets, and worship their saints as they themselves chose. That they could not do these things—that they were finally slaughtered for trying—is not so much evidence of passivity and submissiveness on their part as of the inhumanity of those who regarded them, not as people, but as objects, "resources," to be fought over and controlled.

Notes

Abbreviations

AGCh	Archivo General de Chiapas, Tuxtla Gutiérrez, Chiapas
AHDSC	Archivo Histórico Diocesano de San Cristóbal, San Cristóbal, Chiapas
BFB	Biblioteca "Fray Bartolomé de las Casas," San Cristóbal, Chiapas
CM	Colección Moscoso, San Cristóbal, Chiapas
TC	Tulane Collection, Latin American Library, Tulane University, New Orleans (microfilms of nineteenth-century Chiapas newspapers)

1. Vicente Pineda, *Historia de las sublevaciones indígenas habidas en el estado de Chiapas* (San Cristóbal, 1888); Flavio Paniagua, *Florinda* (San Cristóbal, 1889); Cristóbal Molina, *War of the Castes: Indian Uprisings in Chiapas, 1867–1870* (New Orleans, 1934; English translation of a contemporary memoir). Also see the serialized account of the war published in *La Brújula*, newspaper of the San Cristóbal conservatives (Aug.–Oct. 1869) (TC).

2. See, for example, Victoria R. Bricker, "Algunas consecuencias religiosas y sociales del ativismo maya en el siglo XIX," *América Indígena* 33 (1973): 327–48, and *The Indian Christ, The Indian King* (Austin, 1981). Also see H. Favre, *Changement et continuité chez les Mayas du Mexique* (Paris, 1971), pp. 269–306; G. H. Gossen, "Translating Cuzcat's War: Understanding Maya Oral Tradition," *Journal of Latin American Lore* 3 (1977): 249–78. Finally, see Carter Wilson's novel, *A Green Tree and a Dry Tree* (New York, 1972).

3. For political aspects of the lowland-highland division, see Manuel Trens, *Historia de Chiapas*, books 3–7 (Mexico City, 1957). Unfortunately, there is no reliable socioeconomic history of nineteenth-century Chiapas as a whole, although some aspects are covered in R. W. Wasserstrom, "White Fathers, Red Souls: Indian-Ladino Relations in Highland Chiapas, 1528–1973," Ph.D. dissertation, Harvard University, 1976.

4. Flavio Paniagua, *Catecismo elemental de historia y estadística de Chiapas* (San Cristóbal, 1876) (CM).

5. CM, *Colección de leyes agrarias y demás disposiciones que se han emitido en relación al ramo de tierras* (San Cristóbal, 1878); AGCh, "Prontuario del inventario del ramo de tierras" (Tuxtla, 1891).

6. The transformation of the lowlands is reflected in the remarkable growth of the region's ladino population between 1819 and 1860. For the highlands, it is easily traced through the entries of the "Prontuario del inventario del ramo de tierras" (AGCh).

7. AHDSC, Enrique Mijangos, párroco of Chamula, to the provisor of the diocese, May 7, 1855, and "Plan de Chamula," Saturnino Rivas, agrimensor, June 1855. Also see CM, *La Voz del Pueblo*, Dec. 8, 1855, and Feb. 2, 1856. (*La Voz del Pueblo* was the official newspaper of the state government.)

8. AHDSC, Enrique Zepeda, vicario of Chamula, to the Ecclesiastical Government, San Cristóbal, Oct. 27, 1804.

9. CM, *La Voz del Pueblo*, Feb. 2, 1856. There were 637 families of non-Chamulas on the 44 percent of the estate not Chamula. Assuming an even population density on the entire property—actually a conservative assumption, since the Chamula density was undoubtedly higher—this would give approximately 740 families on Chamula's 56 percent.

10. TC, *El Espíritu del Siglo*, Oct. 12, 1862.

11. Chiapas's legislature ratified the national decree of April 28, 1823, which specified many of the duties of the clergy, in 1826. Soon after, measures were adopted for each of the state's own religious subdivisions, as for instance the "Arancel de cobranzas y mensualidades autorizadas para el vicario de Chamula," promulgated on Aug. 10, 1827 (AHDSC).

12. Wasserstrom, "White Fathers, Red Souls," pp. 142–48.

13. Trens, *Historia de Chiapas*, p. 591, gives complete figures for 1856, one of the few years for which comparisons are possible.

14. Trens, *Historia de Chiapas*, pp. 328–30; AGCh, Decreto del 20 del julio, 1831, Gobierno del Estado de Chiapas.

15. Trens, *Historia de Chiapas*, pp. 441–43. Also, AGCh, baldiaje, Decreto del 9 de junio, 1849; and lands, Decretos del 28 de enero, 1847, 24 de marzo, 1847, and 24 de mayo, 1849.

16. Chamula, with 12,000 inhabitants, would have constituted 31 percent of San Cristóbal's total departmental population of 38,000 in the 1850s. Its share of the head tax of 11,552 pesos paid in the department in 1855 would therefore have been approximately 3,600 pesos—or, at 1.5 reales a day for native labor, something more than 19,200 man-days of labor. See population sources in Trens, *Historia de Chiapas*, p. 591; and in CM, *La Voz del Pueblo*, Feb. 2, 1856.

17. 1,460 man-days in personal service, and 15,500 in cash and kind. AHDSC; "Cuadrante de San Juan Chamula" (1855) and "Estados trimestrales de Chamula" (July 14, 1855, and January 14, 1856).

18. In addition to the payments already enumerated, Chamulas were also providing an undetermined amount as stipends for their schoolteacher and secretary. In 1856, these were described as one of the most onerous of the Indians' burdens in *La Voz del Pueblo*, Jan. 19 (CM).

19. Cases involving priests and secretaries were compiled from AHDSC; land cases were compiled from AGCh, "Prontuario del inventario del ramo de tierras."

20. Reflected in AHDSC, "Estados trimestrales de parroquias" (1848–57). This was a kind of report first required of priests in 1848 and discontinued in most of the diocese during the War of Reform in the late 1850s.

21. Wasserstrom, "White Fathers, Red Souls," p. 159.

22. The abolition of serfdom was repealed by the Decreto del 22 de mayo, 1851, and the controls on agricultural exports established by the Decreto del 8 de noviembre, 1853 (AHCH). For information about the land laws, see Trens, *Historia de Chiapas*, pp. 522–31.

23. Trens, *Historia de Chiapas*, pp. 515–60.

24. For general background of the Reforma, see Luis González, "La Reforma," in Daniel Cosío Villegas et al., *Historia Mínima de México* (Mexico City, 1974), pp. 104–14.

25. González, "La Reforma," pp. 111–14.

26. Trans., *Historia de Chiapas*, pp. 565–83.

27. According to *La Voz del Pueblo*, Feb. 2, 1856 (CM), Mitontic, Chenalhó, and Tenejapa were asked to pay 3,000 pesos to redeem their shares of "Nuevo Edén" in 1855—a total of some 16,000 man-days of labor. Chamula reportedly made a deal for some 5,000 pesos—26,666 man-days—slightly earlier (AHDSC, "Estado de Chamula," 1855). Whether any of these amounts were ever paid is unknown.

28. The case for the Chamulas helping the conservative insurgents is largely circumstantial. From the start of the War of Reform in Chiapas near Ixtapa in mid-1856, through Ortega's final defeat near Chanal in June 1860, most of the fighting took place across the Indian townships of the central highlands, and the priests of several of these communities were among the conservative sympathizers who fled to Guatemala in 1859 (see Trens, *Historia de Chiapas*, pp. 601–24). There is also some evidence to suggest that Chamulas served in the liberal armies during the same period, although it is uncertain whether the charges that the liberals were using "chamulas" referred to the people of that township or to poor and Indian troops in general (TC, *La Bandera Constitucional* (Tuxtla), Oct. 9, 1858).

29. Trens, *Historia de Chiapas*, pp. 608–09; Flavio Paniagua, *Salvador Guzmán* (San Cristóbal, 1891), p. 107. The drop in religious taxes between 1858 and 1861

was recorded in "Cuentas de parroquias" (AHDSC). At this early date, the decline was undoubtedly due more to the flight of the priests than to the 1857 decree outlawing church collections from the poor—a decree unenforceable in Chiapas until the mid-1860s (AHDSC, Decreto del 11 de abril, 1857, México; Trens, *Historia de Chiapas*, p. 617).

30. CM, Decreto de 21 de noviembre, 1861, Tuxtla ("Recaudación de capitación"); CM, Ley Reglamentaria de la Administración Pública de los Dptos. y Municipios, Chiapa, Jan. 15, 1862. The number of soldiers required of the state is from Trens, *Historia de Chiapas*, pp. 627, 630; of Chamula, from the letter from Manuel María Suárez, vicario of Chamula, to the Ecclesiastical Government, July 28, 1862 (AHDSC).

31. AHDSC, Suárez to Ecclesiastical Government, July 28, 1862.

32. AHDSC, Pueblo of Cancuc to the Ecclesiastical Government, April 12, 1863; AHDSC, Juan M. Gutiérrez y Aguilar, párroco of Cancuc, to the Ecclesiastical Government, April 19, 1863.

33. AHDSC, "Cuentes de Chamulas, varios años."

34. Trens, *Historia de Chiapas*, pp. 661–88; M. B. Trens, *El Imperio en Chiapas* (Tuxtla, 1956); CM, "Manuscrito del Sr. Villafuerte" (contemporary diary).

35. Trens, *El Imperio en Chiapas*, pp. 18–27, 33; CM, "Noticias de las personas que . . . prestaron servicios a la facción intervencionista," *El Espíritu del Siglo*, May 21, 1864.

36. Trens, *El Imperio en Chiapas*, pp. 33–43; Trens, *Historia de Chiapas*, pp. 661–65.

37. Trens, *El Imperio en Chiapas*, p. 39; AHDSC, Enrique Mijangos, párroco of Zinacantan, to the Secretary of the Ecclesiastical Government, Oct. 19, 1863.

38. AHDSC, Superior Gobierno Eclesiastico to Prefecto Superior, Gobierno Imperial, Nov. 10, 1863; AHDSC, J. Agustín Velasco, párroco of Tenejapa, to the Ecclesiastical Government, Oct. 12, 1863.

39. AHDSC, "A los habitantes del departamento de San Cristóbal Las Casas" (a flyer), Manuel Arévalo, San Cristóbal, Jan. 26, 1863.

40. AHDSC, Manuel María Suárez, vicario of Chamula, to the Ecclesiastical Government, Sept. 22, 1863.

41. TC, *La Brújula* (San Cristóbal), April 23, May 28, and Sept. 24, 1869.

42. C. C. Cumberland, *Mexico: The Struggle for Modernity* (New York, 1968), pp. 163–66; Trens, *Historia de Chiapas*, p. 675.

43. Trens, *Historia de Chiapas*, pp. 672–80.

44. Ibid., pp. 680–92. Domínguez was elected on Oct. 29, 1867, and took office constitutionally on Dec. 1.

45. CM, "Correspondencia interceptada a los traidores y mandada publicar de orden del c. Governador," *Espíritu del Siglo*, April 9, 1864. *Espíritu del Siglo* also carried lists of "traitors" "con expresión de sus bienes sobre las cuales debe racaer la pena de confiscación" on April 21, May 28, and June 4, 1864.

46. TC, *La Brújula*, April 23 and Sept. 17, 1869; AHDSC, Enrique Mijangos, párroco of Mitontic and Chenalhó, to Manuel Suárez, vicario of Chamula, Sept. 16, 1864; AHDSC, J. Agustín Velasco, párroco of Oxchuc and Huistán, to the Ecclesiastical Government, June 21, 1865.

47. During 1863–64, the government had been able to collect only regular head and property taxes in the departments of Chiapa, Tuxtla, and Pichucalco. With Ortega's defeat in 1864, it also began to extract revenues from the highlands in the form of forced loans, but when the head tax was again enforced in the region

in 1869 it was decried as a "new" tax (Trens, *Historia de Chiapas*, pp. 674–75; CM, "Manuscrito del Sr. Villafuerte," pp. 8–9; TC, *La Brújula*, April 23, 1868).
48. Justo Sierra, *Juárez, su obra y su tiempo* (Mexico City, 1905), pp. 428–32.
49. Supremo Decreto del 22 de julio, 1867, México (reported in Vicente Pineda, *Chiapas: Translación de los poderes públicos* (San Cristóbal, 1892).
50. Trens, *Historia de Chiapas*, p. 692. (Domínguez took office on Dec. 1, 1867, and ordered the capital moved on Dec. 31.)
51. The escalation of these measures is reflected in the following: AHDSC, Bruno Domínguez, párroco of Zinacantan, to the Ecclesiastical Government, June 4, 1867; AHDSC, Domínguez to the Ecclesiastical Government, Feb. 26, 1868; and AHDSC, Enrique Mijangos, párroco of Mitontic, Chenalhó, and Chalchiguitán, to the Ecclesiastical Government, May 15, 1868. In his letter of Feb. 26, the priest of Zinacantan wrote: "The *ayuntamiento* and *maestro* of this pueblo have just informed me for the second time that the state has decreed, among other things, the complete dissolution of the *mayordomos* who serve in this holy church, as well as the abolition of the position, and since without these it will not be possible to preserve organized religion, much less provide for the subsistence of the minister, and since it is possible to see behind this decision the purpose of driving the priest from the town, I ask that I might be removed from here as soon as possible in order that this community might understand how sorely it will feel the absence of a priest."
52. AHDSC, M. Francisco Gordillo, párroco of Oxchuc and Huistán, to the Ecclesiastical Government, Oct. 27 and Nov. 15, 1868; AHDSC, Enrique Mijangos, párroco of Pantelhó, to the Ecclesiastical Government, Feb. 13, 1869. In the last of these letters, Mijangos reported that in Pantelhó "the native justicias rejected me, demanding to know who had sent for me. After calming down a bit, they unanimously confessed that the maestro had instructed them to act as they did."
53. For Zinacantán, Chalchiguitán, Mitontic, and Chenalhó, see note 51; for Oxchuc, Huistán, and Pantelhó, note 52; for Tenejapa, AHDSC, Manuel Suárez, párroco, to the Ecclesiastical Government, Nov. 21, 1868.
54. AHDSC, M. Francisco Gordillo, párroco of Oxchuc and Huistán, to the Ecclesiastical Government, Oct. 27 and Nov. 15, 1868. In the second of these letters, Gordillo wrote: "I am just now returning from a fiesta where the damned Indians acted vilely, refusing even to pay twelve pesos for the service without threats. I wanted to raise the prices for baptisms and marriages to compensate, but saw that if I did they would not baptize anybody."
55. AHDSC, Manuel Suárez, párroco of Tenejapa, to the Ecclesiastical Government, Nov. 21, 1868.
56. R. F. Wasserstrom, personal communication.
57. AHDSC, Anselmo Guillén, párroco of Chamula, to J. Facundo Bonifaz, Secretario of the Ecclesiastical Government, April 8, 1870; "Cuentas de Chamula, varios años" (AHDSC) contains both accounts and notes for 1865–69; TC, *El Baluarte* (Tuxtla), Oct. 1, 1869.
58. Molina, *War of the Castes*, p. 365. According to Paniagua (*Florinda*, pp. 4–10), the cult was started by Checheb in October 1867 and by the time of Cuzcat's first visit was already flourishing. Pineda (*Historia de las sublevaciones*, pp. 71–72), on the other hand, says that Cuzcat and Checheb made a clay idol together in late 1867 and that their intention throughout was to start a lucrative new religion.
59. Molina, *War of the Castes*, pp. 365–66.

60. AHDSC, Enrique Mijangos, vicario interino, "Estado trimestral de Chamula," July 14, 1855.

61. AHDSC, Mijangos, "Estado trimestral."

62. Molina, *War of the Castes*, p. 367.

63. Ibid.

64. Ibid.; CM, "Manuscrito del Sr. Villafuerte," p. 8.

65. TC, *La Brújula*, June 11, 1869. CM, "Manuscrito del Sr. Villafuerte," p. 8. According to Villafuerte, San Cristóbal began frantic preparations for an expected Indian attack on May 1, 1868, all able-bodied men being organized into military companies under jefes militares.

66. Molina, *War of the Castes*, p. 367; CM, "Manuscrito del Sr. Villafuerte," p. 8; TC, *La Brújula*, June 11, 1869.

67. Molina, *War of the Castes*, p. 367. The three priests were Manuel Suárez, Bruno Domínguez, and Enrique Mijangos.

68. Ibid., p. 368. Melchor Gómez, a scribe from the ayuntamiento of Chamula, was named mayordomo—an office outlawed in the Indian pueblos by the state government.

69. Ibid.

70. Ibid.

71. Ibid., p. 368–69; TC, *La Brújula*, July 9, 1869.

72. E.g., TC, *La Brújula*, April 23 and May 28, 1869. In answer to the carping of the highlanders, the liberal newspaper of Chiapa, *El Baluarte*, ran a long series during 1868–69 on the political "crimes" of the conservatives during the 1860s: "La lucha contra el llamado 'Imperio Mexicano' en Chiapas."

73. TC, *Espíritu del Siglo*, May 9, 11, and 23, and Dec. 3, 1868.

74. Ibid., March 27, 1869; TC, *La Brújula*, April 30, 1869.

75. TC, *La Brújula*, May 28, 1869; TC, *El Baluarte*, Oct. 1, 1869.

76. Galindo's history and motives are discussed in Molina, *War of the Castes*, p. 360; TC, *La Brújula*, Dec. 17, 1869; and TC, *El Baluarte*, Sept. 22, 1870. San Cristóbal's mood during this period can be detected in *La Brújula*, April 11 and June 11, 1869—indeed, the issue of June 11 was already talking about a "caste war," this several days before the outbreak of violence that supposedly started the "Caste War of 1869."

77. Paniagua, *Florinda*, pp. 32–34; Pineda, *Historia de las sublevaciones*, pp. 78–79. Galindo's construction of the facts is from his testimony at his trial, "Proceso instruido contra Ignacio Fernández de Galindo, 23 de junio, 1869," reprinted as Note F in Paniagua, *Florinda*.

78. CM, "Manuscrito del Sr. Villafuerte," p. 9; Molina, *War of the Castes*, pp. 372–73. At Galindo's trial, it was reported that he had been present at three killings, to which he replied that he had only gone along to try to restrain the Indians, to prevent killing ("Proceso," in Paniagua, *Florinda*).

79. Molina, *War of the Castes*, p. 375; CM, "Manuscrito del Sr. Villafuerte," p. 9. From other sources, it can be calculated that a total of sixteen ladinos died in these two fights. How many Indians were killed is unknown (see note 81).

80. TC, *La Brújula*, July 25, 1869; Molina, *War of the Castes*, p. 375.

81. TC, *El Baluarte*, *Alcance #5*, June 22, 1869; CM, "Manuscrito del Sr. Villafuerte," p. 10. Paniagua (*Florinda*, Note C) and Pineda (*Historia de las sublevaciones*, p. 82) later claimed that many more ladino civilians were killed in "brutal attacks" that lasted through June. Paniagua even provides a list of supposed "victims," although he provides no dates or places of death, or even, in

most cases, complete names. From the lists of casualties published in *La Brújula* (July 9 and 25, 1869), however, it appears that 79 ladinos were killed in the entire "Caste War," of whom 47 were combatants, 16 were accounted for individually (see notes 79 and 80), and 16 were apparently killed in the attacks on "Natividad" and "La Merced" in mid-June.

82. Molina, *War of the Castes*, p. 375.

83. Pineda (*Historia de las sublevaciones*, pp. 87–93) argues that Galindo was tricked by the "extreme cleverness" of San Cristóbal's *jefe político* into turning himself over. Paniagua (*Florinda*, p. 48), on the other hand, has it that he thought the Indians would soon attack to free him—though why he, the supposed military leader, would have turned over the army to Cuzcat if an attack was eventually going to be necessary anyway is never explained. Finally, a lowland commentator, José M. Montesinos—an enemy of Governor Domínguez—claims that Galindo was an agent provocateur of the governor and fully expected the governor to ride to his rescue. *Memorias del Sargento, 1866–1878* (Tuxtla, 1935).

84. TC, *El Baluarte*, July 9, 1869.

85. Ibid.; TC, *La Brújula*, Dec. 17, 1869.

86. Molina, *War of the Castes*, p. 376; TC, *La Brújula*, June 25, 1869. From the internal evidence, it appears that *La Brújula* was often published up to a week earlier than the date it bore, so the number of June 25 may actually have come out any time between June 18 and 25.

87. TC, *El Baluarte*, June 18, 1869. Later it was claimed that Domínguez had been organizing a force to defend San Cristóbal as early as June 14—and, indeed, among the forces that bargained with Galindo on June 17 were twenty-five troops sent from Chiapa as observers three days earlier. There is no evidence that he intended to take any further action, however (TC, *La Brújula*, June 18, 1869).

88. Montesinos, *Memorias del Sargento*, p. 66; see also the letter from Tuxtla correspondent of *La Brújula*, July 16, 1869 (TC).

89. Molina, *War of the Castes*, p. 377; TC, *La Brújula*, July 2, 1869; TC, *El Baluarte*, July 9, 1869. From contemporary sources, it appears that the Indians actually fled when confronted by the lowland soldiers and that the only ones who fought back were those who were cornered against steep hills with no escape possible. One such group, in its desperation, ran directly toward the lowland cannons, causing the wild firing that accounted for most of the ladino casualties. (Even Pineda [*Historia de las sublevaciones*, p. 101] concedes most of these facts.)

90. TC, *La Brújula*, July 2, 1869.

91. Reported in *La Brújula*, July 9 and 16, 1869 (TC). Domínguez's circular to the officials around the state was dated June 26.

92. TC, *La Brújula*, July 9, 1869.

93. As reported to his nephew, J. M. Montesinos (*Memorias del Sargento*, pp. 61–62).

94. Molina, *War of the Castes*, p. 379; CM, "Manuscrito del Sr. Villafuerte," p. 10.

95. Molina, *War of the Castes*, p. 379.

96. F. Paniagua, "Guerra de castas," *La Brújula*, July 9, 1869 (TC). As evidence of the tone of the discussion, an unsigned editorial in the same number suggested exiling the highland rebels to the Soconusco, where they could become a permanent work-force, and still a third piece, on July 16, 1869, argued that the rebels should be defeated utterly, killed to the last man, as an example to those who remained.

97. TC, *El Baluarte*, July 23, 1869. Some lowland troops were released after July 3, but most were assigned to the highlands indefinitely as of that date. This probably accounts for the "dissatisfaction" noted in *El Baluarte* on July 23.

98. TC, *La Brújula*, Sept. 17, 1869. *La Brújula* of July 16, 1869, says the Indian dead were too numerous to count, and "El Manuscrito del Sr. Villafuerte" (CM, p. 10) says there were no fewer than 300.

99. "Informes del comandante militar," July–December 1869 (collected in Paniagua, *Florinda*, Note G–J). In a letter to *La Brújula*, published Sept. 24, 1869, Victor Domínguez, owner of one of the ruined farms, described the Indians as "monsters of ingratitude."

100. "Informes," in Paniagua, *Florinda*, Notes I–J; TC, *El Baluarte*, Aug. 13, 1869. On August 24, 1869, a crowd of fugitive Indians from Chamula, San Andrés, and Santiago took their revenge on one settlement of such "loyal" Indians in San Andrés, killing twenty of them and burning their houses (TC, *La Brújula*, Sept. 3, 1869).

101. Rosas to the state government, Nov. 13, 1869 (published in TC, *La Brújula*, Nov. 19, 1869).

102. TC, *La Brújula*, Dec. 24, 1869; "Informes," in Paniagua, *Florinda*, Note K.

103. Flavio Paniagua, *Catecismo elemental de historia y estadística de Chiapas* (San Cristóbal, 1876).

104. Molina (*War of the Castes*, p. 379) reports executions of "rebel leaders" turned over by Chamula's ayuntamiento on July 26, 1869 (five), and October 3, 1869 (three). In addition, the "Manuscrito del Sr. Villafuerte" (CM, p. 11) reports that the presiding officer of Chamula brought the head of one rebel to San Cristóbal on July 10, 1870, and two more on August 4. Ladino forces also intervened directly in the native communities through 1870, attending all the major fiestas, and on July 7 arresting and summarily executing a Chamula scribe who had tried to arouse a protest against the head tax (Molina, *War of the Castes*, p. 383; CM, "Manuscrito del Sr. Villafuerte," p. 11).

105. Many of those who fled during the summer of 1869 settled in San Juan Chamula El Bosque, a settlement north of Chalchiguitán that also became a refuge for émigrés in 1870–71. That groups of "rebels" were also exiled by the government is known from the letter from Agustín Velasco, *párroco* of Chamula, to Dr. Feliciano Lazos, lector of the Ecclesiastical Government, Jan. 15, 1864, in which he inquired about religious jurisdiction over the children of exiles from the state of Veracruz (AHDSC).

106. The first steps of this process can be detected in the "Manifesto del indígena c. Domingo Pérez" (TC, *La Brújula*, Nov. 26, 1869), in which Pérez, apparently a Chamula, refers to the "rebels" whom he was then pursuing as "barbarians whose wish it is to eliminate the ladino class and sow their own deprived vices among their fellows." By the 1870s, the surviving stories in Chamula had it that Cuzcat and his followers were entirely to blame for the violence they brought down on the community (see Gossen, "Translating Cuzcat's War"), whereas in Chalchiguitán, for instance, Chamulas in general were blamed (Ulrich Köhler, personal communication). Only in such out-of-the-way villages as Magdalenas did versions of the events survive in which Cuzcat and his followers were depicted as "good" and the persecution of them unjust (Amber Past, "Lo que cuenta una mujer de Magdalenas," in J. Burstein and R. Wasserstrom, *En sus proprias palabras: Cuatro vidas tzotziles* (San Cristóbal, 1979).

107. Pineda, *Historia de las sublevaciones* (1888); Paniagua, *Florinda* (1889). Vicente Pineda also wrote the most important of the subsequent articles, "La traslación de los poderes públicos del estado" (San Cristóbal, 1892), a pamphlet (AGCh).

108. The citation is from Pineda, "La traslación de los poderes," who went on to argue that "the capital must remain where there are the most individuals to govern, direct, repress, educate, civilize, and enlighten." The first two appendices of Paniagua's *Florinda* were about the transfer of the capital to Tuxtla in 1867 and its supposed consequences (Note A) and the cultural and educational advantages of San Cristóbal (Note B).

109. Galindo is identified as an imperialist in Paniagua, *Florinda*, p. 12. The first mention of the supposed crucifixion is in Pineda, *Historia de las sublevaciones* (pp. 76–77), and the exaggerated battles are to be found in Paniagua, *Florinda*, pp. 48–74, and Pineda, *Historia de las sublevaciones*, pp. 94–116.

110. Transfer of the capital: AGCh, Decreto del 11 de agosto, 1892, Tuxtla. Formation of the Partido de Chamula: AGCh, Decreto del 24 de abril, 1896, Tuxtla.

111. Frederick Starr, *In Indian Mexico: A Narrative of Travel and Labor* (Chicago, 1908).

112. Antonio García de León et al., *La violencia en Chamula* (San Cristóbal, 1979); Juan J. Manguén et al., *La Guerra de Castas, 1869–1870* (San Cristóbal, 1979).

II

Popular Religion and "Folk Catholicism"

3

Emerging from the Shadows: A Visit to an Old Jewish Community in Mexico

Allison Gardy

Latin America has long had a sizable Jewish population, although until quite recently Jews tended to keep their faith hidden for fear of persecution and recrimination. Although their history, like their identity in Latin America, is intentionally obscured, Jews apparently came to the region in fairly large numbers during the colonial period, both in violation of and in escape from the Spanish Inquisition. Many Jews, known variously as conversos, *"New Christians," or, derogatorily,* marranos_(swine), *fled to the New World over the course of the colonial period. Although the Inquisition also exerted its control over Mexico and Peru, the New World Inquisition was generally not quite so preoccupied with the "Jewish heresy" as its Iberian counterpart. Even so, Jews tended to settle in parts of the New World where Spain's authority was the weakest, such as on the remote northern frontier of what is now called New Mexico, or in what was considered to be generally undesirable territory, such as Costa Rica. Many Jews also rebuilt their lives in viceregal centers such as Mexico City and Lima.*

Despite what were in some areas fairly sizable Jewish populations, the exigencies of secrecy and isolation meant that with the passage of time, Latin American conversos *tended to lose their distinctly Jewish identity, while others maintained such customs as the overwhelmingly Catholic culture would permit. In many areas, the descendants of the Sephardim are only dimly aware of their own families' origins, but for others the*

From *NACLA Report on the Americas* 27, no. 2, *Peril and Promise: The New Democracy in Latin America* (September–October 1993): 10–14. © 1997 by the North American Congress on Latin America, 475 Riverside Drive, #454, New York, NY 10115-0122.

Jewish faith still runs deep, as this article on a Mexican community illustrates.

Allison Gardy is a freelance journalist who has published articles in such national publications as NACLA, *from which this chapter is taken.*

The Jews of Venta Prieta say that their ancestors accomplished the impossible. They remained Jews throughout the Inquisition, even though they had no synagogue and no rabbi to instruct them during the long centuries of hiding.

It is easy to miss Venta Prieta. There is no welcome sign, no landmark visible from the road. It appears at first to be nothing more than a cluster of small stores, unpaved streets, and low flat houses hiding among the dry brown and yellow hills on the outskirts of the old mining city of Pachuca in central Mexico. But visitors keep coming—journalists, anthropologists, curiosity seekers. If it could choose, Venta Prieta would remain anonymous. Go away, say a man's eyes when a visitor asks if she is in the right place. Leave us alone. And then with words, "We are not objects in a museum."

Founded in the 1850s, this small Mexican community lived through its first century guarding a deep secret—its Jewish identity. Its founders and most of its inhabitants were descendants of families who had spent three hundred years hiding in Mexico's mountains after escaping the Spanish Inquisition. The community's founders, a couple named Tellez, settled in Venta Prieta when it was just an outpost, a ghostly presence that came to life with the visit of the occasional traveler. Today the village sits in the shadow of a giant new shopping mall across the road, and its secret has been out in the open for thirty years. But secrecy is an old habit, a vestige of a survival skill that kept the community alive for centuries.

The story really begins with the expulsion of the Jews and Muslims from Spain in 1492, during the Inquisition. The Holy Office of the Inquisition, established by King Ferdinand and Queen Isabella in 1478, had already burned thousands of Jews at the stake in the decade before the expulsion decree. In the half century following the expulsion, roughly a third of Spain's Jews were burned at the stake, a third fled, and another third were forcibly converted to Catholicism. Of those who converted, many maintained Jewish customs in private.

Many Jews left Spain on ships bound for the New World, where they hoped the Inquisition would be less severe. So many took this path of survival that by 1550 almost 25 percent of Mexico City's Spanish population was known to be Jewish, and the community had its own Grand Rabbi. The number might have been even larger, since many Jews disguised themselves as Catholics. "The great majority of Mexicans today have Jewish blood, though very diluted," says Orthodox Rabbi Abraham Bartfeld of Mexico City.

New Spain was not the haven Jews imagined. In fact, the Inquisition there lasted longer than it did in Spain, where it was finally suppressed in 1808. In Mexico, the Spanish authorities established a Tribunal of the Inquisition in 1571 which existed until the colony's War of Independence in 1821. During the war, the Inquisition accused the revolutionary priest José María Hidalgo y Costilla, the father of Mexican independence, of practicing Judaism, among other "crimes." By then the Inquisition had become so despised by the general population that it was commonly referred to as the "Unholy Office."

Historians have contended that Mexico's colonial Jewish population was either wiped out or converted. But the Jews of Venta Prieta say that their ancestors accomplished the impossible—they remained Jews throughout the Inquisition, even though they had no synagogue and no rabbi to instruct them during the centuries of hiding. In the last fifty years they have built their own temple, bought their own Torah, and, in keeping with biblical tradition, have had an eternal flame of olive oil—which requires constant attention—burning inside the temple.

But Mexico's orthodox rabbinate, wary of the long centuries that the Inquisition's refugees spent underground, disputes Venta Prieta's claim that it is Mexico's oldest Jewish community. "They can't prove their ancestry goes back to colonial times," says Orthodox Rabbi Bartfeld. While he admires their "spirituality," Rabbi Bartfeld considers the heritage of the people of Venta Prieta to be as much Catholic as Jewish. He believes the only legitimate Jews in Mexico today are twentieth-century immigrants from Europe and North Africa and their descendants. Mexico's entire Jewish population numbers about fifty thousand, 80 percent of whom live in Mexico City.

Conservative Rabbi Samuel Lerer disagrees with the orthodoxy. He met the Venta Prieta community in 1968, the same year he left the United States for Mexico. He found that they had recognizably Jewish characteristics: they did not eat pork or mix milk and meat, and virtually all the men were circumcised. What's more, says Rabbi Lerer, "they can trace their lineage back to the early nineteenth century. How many Jews can prove they are Jewish beyond three generations?"

It was Rabbi Lerer who piqued my curiosity about Venta Prieta. He showed me a few articles about the community published in the United States and Mexico, and complained of their inaccuracies. None of the articles explained Venta Prieta's history. The rabbi then sent me to the one man who knows the community's story.

His name is Rubén Tellez. He is a direct descendant of the community's founders and, at 53, he is Venta Prieta's reluctant elder spokesman. He is withdrawn and embittered, and he hates journalists. He could not care less about what Mexico's Jewish community or any other outsiders might think of Venta Prieta.

He runs a little store out of the back of his house on the only paved street in town. Its sign says La Paz. Peace. But inside, it is too peaceful. While the shopping mall across the road hums with activity, the only person to walk into his store all afternoon just asks to use the telephone. Tellez sits in a corner, wearing a plaid shirt, a baseball cap, and dark-green sunglasses. He leans back on a folding chair with one knee up against a rusted card table. Above his head hangs a collage of Coca-Cola ads. He closes a book, its title concealed by a dust jacket, and looks up.

"So you want to write a story? Isn't that nice. Do you expect me to drop what I'm doing to attend to you just because you want to write about us?" he asks. "Don't you understand how tired we are of strangers poking into our intimate lives with questions and criticisms, trying to see if we really exist, if we're really who we say we are?"

I tell him I would be happy to come back at a more convenient time. "There is no convenient time to talk to journalists," he says. "They stay at a hotel in the city, then come here for a few hours to stare and dig up our past. They write lies about us and never send us the articles. They promise everything and deliver nothing. It's a waste of time. I may look like I'm just sitting here, but it's my time."

"Rabbi Lerer sent me." I show him the rabbi's card.

"The rabbi has done wonders for us and we owe him a lot, but with all due respect, he is sometimes too openhearted."

"Could I at least attend tonight's Sabbath service?"

Amazed I am a Jew who wants to attend his synagogue's services, and impressed that I actually know how to pray in Hebrew, he relents. He even offers to put me up at the community's guest house, "as a guest, but not as a journalist." Then, having granted me permission to write, but not to ask questions, he dismisses me. "You've already wasted enough of my time," he says. "I have to read the Torah portion for this week. Goodbye."

Venta Prieta's synagogue stands behind a forbidding white wall, but a little door opens onto a courtyard filled with bouncing children, whose faces represent a cross-pollination of continents: Europe, North Africa, Indo-America. Rough blue-and-yellow stained-glass windows with elongated Stars of David ring the small temple. Inside, rows of old wooden pews with separate chair backs and armrests seat about one hundred people. The Sacred Ark, which houses the Torah, is made of marble and onyx. A white polyester curtain with two fierce lions of Judah sewn in sequins covers the Sacred Ark. Next to it, a flame flickers in a silver bowl filled with olive oil.

Replicas of [Marc] Chagall's *Twelve Tribes of Israel* hang around the wall where the Stations of the Cross would be in a Catholic church, and outside the temple door sits a box for donations. Other hints of Catholicism appear during an otherwise standard service. The women, for example, touch the Torah's cover with their hands (instead of with a prayer book), then touch their fingers to their forehead and lips, a hand motion not too unlike the sign of the cross. Also, when the Sacred Ark is opened, congregants raise their hands, a gesture seen in church but not in synagogue. Rabbi Lerer once mentioned that when he visits Venta Prieta, they touch his robe and kiss his hands, even though such behavior goes against Jewish custom.

"Some criticize us for these customs and say they're Catholic," says Miguel Copca, Tellez's 20-year-old nephew. "But these are not Catholic traditions. They are our traditions and we're not going to change them. What's important isn't where your hands are, but where your heart is."

Saturday morning prayer begins at eight and lasts until 11:30, with most of the thirty congregants trickling in halfway through. Tellez watches me read and listens to me sing in Hebrew. The melodies are Sephardic— from sixteenth-century Spain. After lunch, he goes to see about getting more streets paved in town. While his wife and children do errands, I wash several days' worth of dishes. It is the least I can do before returning to Mexico City that evening. Before I leave, Tellez reluctantly agrees to speak with me again. "If you're really interested," he says, "come back when I have time, and bring a short list of questions." We agree to meet in five days.

When I return, he is in the same position he had been in when I first met him, wearing the same baseball cap, leaning back in his chair, and reading the dust-jacket Torah. "I was hoping you wouldn't come," he greets me, "because frankly I don't feel like answering any questions today. I was thinking how much your visit reminded me of going to the dentist." He tries to hide a faint smile. "I'm writing my own book about the family," he adds. "It's called 'The Lost History.' I just need a few more documents to finish it."

"Once you publish it, you'll never have to talk to a nosy stranger again."

"That's the idea."

We talk about everything but Venta Prieta. He asks me what I am going to do with my life, and gives me marriage advice. He says his father died when he was young, and he had to drop out of school to support the family. "Let's hear the questions," he says abruptly. At first he gives terse, vague responses. "What we have are several plausible versions of our earliest history," he says. "If there were any written proof of our antiquity, all of this would have been written up years ago in the United States." But his answers gradually unfold into a narrative, and, together with Miguel's anecdotes from my first visit, they tell a story.

A family, under the original name of Tellezgirón, most likely arrived in Veracruz in the sixteenth century. During the Inquisition, they escaped to Zamora, Michoacán. Then, "fleeing as usual," they settled in the mountains of Hidalgo where their name was shortened to Tellez. By the 1850s, the family withered away to a single couple and their Jewish secret. They emerged from hiding and founded Venta Prieta.

Tellez can plot the family's genealogy directly to this original couple. Descendants of this founding family intermarried with their Catholic neighbors and with their Catholic and Jewish cousins. "Today the family has divided into two branches: Jewish and Catholic," he says. "We get along as a family. We just don't talk about religion, politics, or anything." Miguel's brother and father are Catholic, for example, while he and his mother are Jewish.

Rubén Tellez's great-grandparents farmed the land and gathered the family to pray in a little room. So as not to attract attention, the Sabbath service was shortened and people came and went one by one. "When we asked our elder uncle what something meant in Hebrew," Tellez recalled, "he would only say, 'Shh! Shh!' and turn the pages of the prayer book."

In 1923, when the family grew too large to fit in the elder's little room, they built a small temple. During World War II, a rumor spread that Palestinians were coming to kill the Jews of Venta Prieta. The family dismantled the temple and returned to conducting services in the home of an elder. Meanwhile, a pro-Nazi movement in the nearby town of Tulancingo scattered the Jewish community there. Today, the only nonfamily members of Venta Prieta's synagogue are from Tulancingo.

Miguel's mother remembers that a terrible *viruela negra* (black plague) struck Venta Prieta in her childhood. The Catholic population died in such numbers that corpses were loaded onto carts and hauled away. Only one Jew fell sick, but did not die. A rumor spread that the Jews had medicine and were hiding it. Miguel's mother remembers angry townsfolk entering and searching their house and remaining suspicious until long after the plague subsided. Miguel wonders if their dietary laws might not have protected the Jews from the virus.

The community built a new temple after the war, and a bigger one in 1967. In the 1960s they openly identified themselves as Jewish for the first time. "The new generation felt more secure," says Tellez, who, along with Miguel's mother and other young people at the time, began seeking

Hebrew books and schooling. "The only Hebrew the elders could read was the Hebrew of the prayers," he says. "We wanted to know more."

The community learned to speak Hebrew in Miguel's generation, and young people began taking trips to Israel through international Jewish organizations. Returning with language and knowledge, the young instruct the old in ancient tradition. "Likewise," says Miguel, "the next generation will correct us."

A few months ago, a Hebrew teacher from Mexico City was transferred to Pachuca and has volunteered to give language classes in Venta Prieta. Children training for their bar mitzvah (coming-of-age) ceremony take lessons with Rabbi Lerer in Mexico City every other Sunday, making a four-hour round trip for a one-hour lesson. Because the 71-year-old rabbi has his own congregation to attend to on the Sabbath and is busy during the week, he performs mass weddings and bar mitzvahs in Venta Prieta on the two or three Sundays in the year that fall on the first day of the lunar month, which is when the Torah can be read.

Miguel's generation is more career-minded than previous generations. So far, they have found work in the rapidly developing city of Pachuca. "But if my job takes me to another state," Miguel says, "I'll go." Tellez does not worry that the younger generation's quest for upward mobility could lead to a flight from Venta Prieta. "Why should they move away?" he asks. "Life is comfortable here. There is no hunger anymore. We even have luxuries. Besides," he adds, "people have property here and a cemetery, and they can't take either with them."

I ask Tellez when he plans to finish his book and tell the whole story of Venta Prieta. He says the documents and photographs he needs are in the possession of the oldest member of the community—a man almost 80 years old and filled with stories. But an accident several years ago left the man deaf and babbling incoherently. He forbids people to look at the family records and goes into a rage if someone tries to borrow them. "I cannot finish the book until he dies," says Tellez.

I want to take a photograph of the schoolroom before leaving Venta Prieta. "Later, later," says Tellez, until it is too late and I have to run to catch my bus. There are questions I have not asked. There are answers he has not given. But I have gotten enough. I came to see Venta Prieta and have learned it does not quite resemble what has been written about it.

Our handshake is warm and firm. "I wish I'd taken that photo," I say. "You'll have to come back," he replies. I glimpse a hint of a smile.

4

The Metaphor of the Day in Quiché, Guatemala: Notes on the Nature of Everyday Life

Duncan Earle

The first decades of independence brought considerable stress to the institutional Roman Catholic Church, resulting in a greatly diminished presence of the official Church on the social landscape in Latin America. But while the Church as an institution slowly vanished from the distant countryside as the nineteenth century progressed, Catholicism both as a system of belief and as a way of life did not. To the contrary, a type of popular Catholicism as practiced and interpreted by an enthusiastic local laity quickly emerged to supplement and eventually replace orthodox Catholicism in many indigenous regions and also on the far geographic frontier, where it developed spontaneously and thrived without the knowledge or blessing of the Mother Church. For many authors, the result was what many call "folk Catholicism"—a syncretism, or blend, of indigenous and Catholic beliefs that were specific and resonant to a given locality and community.

Duncan Earle, however, rejects the notion that local indigenous spirituality can be classified as "folk Catholicism" or "syncretism," noting that it is impossible to believe simultaneously in one God (as Catholicism demands) and in many deities, as is common in Maya tradition. He also argues that while Catholicism constitutes an element within Maya indigenous spirituality, it is only one of many components. In Earle's view, "folk Catholicism" is neither a type of poorly understood Catholicism nor a subversion of native forms beneath a Catholic façade. Rather, it is a

From *Symbol and Meaning Beyond the Closed Community: Essays in Mesoamerican Ideas*, ed. Gary Gossens (Albany, NY: SUNY Institute for Mesoamerican Studies, 1986), 155–72. Reprinted by permission of the SUNY Institute for Mesoamerican Studies.

fusion of Christian and indigenous belief, internalized and contextualized within a Maya worldview in such a way as to have internal logic and essential meaning to believers.

In addition to conducting extensive field studies as a professional anthropologist, Earle served for a time as an apprentice to a Ki'ché Maya shaman, so his work is informed by both an etic (outsider's) and emic (insider's) perspective. In this chapter on the Quiché in Guatemala, Earle explicates the Maya worldview from a study of beliefs centered around a common human experience, one day—that essential unit where time and place, sacred and profane, converge.

Duncan Earle is currently director of the Center for International Border Studies at the University of Texas, El Paso He is the author of several articles on continuities and change in contemporary Maya society.

> I was in the graveyard. Everyone was dressed like before, the men with their white pants, their aprons of wool, their sandals. When I arrived there they gave me a bed to lie in, just like the others. The men and the women were all separated, men over here, women over here (gesturing). The men kept busy mending their clothes, while the women were grinding corn and weaving.
>
> Then a man came up to me. He was the man in charge. He told me that I had come too soon, that it was only noon, and that I should come back at four in the afternoon. So I said goodbye to all my departed friends and godbrothers, it was very sad to see them all. That was all of it, all of the dream that came to me.
>
> Oh, that he might have said five o'clock, that would have been 100 years of life for me. As it is I should last to 80. You see, at 50 years old, like I am now, that's when I was at the graveyard, that's like the middle of the day.
>
> —A portion of notes on a dream told to me by Lucas Pachaac in his home on July 25, 1979, Chinique, Guatemala

A major contribution of the symbolic and structuralist approaches to the study of human cultures is one of giving order, of providing conceptual bridges between diverse categories of cultural phenomena through establishing overarching principles. These principles provide the ethnologist with an analytic framework for making more intelligible classes of field data that have escaped a holistic analysis based upon more standard categorizations. The weakness, however, of many structuralist approaches has been an overemphasis upon presumed universal principles and insufficient attention to the specific principles of the culture under study.[1] In this study I explore the daily world and worldview of the Quiché rural farmer of the highlands of Guatemala to discover basic structural and symbolic principles of particular force in their cultural system. It is instructive to identify general binary oppositions, but it is the specific symbolic content of the poles, and in what "symbolizing" forms they are embedded in everyday life, that is most central to this inquiry.

To obtain a sufficiently holistic perspective on the daily life of the rural Quiché of highland Guatemala, it was necessary to take up a methodological approach not often employed in structuralist studies, but one which when used has shown great promise.[2] I began my investigation by taking up residence in a rural Quiché home and participating, when possible, in the activities that took place there. Two types of inquiry were employed. One was descriptive, recording objects and their location in the family's immediate surroundings. The other was communicative, dealing with people's impressions of the surroundings, their roles in life, and their beliefs about the nature of things outside the world of the objectively observable. On the basis of these two modes of inquiry, I formulated certain preliminary analytical ideas about the central conceptual principles that appeared in diverse domains of rural life among these Quiché agriculturalists.

These ideas were then taken back to the more articulate members of the family for their views on my analysis. The important work by other ethnographers in the area, especially Ruth Bunzel (1952) and Barbara Tedlock (1978), were also used for comparative purposes.[3] I also discussed my thoughts with a number of other Quiché Indians from the area, some like the family, followers of the old traditional (or Costumbrista) religion, and others who were converts to Reform Catholicism.[4] On the basis of this second phase of inquiry, and the various forms of confirmations I received in the course of it, the initial concepts were further clarified and my certainty of them reinforced.

Studies of the Maya have frequently made reference to their tendency to link concepts of time and space (León-Portilla 1968; J. E. S. Thompson 1970; Gossen 1972b, 1974b). It is not surprising in light of this to find time-space relations important among the Quiché Maya as well. More specifically, Gossen in his work with the Chamula Tzotzil of Chiapas has discovered that the sun is "the initial and primary symbol of ethical, spacial, and temporal order in the Chamula universe" (1972b:136). For the Quiché, a similar principle seems to be operating. More precisely, it is the solar temporal cycle that provides the primary and irreducible unit for the conceptualization of time, and it is the habitual actions and the contexts for those actions that occur in the course of a day that provide the basis for conceiving of larger and more abstract temporal and spatial domains. The primary spatial manifestations of the day cycle are the human body and the household area, as it is interaction between the people and their most immediate environment that defines the spatial context of activity on a daily basis. Thus it is the space experienced in the daily round that links space to time. Activities are defined and determined by the position of the sun, the indicator of the chronology of the day; what time it is determines what space one occupies.

This temporal cycle and its spatial connections are structurally related to larger units of time and space. The cycle of the year and of a human lifetime are metaphorical "expansions" of the day cycle, and larger spatial domains are extensions of the immediate daily ones. This tendency to link smaller units of time and space to larger ones has been noticed by Vogt (1969) and Gossen (1972b) in their studies of the Tzotzil, and can be formalized for this study by identifying two general characteristics of it: (1) larger units are made up of the smaller ones (e.g., the year is made up of days), and (2) the organizational principles structuring the smallest units will also be the organizational principles structuring the larger units.[5] In order to demonstrate how these structural principles operate, I will first explore the environment of the Quiché and describe how a day is experienced by them. From there larger domains of time and space will be presented, including religious concepts as they are spatially and temporally expressed and explained. Basic principles that structure the day will be defined and I will identify this same configuration in the "expanded" levels. Before proceeding with this analysis, a descriptive introduction to the Quiché is in order.

The Setting

The Quiché are one of over 20 linguistically differentiated Maya groups in Guatemala (Kaufman 1974: 85). They are the largest group, with over a million speakers (most of them located in the western highlands). My investigation focused primarily on the area called the Central Quiché Basin, an area circumscribed by mountains to the north and south and descending, heavily interrupted lands to the east and west.[6] Near the center of the basin, at the edge of the northern range is the *municipio* or township of Chinique, where much of my research took place. It shares with seven other *municipios* the relatively rich and extremely deep volcanic deposits that make up the majority of the surface of the basin. These unstable, differentiated soils form large "layer cake" mesas surrounded by canyons and gulleys that have been formed by the local river systems, and by steep and infertile mountain slopes. This triple division of Quiché topography, canyon (*siwan*), elevated plain (*jyup-tak'aj*), and mountain (*jyup-quichelaj*), provides the regional ecological context for the rural people.[7]

Rural Chinique, like so much of the western highlands, is predominantly occupied by dispersed settlements of subsistence farmers of the maize-beans-squash complex, a complex known throughout Guatemala as *milpa* agriculture. These agriculturalists are mostly native American descendants of the pre-Hispanic Quiché kingdom, and their lifestyles reflect a strongly continuous cultural heritage.[8] Income is supplemented by the raising of turkeys, pigs, and chickens, as well as the sale of surplus maize. Most Quiché farmers today do not have sufficient land to provide them with necessary income for the purchase of salt, sugar, chile, coffee, clothing, utensils, religious offerings, and other materials not provided by the land itself. For this reason many seek day labor locally or seasonal work on the coastal plantations to the south and southwest. Others have specialized, providing services, craft items, or items for town consumption (e.g., firewood), and/or working as petit merchants moving between the regional market towns. Sometimes a single family will have members engaged in *milpa* farming, local marketing, coastal work, local skilled specializations, and the maintaining of a neighborhood store. Rarely, however, are the families completely divorced from rural, agricultural life.

The basin has a marked rainy and dry season, typical for high altitude tropics (approximately 2000 m) at these latitudes. It rains vigorously from May to September, tapering off in the months of October and November. The rest of the year has almost no rainfall at all, except in the high mountains, and the *milpa* fields are dormant during this period. Only in a few, naturally irrigated areas can *milpa* be planted out of season.[9] The great majority of the population live on the basin surface (the *jyup-tak'aj*), where the only fallowing is the dry season itself. Higher, on the mountain slopes and ridges, the poor soil requires farmers to follow long fallow regimens. This fact, combined with the scarcity of running water, counteracts any advantage that a longer rainy season might provide in the mountains, so that the higher regions are very sparsely settled.

The canyons have a plentiful water supply but are as unsuitable for farming as the high mountain slopes. The extremely steep slopes do not allow sufficient amounts of sunlight into them, and the soils are highly eroded. The streams serve as a place to wash clothes and to bathe, and the water holes that form in the canyon banks provide a source of drinking water, so vitally important in the dry season.

The ideal rural settlement pattern places the house in the middle of the cornfield, in the center of one's property, although occasionally close kin will have houses clustered together. Houses are usually constructed with adobe brick, made from the soil in the immediate vicinity and dry pine needles, with a pine beam and tile roof. The wood is usually brought from the mountains (*quichelaj*), and a special pine with a high resin content (*quiek'chaj*, "red pine") is sought for the main beams of the roof frame. House compounds usually have a separate kitchen room, and invariably a porch or portico with a small yard in front of it provides outdoor space within the domestic arena.

Chinique township is unusual in that even the rural areas once had been in the hands of the non-Indian Ladinos, and much of it has only recently been acquired by the Quiché. Since the massive depopulation of the Santa Cruz del Quiché area shortly after the Conquest, the native population of Chinique has always been less there than in areas to the west.[10] In this century, people began to migrate from the more populous areas and to settle in Chinique. Many came to work for the local Ladinos, now a minority in the township but still strongly in control of it. Quiché influence in the town is virtually nonexistent. Unlike most "Indian" towns, the Chinique town center no longer serves as a central focal point for the periodic religious activities of the traditionalists. Poor interethnic relations combined with the control of the church by a large group of Reform Catholics (*Acción Católica*) has left the traditional Catholics of the "old ways," those who practice a religion firmly based in pre-Hispanic concepts, alienated from the town. Their religion remains rurally vital. They maintain shrines of veneration in their houses and in the hidden folds of the hills, gullies, and mountains. Here, in the home and in the shrines of the wild, the Maya church is maintained. Only in the graveyard do the different theologies come together in a single public place, as there is common respect between the living while amongst the dead.

Near the graveyard is the *cantón* or "neighborhood" of Mukunajá, as it is called. In it lives the family with whom I lived, a family I will refer to here as the Pachaacs. The patriarch, Don Lucas, is a well-respected *chuchkajau* or shaman-priest, and he heads a large and healthy family.[11] Through years of arduous labor on coastal *fincas*, he accumulated enough capital to buy a sufficient amount of land to support himself and his three adult sons with their families. When I first arrived in 1976, they were all living essentially in one house, with two of the sons not yet married and not living at home. Now there are four households, in four houses clustered close together in a line. Due to the general closeness of the family, meals are still frequently taken as a single group, at the father's home. The lack of strife between the father and the sons keeps the family from a more abrupt and total fissioning, as sometimes occurs in Quiché households.

The Structure of Action

This traditional rural Quiché family in the process of reproducing itself provided an ideal setting for grasping the nature of the daily, yearly, and life cycles. Before I describe these cycles and the human actions in them, an analytical distinction should be made between the structure of experience based upon the perception of "fixed" objects and processes, and that based upon "relational" circumstances. That is, while certain phenomena are seen in the same way by all family members in a fairly uniform way, others are viewed from different perspectives by people in different roles or domains of habitual action. Gender and age are the two main variables in the family's division of action, and these will alter their "relational" perspective in certain categories of experience. This distinction is often missed in structural analyses that are themselves positioned outside the daily life of its subjects, or in which only one action domain (adult males, usually) are represented.

The division of labor in the household is strictly maintained along age and sex lines. The most central chore of the men is working in the *milpa*, planting maize, hilling and weeding it, and overseeing its harvest. Women usually participate in field labors as they relate directly to household matters (the gathering of fodder for animals and wild plants for food supplements).[12] Women are called in Quiché the *rajau ja*, literally "owners of the house," not because they legally own the physical place but because it is their action domain. Women do leave the house, to haul water, collect plants, wash clothes, and gather kindling, but all these labors have their starting place and purpose firmly rooted in household activities. If a woman has no adult males in the house, she will usually raise money to pay for a man to work her land; such households are rare. Men, on the other hand, rarely are involved in food preparation. With no hesitation, Don Lucas once held up his hands and said, "See these . . . they do not know how to make tortillas (corn cakes)." The complementary interdependency of the sexual division of labor provides a strong economic basis for marriage.

Divisions of labor by age will be discussed presently. In order for the Quiché household to survive, it must maintain these divisions, and this division in "practices" (Bourdieu 1977) conforms to a basic principle that runs through all the conceptual domains of Quiché life. For this reason, qualities of maleness and femaleness are associated with many things that have no inherently sexual status. Similarly, age associations are attributed to processes and concepts as well. This basic structure involves a dialectical relationship between two elements: *static constancy* and *cyclical growth and decline*. Things that are unchanging are conceptually juxtaposed to those things that change, things that grow and die. The process of separation, complementary opposition, and reintegration of these two concepts characterizes the Quiché view of daily life and their beliefs about the nature of the temporal and spatial world. The sexual division, the distinction between daytime and night, the separation of the mesas from the mountains and canyons, the opposition of cornfield to forest, even the arrangement of the religious cosmos share this structural form. How this principle operates is most clearly seen in the process of a single solar cycle, and the human practices that occur in it. How the day is divided up anticipates all of the other divisions and their relationships.

The Day

The movement of the sun through the day provides the rural Quiché with a clock, an unerring and universally experienced habitual process. The beginning of the day cycle is experienced prior to dawn, in the *nim ak'ab* or "big night," when the women rise. If Venus is in its morning position (when it is called Ixtamalera, a proper name), it shines brightly in the high altitude atmosphere. As dawn approaches, frequently a mist appears, with dense fog filling the canyons and low forests. This is the coldest time and is quite chilly even in the warmest months.[13] The mist and volcanic dust often cause the sunrise to be very red as the sun crosses the horizon. It appears to come from the arid canyons and low mountains to the east, from the perspective of the Quiché Basin, and as it illuminates the region the heat burns away the fog and warms the land. As it climbs to zenith, it becomes increasingly strong and sunny areas become sharply warmer than shady ones. From its midday position, its strength begins to wane as it descends to the western horizon. If it is the rainy season, the clouds generally move in after noon but before dark, leaving a clear sunset. The sun finally "dies" and "goes into" the earth, as they say in Quiché, bringing back the darkness.

This process seen in the cosmos has its earthly counterpart in human activities. The wife wakes in the predawn chill and brings the hearth fire back to life from the coals of the previous night. The women begin to grind the kernels that have cooked all night on the grinding stones and slap together tortillas, as the men rise with the sun. After a light breakfast, the men warm themselves and leave for the fields. They don their thick straw hats against the sun's strength, and begin to work the land with their broad hoes. The women generally stay close by or in the shaded house, leaving principally to haul water or to wash clothes in the canyon. If the men are far from home, they will bring them their lunch in the fields. Otherwise the men return home to eat the noon meal.

As the sun wanes in the afternoon, or as the rain moves in, the men return home. Their strenuous physical labor, in their field or working for others, has made them tired and weak. The adult women are still active, preparing the evening meal, preparing the corn and lime for the next day's dough, and tending to the children. Their work is not as intense as that of the men, but it is more continuous. In terms of their domains of action, men are like the sun, while women are more akin to the earth, observing and complementing the solar path. The adult man's active role is one that follows a pattern of cyclical increase and decline, and his domain, the field, itself experiences an increase and decrease in heat as the day transpires. The women, on the other hand, remain predominantly around the dark and unchanging house and canyon, insulated from the sun. Their work is constant, unchanging from day to day, season to season; regardless of the time, they must keep the house swept, the water jar full, the children fed and the food attended to. Thus the complementary opposition of male cyclical and female constant action is in the day cycle analogous to daytime and night or, alternatively, sun and earth. This pattern will again emerge in the course of a year.

The Year

The solar year is defined within a framework of cyclic solar movement as well, as the visible point on the horizon where the sun appears and disappears moves northward and southward. Beginning with the period when night is longest, the increase in day length is marked with a northerly progression of the sun. The sun passes true zenith in early May at this latitude, bringing on the rainy season. It continues north until the summer solstice, then returns for a second pass through the zenith in early August, marking the end of the heaviest rains and the most arduous agricultural labor. Here the days begin again to become "shorter," with less daylight time each day until the sun has moved to its December position. As I have said, the rainy season and the dry season are very sharply divided, with the times of the longer days associated with the rains and the period with long nights associated with the dry, agriculturally dormant season. The active part of the year is conceptually linked to the active part of the day cycle, while the dormant portion of the year is associated with the night. As we shall see below, this is not just an outsider's association, but one frequently expressed by the Quiché.

In late February the first thunder is heard in the eastern mountains, signaling the coming of the rains three months later in the year. The rumbling is said to be associated with the drying up of the springs. The mountain rain spirits are said to pull the water from the ground, loading the clouds with it until the rainy season, in the nearby mountain peaks. At this time, the clear sky begins slowly to fill with dust and the smoke from the burning of fields. At this time the year is very old (*nim' rij*, "big, mature"). The changing of the Mam or year bearer happens at this time as well.[14] The very first sprinkles reach the basin about the time of Easter. After a pause, the rains arrive in earnest in late April or early May. The "Day of the Cross," May 3, is considered the ideal time for the rains (this is the approximate day the sun reaches first zenith at these latitudes), but the farmers will wait to be sure the *nim jab* or "big rain" has come, by seeing if the rains continue several days in succession.[15]

With the coming of rain, the new "young year" begins (*alaj junab*). The first three months have the heaviest rainfall, which tends to be almost daily (in the afternoon), with two 8–10 day dry spells in July and August. By late August, the volume of rain decreases, and the pattern of afternoon rain begins to be replaced by rain at night. The days begin to become shorter and with frequent periods of mist and drizzle in the months of September and October. By the end of October or early November, around the "Day of the Dead," the rain abates and the long drying-out process begins.

Solar rebirth is associated with Easter by the Quiché, for it is the time when Jesus (the sun spirit or bearer) ascends into the heavens and reinstates the correct moral order (see the story of Jesus below). The year becomes young again, as the hard rains fall (rain is conceived of as masculine), to die in the fall when the Quiché honor and "feed" their dead. The month of October is the time when the dead walk about on the earth, observing the living. This will be discussed further below. It is apparent already that the year is conceived of in terms of day and lifetime metaphors.

The labor domain division along lines of gender, separating the male increase/decrease from the constant female, is present in the yearly round. Adult men begin the agricultural year with the light work of burning the old cornstalks, just before the rain. Then with the rains, they must put out tremendous amounts of labor, working to keep pace with the growing corn. To fall behind, to plant a week late, to weed too late, these errors could have great consequences for the maize crop later on in the year. Only proper timing will guarantee a good yield. By mid-August, the corn has reached its full height, and little more work is needed. No more weeding is necessary for it would disturb the roots.

During the dry season, apart from working for others, there are few chores for the men. This is the time when new houses are built and old ones repaired. This is when large wood is cut and cleared. With the exception of a few moist areas, there are no plants grown in this time period. At least since colonial times, this "work drought" has helped to encourage highland people to migrate to the coastal plantations of the piedmont, to pick cacao and later coffee, cane, cotton, and other tropical products.[16] By Easter, the time when families are reunited, everyone returns to prepare their fields. For many years the Pachaac family followed this pattern.

The women have few chores that are differentiated by the seasons. Child rearing, food preparation, cleaning, and hauling water are constant throughout the year. They may help the men in the fields by gathering and sorting weeds, but food-gathering activities are as constant as the supply, one week mustard, one week mushrooms, a third week blackberries. Women tend to weave in the dry season more frequently, for there is more time and it is more pleasant when there is no mud about. But most of the scheduling of female activities is not correlated with the solar year, for they are either daily or determined by the cycles of infants or the moon (as will be seen below).

Women do sometimes participate in the planting, but they never plant maize. They will follow behind the men and plant companion plants like squash, beans, and potatoes. They never handle the broad hoe but use a pointed stick instead. The Pachaacs plant seven varieties of maize, being careful to keep the seed types segregated. This is important because each type has a slightly different growing season, and work time must be spatially scheduled in the field. Fast-growing varieties are planted in the soil that is most elevated and exposed to the sun, while longer types are planted in lower, moister areas with more shade. Two types, a very fast and a very slow (called *cuarentena* and *sakpor*), are planted close to the house to prevent theft. White varieties are generally the first to be harvested, then the yellow types, and finally the pinto and black ones.

Seeds are planted in rows demarcated by the old ones, with the old ridges becoming the spaces between the new ones. This utilizes the topsoil washed away from the old hills as the base soil for new seedlings. The troughs formed by the old rows also provide a water catchment to channel the new rains to the seeds, and to prevent erosion of the soil and the fragile new plant. It is not until the plant is some 30 cm high that the old ridges are scraped up and piled around the base of the new plants, forming new ridges. Approximately five seeds are planted together in each hill, with one meter between plant clusters. The roots intertwine as they grow, making the plants resistant against strong winds, and the space between them allows the companion plants and the useful weeds to grow.

Two weedings, the *nabe chac* ("first work") and the *camul*, are done to pile up earth to form new rows and to selectively weed out the unwanted plants, turning them into the soil. This is the most difficult task of the *milpa* labors of the men, for not only must they move large amounts of moist, muddy earth, but they must be increasingly careful not to destroy wanted weeds. They must be sure that no area gets too far behind in the weed cleaning either, or the corn will suffer.

Harvest begins in November (except the very early varieties, which are a recent innovation) and extends through early January. At harvest time maize, like men on a daily basis, returns to the house, where it is stored in the attic, called the *tem*. *Tem* literally means "seat," and it is the same term as is used for the chairs that men sit upon in the house. The corn "sits" in the house through the dry season, providing the major food source for the year and the seed for future years. The Pachaacs use their own corn for seed and do not purchase any, for they understand that each corn type becomes acclimatized to a specific ecological niche, and does not do well in foreign climes.[17] Over twenty-five different seed types are in this one municipality alone.

The coming of the rain in the year cycle, like the coming of the sun in the day cycle, introduces the active, cyclic growth-and-decline element into the previously static, dormant, and constant environment. The rain appears to play an analogous role in the year to the sun's role in a day. That is, to start weakly at the beginning, then to become strong in the middle period, and wane at the end. During the rainy season, people will say that the strong and hot sun will call the greatest rains, which will arrive right after the sun's greatest heat. Similarly, the greatest heat of the year just precedes the cooling rains.

In the context of the agricultural cycle, the dry season is like night, and the rainy season is akin to the dynamics of the day. Similarly, the life cycle of an individual has its dormant and dynamic periods, so that metaphorically the solar daily round encompasses a lifetime. This may seem to crosscut the division of men into solar and women into night/earthy domains, but none of these semantic domains is neat and tidy. Very often two organizing schemas will collide or contradict each other, which becomes a problem for the analytic interpreter. It does not seem to be a problem for the people, however. The fact that women are both constant as housekeepers and dynamic as producers of children is resolved by the existence of a second calendar, one which is divorced from the patterns of the solar year. While the solar year measures the growth cycle of maize, this "human" calendar measures the gestation cycle of people.[18]

Human Lifetime

This calendar of the observed time of human gestation is also based upon days, but a complete cycle of them is only 260 days long. This calendar, well known to scholars of the Classic Maya and Contact-period Mesoamerica by the name of *tzolkin* or *tonalpoualli*, combines 20 day names or *rajau k'ij* ("lords of the days") with 13 numerical coefficients. Since they are not multiples, every combination is made once and once only before the 260-day round is complete. This calendar, called by the Quiché the *ajilabal k'ij*, "the count of the days," or *uwach k'ijal*, "the face of the days," has two major uses for the Pachaac family. One, as I have said, is to determine the date of delivery for pregnant women.[19] The moon is said to determine menstruation (*retal ic'*, "the sign of the moon"), and the day that the sign does not arrive with the moon will be the same day name of the calendar as the child's birth date. Midwives, like Lucas's wife, utilize this calculus to prepare their clients and themselves for the birth process.

The day one is born on has great meaning for the Quiché, for one's fate is determined by it. In keeping with the primary principle of the day, one's birthday is a condensation of one's lifetime. The characteristics of the day "owner" or "ruler" and its number will determine the nature of the newborn child. A girl born on 3 *came* is said to be a good midwife, a man born on 8 *batz* could become a great diviner, it is said. Divination is the other major use of the calendar—not just to assess one's character on the basis of the date of birth, but to divine with a system of sortilege which days are involved in one's future circumstances.[20]

Shamans are diviners. Called *chuchkajau* ("mother-Our-Lord") or *Ajk'ij* (profession marker + "the day," "day-man"), they act as both priestlike officiators at religious events of all description and as curers. Their curing power derives from their divining talents, which they learn to develop if it has been determined that they are to be initiated. Election to this role can be divine, with signs being derived from illness, dreams, or a birth date that determines the calling. Some, like Don Lucas, inherited the role, but usually other divine confirmations are necessary before a father will initiate a son or daughter. Don Lucas claims he was saved from a life of alcoholism by the call of the "beans."

The beans are little red seeds from the *tzite'* tree (*palo pito* in Spanish, *Erythrina corallodendron L.*), which are wrapped in a little bundle with quartz crystal stones, coins, jadite pre-Hispanic artifacts, and other indestructible items. This bundle is formally presented to the diviner upon being trained and initiated, and it is this paraphernalia he (or she) will manipulate to assess the particular days that speak to the issue at hand. Barbara Tedlock (1978) thoroughly discusses the divination process in the Quiché town of Momostenango, and it is very similar to Chinique.

The divining process is somewhat long and involved, but a basic outline goes as follows: The *tzite'* seeds are separated from the other objects (which act as witnesses) and are put in a pile. A prayer is said, and a handful of the seeds are separated from the pile. These are spread out on the divining surface, always a little table with a cloth covering it, and then counted out in groups of four, like a bank teller counting pennies. Each bean is a corner of a day, and each cluster represents a whole day. If the count comes out with the last group being two or, ideally, four, then the beans wish to speak.

With the "faces of the days" laid out, the diviner begins to count through the calendar, starting with the current day, the day of a portentous dream, or some other significant day. When he gets to the last day, this is one indicator of the meaning of the response. This is usually done four times, and it is the combination of the four day names and their corresponding numbers that provides the core of the diviner's interpretation. *Caipa'* or heat lightning is said to jump in the diviner's body when counting through certain days, signifying certain additional messages pertinent to the outcome. On the basis of these day meanings and a knowledge of the condition of the patient, the *chuchkajau* is able to discover the nature of the problem his client has, and can offer help in resolving the difficulty. Diviners are used by the traditionalists to decide upon issues relating to marriage, travel, illness, business, unusual occurrences, even to interpret dreams.

Through divination, the "human calendar" not only charts out the birth fate but the nature of one's fate throughout a lifetime. While the fortune of corn is measured by the Christian calendar of saint days, the fortune of the people is measured out with the diviner's bundle.[21]

Like the wee morning hours when the family wakes and warms up around the fire, like Easter when the family is together, the earliest years of a Quiché child are spent in the protected environment of the home, with the women. Sunrise and the onset of the heavy rains are analogous to the division of the sexes in early adolescence. As a child, one is allowed to play a great deal, free from adult labor roles. Most tasks assigned to small children are undifferentiated by gender, chores like looking for berries, gathering mushrooms, carrying weeds for the animals (Lucas has some pigs), or tending other smaller children. Generally these roles are in the female labor domain, however, and boys are not differentiated in terms of action domains until they begin to help their fathers in the fields.

As adolescent boys learn the tasks of farming, young girls learn the female tasks. Each becomes familiar with a distinct and complementary action domain. Each day the young man leaves the house, to work for his father—eventually he leaves the household altogether to form his own. Most young women marry and leave, to set up their model of the past home. In this way the productive and reproductive aspects of the domestic unit form themselves anew. The dialectical interaction of the solar male and lunar and earthly female create the conditions for fertility. The sun is strongest at noon, the rain is fiercest in June and July, and the productive and reproductive potential of the couple is strongest in this parallel period. From puberty to the late thirties the central concern of a rural Quiché couple is corn and child raising. Here the opposition of labor domains is most pronounced.

The birth of the first son marks the beginning of a change in adult roles. This first grandson is called *caxel*, literally "replacement," and is thought to inherit attributes of the patriarch. This also occurs in the case of women. Just as Don Lucas and his wife became grandparents, his labor output began to wane somewhat, and she stopped bearing children. By the time the *caxel* was five years old, three of his four sons had gotten married and had settled close by. His wife was not going to have more children. It was time to divide up the land.

Land inheritance is a very touchy issue among the rural Quiché, especially in these times of high population density, high land prices, and general land scarcity. In order to help maintain harmonious relations between the children and to prevent the splitting up of kin groups, it is frequently the custom for a man to divide up his land as soon as the majority of his children are grown and married. This tends to dispel the tension between father and grown sons, which can become great due to the conflict between working for wages outside the family and working in the family for only the promise of future inheritance.[22] In most Quiché families, only men inherit their father's land, but in the Pachaac case there were sufficient holdings to assign a piece to each of his two daughters. These parcels were smaller than the one given to the oldest son, who typically inherits the ancestral house and the largest plot.

So, one sunny day in March, Don Lucas got out the rope cord and measured out square *cuerdas* of land (thirty *varas* of 33 inches to a side), making sure they were true squares by measuring diagonals from the opposed corners. He was careful to be sure that each lot had all the varieties of soil and incline, and that all the pieces had wooded areas. In this way, the patriarch left himself landless. In a sense, Don Lucas had renounced the domain of the field and sun, to return again to the domain of the house, devoting much of his time to shamanistic activities in service to the community, and less to the direct productive role now inherited by his children. In parallel fashion, his wife renounced the reproductive domain to exert more authority over the family and to dedicate herself to her community duty as a midwife.

In the old couple's divestment of their productive and reproductive roles, they begin to act as intermediaries between the spiritual Mundo or sacred earth and the productive community. She dedicates herself to the sacred calling of bringing new infants into the world, and to curing with herbs and the sweat bath, and he to spiritual curing, divining, life-crisis officiation, and the mediating between the living and the place of the dead. All of these roles are associated with the constant, the dormant, nighttime world, the dry, the dead, the house principle, all those things juxtaposed to the male principles of sun, rain, maize field, and overt masculine physical strength, and the complimentary and corresponding female role as child producer. In this way they return to the domain of the earth metaphorically before they return to it in death literally.

The androgeny of youth returns with old age. Old people are said to be "dry," like the dry season, like the late-in-the-day sun. The polite way to discuss those who have died is to say *xcopan ruk'ij*, literally "it arrived, over there, his sun (or day)," or "his sun has set." The dead are conceived of as being in the west (the location of graveyards with respect to town centers in the Quiché area) where the sun sets, and the unborn are "up" in the east, where the sun and rainy season rains are "born." While the old women return to receive the newborn as midwives, the old men return to mediate the fate of humans from their birth to the end of their lives, paying the sky and earth deities to not "shorten the day" of their clients.[23] In their role as community as well as family grandparents, they prepare themselves for return to the sacred domain of the earth, divorced again (like children) from the realm of sexual and sensual desires and ready to become an earth ancestor. I will return to this topic in the context of the discussion of religion.

At death the cycle is complete, just as it becomes complete with sleep, and with agricultural dormancy in their respective temporal levels. The dead leave completely the material world of the flesh and become just spirits, living in the darkness like stars in the heavens. As the dry maize ears are laid up to be stored through the dormant season, this is the time to travel to the cemeteries and address the Lord of the Dead (*rajau tak xcam winak*) and the deceased relatives. One serves an offertory "meal" of candles, incense, and liquor to pay back the dead for their aid in cajoling the sacred earth to allow a good yield. At the end of the agricultural year, the earth spirits in charge of the bringing of the rain, the solar avatars (Jesus and the saints, the ancient Quiché heroes), and the Earth itself are "paid," "fed" for their aid in sustaining another year of life. In death, a lifetime is paid back to the Mundo by the feeding of the body to it.[24]

Beliefs about death will be discussed below, but one thing should be made clear at this time. Not only do they believe that the dead "feed" the Mundo, bringing each member of the population out of this world and into the other one, but they point out that the end of a day here on the surface of the earth is the beginning of a day for the dead. This underground "mirror" place of the night sun preserves the authority structure of the surface world, so that those elders who have attained advanced office in the community will maintain it after death. Their office, their sacrifice to the community, is viewed as a form of purification—one necessary for a smooth transition. Those who know no prayers have a chicken killed at the time of their funeral, because it is said that the chicken has no sin, no errors, since it does not "mistreat" anything. It is like an infant. At the time the dead person arrives at the entrance to the other world, the chicken can "call" a prayer that will allow them to pass through. So not only do people become physically and behaviorally more like infants at the time of old age and death, but it is their ideal that one should become pure like a child at the time of death, in order to return to the sacred earth. If one follows this cycle correctly, there is the promise of power in the afterworld. Those who have learned the prayers and obligations, the calendar and its esoteric knowledge, are the most prepared for their journey to the west.

Before discussing Quiché religious beliefs in greater detail, I wish to introduce briefly the spatial domains of daily life. These domains appear to recapitulate the basic principle of the solar cycle, in ways similar to the temporal ones. Divisions manifest in space tend to reflect this same opposition of the constant to the cyclical and changing, at the level of the human body, the house and household, and the larger ecological setting as well. Mention has already been made of this topic with regard to east-west orientation, and the contrast of the earth surface to both the sky and the Underworld place of the dead. The immediate places that act as the setting for daily life will also serve as a framework for the understanding of spatial relationships in the Quiché religious cosmos.

Spatial Domains

The first and most reduced spatial domain is the human body, and its primary domain of action is the house and household area. The body is used as a spatial referent with regard to fixed things, including the house parts. For example, the door of the house is called *uchi ja*, "the mouth of the house," and the porch posts are called "legs" (*racan ja*). The house as a spatial metaphor tends to operate more as a representation of relational domains of space, one that is viewed within the context of changing relations of age and gender. An example of this would be the association of the house with the female action domain, as something viewed from within by women and from the outside by adult men. To the very young, the house is the first spatial universe of experience outside of the body itself. For the old man, it is where one is received again when the domain of the fields is passed on to children.

The body is divided into an upper and lower part, with a "path" connecting them running from the mouth to the anus. In the upper part, air circulates down through the mouth to the heart (*ucux*) and back out into the sky. The lower body has air coming up through the feet and legs, which also circulates through the heart, and then returns to the ground. The heart is considered the location of the spirit or soul, and is kept in contact with the upper and lower deities. In fact there are two souls, one on the front side (*angele ajmac*) and one on the back (*angele chijenel*), the first a sinner and the latter a guardian. These two souls play important roles in the dream state and in death, as will be described below.

The body is also divided into left and right sides, the left being *u mox* (*u* = possessive "its," *mox* = "crazy, stupid") and the right, *uwiquik'ab* (pos. + *wi* = "the head, chief," *quik'ab* = "hand"). In certain contexts, such as divining, signs on the body are associated with a negative outcome when on the left and a positive outcome when on the right. The diviner's body acts like a microcosm of the world body, picking up little heat lightning signals in the divining process, along the surface of the skin. The directional terms are the same as those for the body, with north being the right and south being the left. As we shall see, this arrangement fits the ecological, historical, and cultural order of Quiché spatial relations.

The house (*ja*), with its anthropomorphic parts, is believed to be possessed by a living spirit. The current residents of a rural, traditional Quiché home believe that the house still belongs to its original owner, to whom they pay rent in the form of offerings of candles and incense. Only in this way can peace be made with the house spirit, so that it will not harm them. They claim that without occupants to provide gifts to the ancient owner, a house "dies" and collapses. Since the presence of the smoky fire and the cleaning activities of the women are what prevent major insect infestations of the roof timber, they are correct in their observation.

The house is the first area of experience for the newborn child (beyond the mother's body), and it is the location of most major social events. It is the spiritual seat of the family, as well as the storehouse of its material possessions. For the Pachaacs, it serves as a place for sleeping, storing maize and belongings, cooking and preparing food, as a shelter against the rain, and as a "church" at the family level. For the child, the four walls and corners of the house, with the earthen adobe walls and its beam roof, are the prototype of larger spatial domains.

The Pachaac family houses all follow the same general floor plan, and the spatial orientation of the houses is virtually identical to the other rural Quiché homes in the area and in most of the basin.[25] There is usually one main room and a kitchen, the kitchen either attached to an outer wall of the main structure or as a small room integral to it. This second design is employed by the Pachaacs. It is a rule without exception that the residence has its door(s) facing the west or, alternatively, the south. If the kitchen is part of the main structure, it will invariably be on the left side, as one faces the house. The fact that the norm is to put the back of the house to the east or north, even when it means ignoring a beautiful view, indicates that there is some point to the orientation.

Two factors are involved here. First, there is a functional ecological consideration. Much of the strong wind and rain in the basin runs along the solar path, coming out of the east or northeast. To avoid exposure to the predominant winds, the logical house position is to face to the west or south. Also, during the rainy season, there is usually a late afternoon sun even after a heavy rain and facing the portico towards it would allow for things to be dried in the sun if they were hung in the porch area. If the house is facing west or south, then it would be only logical that the kitchen would be to the left side, so that the wind out of the east would not blow smoke into the main part of the house. These are all explanations offered.

But there are other explanations as well, having to do with making the house strong and orienting it in the proper way. It appears that the ecological functions of house orientation correlate with cultural concepts of directionality that are linked to the solar metaphor. This is not to argue that the ecological circumstances determined, in some mechanistic way, the ideational constructs of the Quiché, nor is it to argue for the primacy of cultural principles of belief as isolated from the environment of material significance for them. It is the long-standing dialogue between the people and their ecosystem that resulted in the dovetailing of environmentally functional and culturally logical constructs. In order to better understand the cultural logic of household space and orientation, more description is necessary. This spatial organization will both fulfill the ecological needs of daily existence and conform to cultural principles that are to be found in diverse domains of Quiché cultural life.

The household space under the tile roof can be divided into four parts: the kitchen, the porch, the altar/storage room, and the attic. The kitchen is the place of most household activities. It is the hearth, the place where all but the most formal meals are taken, where children are born, and where the day begins and ends. All cooking is done over a fire set directly upon the earthen floor. The tortilla griddle (*comal*) sits on three baked clay hearthstones (*xcup*), with pots fit between the stones and protruding logs, to heat water for corn *atol*, coffee, or other beverages. The active nature of this area and its secular or domestic fire contrasts it sharply with the altar room. From the standpoint of the female domain of action, this is the heart or center of the house, and from the perennial position of women, the kitchen is usually on the right-hand side of the house.

From the male position, viewing the house from the *milpa* fields, the right-hand position is taken by the altar room. Here is where the formal meals are taken or outside visitors are received. Festival occasions are celebrated here, with the women congregating in the kitchen but the men always in the room with the altar. It is also where, in the "house seat," the corn is stored. Since only men sit in wooden seats (*tem*), they are linguistically associated with the attic (*tem*, also) and occupationally connected with its contents. Like them, the corn is elevated in the house, on a wooden platform. Here the active, male principle is at rest or in ritual posture before the house saint, and the fire, in the form of candle and incense offerings, is of a ritual nature.

A house altar itself maintains a condensed form of the Quiché cosmos and ecosystem. Like the house, it faces the west/south, with its back ideally to the east. In south-facing houses, it tends to be located in the northeast corner, while in west-facing houses it tends to face due west, and sit in the center of the east wall. Lucas says that all houses have altars, that they are the first thing constructed on a future house site, and that they are the spiritual location of the ancestral owner of the house. It is like a hearth of the primordial, ancestral elements of the home, associated with the resting-place of corn, the night, ritual and public ceremonial occasions (which happen generally at night), and with the sacred Mundo. This is also the place where all activities of the shaman, including divination, take place. With the exception of the maize in the attic, no food is stored here.

The altar consists of a high table covered with colorful material or plastic, on which is placed a wooden box with a glass window in the front. Peering out from within this *tiox ja* ("god house") is an image of a white-faced saint. In front of the box is a series of clay candle holders. Beneath this table, is a second one, just above the floor and attached to the same table legs. Upon this lower table are a group of odd-shaped stones of diverse sizes, called the *tak abaj* (the "stones"), or *camajuiles* (the sacred "idol stones"; prior to the Conquest, this was the name for God in Quiché, but the word was suppressed by the friars and replaced with Dios, or in Quiché *tiox*). As will be seen below, the stones are representations of the perpetual and constant nature of the wilds, the animals, associated with the 260-day calendar, the ancestors and metanymically, with the canyons. The saint house has associations with the solar calendar (celebrations for saints follow the Christian 365-day count), with the celestial path, and metanymically with the high mountain wood from which it has been carved.

Opposite the altar is another, smaller table. Against the west wall is a male figure dressed in a black, Latin suit with a red tie, a bag of money in one hand and a staff of authority in the other. Called San Simón, this saint is associated by the Pachaacs with the forces of the devil and the Ladinos. He is used to address and ward off witchcraft. Being well versed in the ways of evil, he is prayed to when one has been sinful or antisocial in some way, for unlike the pure saints he will understand and sympathize.

It can be seen from the altar complex layout that certain directionally bound themes are being expressed. The saint within his or her house faces the same direction as the house, the town church, even the proper direction for sleeping—with the back to the sunrise and facing the setting sun. This is, as I was told, the direction of life and health. Contrary to this is the direction of death. The dead are buried with their head in this direction, and San Simón is associated with the "dead" Underworld (Xibalbaj).

When looking at the way the house is constructed, this same pattern emerges. First the place must be selected by a local shaman and consecrated with a ritual that establishes the outline of the foundation and the place of the altar. Then the adobe walls are erected. Wooden beams, that have been cut and dried in advance, are then installed, to form the structural support for the roof tiles. All the wood elements have specific names and must be arranged in a certain ordered manner. These names reflect both age stratification and classification by sex. For example, the main beams that run the length of the roof and rest on the triangular end pieces are male, with the lowest being associated with young boys, the second and middle one associated with young men, and the third with the father of the house. But even more crucial to house positioning is the fact that these beams must be directionally oriented. The main beam at the top of the house, called a ridge pole or *rajual ja* ("lord of the house") in Quiché, must be installed with its base (*rakan che*, "leg of the tree") to the east and its point (*wajolom che*, "head of the tree") to the west. This is explained as an extension of the general rule that all posts, tool handles, even corn to be roasted, must be "upright," with the base to the ground or the east. Otherwise, all these things would "stand on their heads" and not be strong.

This feet-east and head-west arrangement is the same as the position for the deceased, and is also how the Santo Mundo, the personification of the earth deity, is said to lie. This is a spatial indicator of the Quiché conception of the house as an entity related to the dead ancestors and the earth deity, and opposed to the solar world of the field and human life. The division within the house between the permanent and primordial altar room and the secular, more temporary kitchen reflects this dichotomy internally. The kitchen is the active and periodically visited domain, where the solar day begins, measures a midpoint, and ends, and where the daily activities of the household most frequently occur. The altar room has static (storage) or ritual roles relating predominantly to the 260-day calendar. (It may be more than coincidence that the stored maize ideally lasts about

260 days, in the attic, between harvest and first corn of the following year.) The altar room, being the base of the house, is the area most associated with the earth deity, even though it is less associated with female activity and more connected to the activities of ritual celebration and offerings overseen by men. While the house as a whole appears in the static and earthbound domain (as opposed to the fields), internally it can be divided between more static and more active areas as well. I will return to the internal division of the house and its relationship to secular and religious functions.

The roof-beam orientation provides a vertical reading of the horizontal plane of the house, again in keeping with the sun/earth dichotomy. The altar room is at the base of the house, the "down" position of the unchanging. The kitchen is in the "up" and solar position, associated with cyclical daily activities. Some kitchens are constructed separate from the main domestic structure. They invariably are to the west, as would be expected from the schema presented here, and face the main house.

The vertical dimension of the house is also present in its very materials. Up to the level of the *tem*, the base of which forms the ring beam that runs around the top of the walls, the house is made of hardened mud, made into adobe from the earth nearby. The only intrusion of wood into this "below" portion of the house is the way out of it, the door leading outside. From the attic floor up to the roofing tiles (tiles replaced the increasingly scarce grass thatch in this century), the structure is all wood. The beams are procured from the *quichelaj*, the mountainous woods that rise above the Pachaac house to the south. The house serves as a place of uniting the physical elements of the earth and the elevated environment of the resin-rich pine trees, just as the altar unites the spiritual domains of the earth and its associated symbols with the elevated, tree-associated domain of the saints. The material universe of the house, the action domains within it, and the ritual microcosm of the house altar within it, these analytically diverse domains weave together to provide the fabric of Quiché daily experience, an experiential process that is perceived and conceived of within the context of the solar cycle and the static earth.

The spatial dimensions of the house extend themselves into larger domains. The house provides a constant part of the agricultural environment, juxtaposed to the cyclically changing *milpa* that rises up and then shrivels in time with the yearly solar round. Houses do not appear with corn but precisely when the corn is dry and the agricultural year is dead, and their construction is governed by the rhythms of human life cycles, not solar ones. At a larger level, the rural lands of the Quiché remain stable and unchanging as compared to the town centers (from which innovations are introduced), and the highlands are more unchanging than the lowlands and the Ladino cities. As I have already suggested, the religious domains of abstract space will tend to follow this arrangement as well.

The spatial expression of the solar metaphor also weaves back into the dimension of time. The direction of the east places it in a temporally prior position, while the west becomes linked with the future, in certain contexts. In daily life, women, who are associated with the lower position spatially, are always up prior to the men.[26] They are also associated with the 260-day birth calendar and the earth stones, symbolically prior to the birth of the sun and moon, as described both in the Conquest period *Popul Vuh* and in contemporary creation accounts, as will be seen below.[27] East and north are prior places for the sun in the day begun at dawn and the year begun at Easter, respectively. The sun then moves west and south in its daily and yearly round, bringing an end to the cycle. It is easy to understand why the Quiché think of the dead as in the west. From the standpoint of the living, the dead are in the "future" place, a place they will visit when this cycle is over.

For Don Lucas, even his outdoor shrine arrangement fits within this spatial order. The main shrine for his household is the *warabal ja* (*waraj* = "to pray in vigil," *bal* = locative, *ja* = "house"), the caretaker shrine for the house. The root of the word is derived from *war*, "to sleep," and the term is related to the concepts of where the house spirit rests, the bed of the house and the foundation of the home.[28] This shrine is located predictably to the north and below the fields and house, in a shallow gully that marks the border of the fields and the woods. The "earth table" (*mesa' rech mundo*) is in the center of the shrine, a rectangular cleared space about a meter-and-one-half wide and a meter deep. To the east, facing west, are a series of stones and one stone cross. These are the *camahuil* stones, representative of the earth spirits. Here Don Lucas asks for protection for those in the house, for abundance, and for the birth of new life. Here the Mundo is witness to the rites of marriage, to the initiation of new shamans, and to the asking for the "birth" of the rainy season.[29]

To the west of this first shrine, above it and facing it, is a second, called the *Ichujyup-tak'aj* or the *pa c'ulel* ("at the mountain-plain" and "at the enemy"). This shrine is much less used, and is basically employed for begging forgiveness for fights, sexual transgressions, lies, and other moral errors that might lead to illness or death. Like its indoor counterpart San Simón, it is also associated with witchcraft.

The reduplication of shrines is common among the Quiché.[30] Just as there is an indoor and outdoor house altar, there are internal and external shrines for the town church, and even for the mountain altar site of *sakiribal*, some four hours walk away.[31] Generally the outside, lower shrine is visited first, but most ritual events requiring the use of the outside site

will use both in series. I am not certain of all of the reasons behind this
dual altar system, but it seems quite in conformity with the dualism related to the day/night, house/field, and cultural space/natural space divisions. The second pair of altars in the wilds do demarcate the border
between the domesticated space of house and fields and the uncultivated,
natural realm of the canyon below and the forests and mountains above.
Since it is equally important to remain in touch with the spirits of the
wild as well as those of the house, fields, and the ancestors, this dual
arrangement may have to do with this. Don Lucas suggests this when, in
response to my questions about the altar locations, he explains that while
the house altar has more sway with his particular *santo* and for minor
family issues, it is the *warabal ja* that has the greatest pull with the forces
of the Mundo. Even though there is a Mundo part of the house altar, the
"earth table" is the place where the earth can be properly "fed." *Kol pom*,
a pine-resin incense of local origin, is only used in the outdoor altar, burned
in a pile in front of the table. Since the use of this incense as a vehicle to
carry prayer is necessary for many rites, and *kol pom* is a transformed
product of the wilds (the only noncultivated, nonmanufactured offering),
this points to the conclusion suggested above. While the home houses the
particular saint (which is above it, and comes down to "visit"), the place
of vigil for the house is the receiving (or "resting") place for the spirit of
the house (which is above it and is called "down"). The material house is
a locally made unification of the elements (water, earth, wood of pine) of
the spiritual earth essence: the spirit of the *siwan* (canyon), the *jyup-tak'aj*
(mountainous plain), and the *quichelaj* (high forest).

This small exploration into the spatial domains of the Pachaac family
is certainly not exhaustive nor complete, but before further discussion of
the Quiché conceptions of space and time can be addressed, more descriptive information is necessary to help the reader grapple with terms
and concepts more and more frequently used. Many aspects of religion
and worldview have been introduced in the course of the presentation of
Quiché rural life. It is time to turn to this sphere of discussion, to attempt
an adequate interpretive translation of Don Lucas's religious beliefs. Some
of these are revealed through direct dialogue with him and his family,
others through the veil of tales, dreams and their interpretation, accounts
of personal experiences and those of others, observations during work
and travel, and even through what is not said.

Religion

The religious belief system of the Pachaac family is complex and, as I
warned the reader above, not entirely systematic nor noncontradictory.

Furthermore, it is a false artifice of the ethnographer to distill out the category of "religious beliefs" from the larger context of beliefs about the nature of the world as a unitary whole containing spiritual and material aspects. This is why terms such as Mundo, *santo*, and *camahuil*, and religious callings like that of the diviner and the midwife have invaded the previous presentation of rural Quiché daily life. However, there is a distinction made by traditionalists like Don Lucas between the description of the material and the spiritual world, despite their close relationship.

First I will present a spatial description of the spiritual world, as it has been described to me. It will be followed by a brief enumeration of the categories of spiritual beings that interact in this space, and finally a paraphrasing of the creation story. This will present the context for a final discussion of Quiché concepts of time and its spatial environs, and how these bring the discussion back to the solar cycle.

The Quiché may be said to have one god, two gods, three gods, and a plethora of gods at the same time without contradiction. In a sense, every dialectical interaction between an active element and its contextualizing environment may be considered deified. Trees, maize, moths, mountains, clouds, even fleas have their "essence" spirits or lords (*rajau*). But fairly clear distinctions can be made between these in terms of their importance to humans, and their centrality to Quiché religiousness. No more central dynamic dualism exists for Don Lucas than the Mundo, the spiritual embodiment of the fertile earth, and the sun, personified as Jesus, with his court of sky-bound companions.

The sky is the uppermost spatial domain, sometimes referred to as a single place (*kaj* or *la gloria*), or as a three-tiered space with three corresponding subsurface levels plus the face of the earth (*uwach uleu*), together called the *wucup ch'u-mil*, the "seven stars." It is the place of Jesus and his kin, a place that the living cannot reach. Below this is the *bendesi'*, the earth surface up to where the clouds travel. Below the surface of the earth is the Santo Mundo, or simply Mundo. This is a layer of fertile or accessible earth, with its special altars located frequently at the tops or edges of raised mounds, hills, or mountains. Certain plains (*tak'aj*), canyons, and caves also have their Mundo shrines. In the Mundo reside the *tak xcam-winak'*, the deceased ancestors, as well as multiple manifestations of the Mundo spirit. Below the Mundo is that barren place made famous by the *Popul Vuh*, Xibalbaj (Don Lucas, in keeping with the local accent, calls it Xbilbaj). There reside the evil saints akin to the devil and San Simón, as well as an evil serpent and the most despicable of souls.

Beyond the distant mountains, beyond the most distant countries Don Lucas can name, lies the sea, in all directions. The sea is the spatial and temporal border. Those who claim to come from across the sea (like many tourists do) are considered to be from another world in a previous creation. This has given rise to a lively mythology about the perennial "gringo" as a creature from another place in time, a survivor from a failed and amoral creation. At the fringes of the Quiché cosmos, time past and distant space meet.

The prior nature of the sea conforms to its location "below" the dry land, and in that the sea is believed to have once covered the fertile ground (see the creation story below). It is also the action of the sacred Mundo of pulling up and filtering the water from the sea that brings rainwater to the spring clouds that hover around the mountain peaks to the northeast of the Pachaacs. Xibalbaj is also prior, for its people once held power on the surface of the earth, before the ascent of the sun.

I have presented this "layer-cake" model of religious space, much as has been presented by other Maya scholars, as a static, synchronic arrangement, which it is not.[32] This is how it is in the daytime, but not at night. For when night arrives here, it is the beginning of the day in the Santo Mundo of the ancestors. Don Lucas remarked that those with urgent prayers for the ancestors can present them with confidence at midnight because the dead are sure to be home eating lunch at that time. The temporal chronology of the day, so precisely perceived by the Pachaacs, dissolves with night as the spatial distinction between *bendesi'* and Mundo also becomes blurred. The dead can sometimes walk among the living at this time, and many an earthbound malevolent spirit is abroad in the dark. The personified spirit of the Mundo, which possesses the body of the *aj mes* (the highest shamanistic rank in the central Quiché area), can only do so after dark, after the sun has withdrawn its territorial laws of order. Then the four earth-lord manifestations can "come down" into the recipient, and act as mediators for community problems and intermediaries between the living and the dead.[33]

People also visit the dead at night through their dreams. The reader may remember from the opening quote that Don Lucas went to the graveyard in his dream, and talked with the Lord of the Dead. The fact that a human lifetime is measured in the course of a single day in the nocturnal world of dreams is not contradictory for Don Lucas to the claims he has made that our night is their day. This is because time cycles themselves shift about at night—many people claim they can travel through time, past or future, in the form of the *angele chijenel*, or guardian soul, while they are asleep. It could be said that every night the spatio-temporal order collapses and the dead and the living intermingle, and that with every dawn the cosmos is put back into its proper order.

Before the arrival of the sun, there was no change. People did not die, nor eat, nor make love, nor even distinguish between the morally good and evil. There was a uniform gray fog everywhere and people trudged about ankle deep in filthy seawater. The first people who tried to "make the creation" were the old couple, Padre Eterno and the Virgen Trinitaria. But they were not able to do it, explains Don Lucas, because they had no strength. They decided that they would try to have their trickster son, Pedro Arimal, try to do it. But he was *"puro animal,"* like a beast, and only went about molesting young women and stealing money. He was finally turned to stone, to become a special *camahuil.*

After the failure of that attempt, the old couple decided to call to-gether all of their offspring, all of the *santos.* They seated them all at a banquet table and chose Jesus and Mary to be the ones to create the pro-ductive world. This immediately roused the ire of the bad saints (among them Satanás, San Simón, Moisés, and the Judios), who began to chase them. While they chased him, Jesus threw back the sea and dried the land out for farming. He also sanctified the work of the agriculturalist, and properly ordered the plants and animals.

By the end of the week, Easter Holy Week, the evil fellows had cap-tured one by one his 13 spirits (Jesus of Nazareth, Jesus on the Cross, Heart of Jesus, etc.) and finally they captured him.[34] San Juan, San Pedro, and other "good" saints tried to help him evade his captors, but he be-came separated from them and was put up on the cross, to be eaten at midnight. The evil saints feared he would try to escape via the cross, and successfully make it to heaven, *la gloria.* So they put two guardians there by the cross, a rooster to the left and a *clarinero* on the right, farthest from the building where the bad saints lived. But the rooster plotted with Jesus, and when the *clarinero* called out at Jesus' escape, Jesus fastened a firefly to the cross and began to climb through the air.

The evil saints rushed out to see what the commotion was about, but found the chicken silent. "What is going on?" they demanded. But the chicken just shrugged and said that the *clarinero* was a wild bird that called whenever he felt like it. "As for Jesus," he said, "he is still on the cross. Look, can't you see the glow of his cigarette?"

In this way the evil saints were fooled until Jesus got to *nik'aj gloria,* "half-way to heaven," where he knew he could not be chased. Then the wily cock called out, loud and clear. When the bad saints discovered what had happened, they were furious, and decided to take the poor chicken for their midnight meal instead. They prepared a great *pul ik'* (chile sauce) and placed the cooked bird on the table just as Jesus was arriving in heaven. But at that moment, the rooster rose and called out his crowing song, flapping his wings, and spraying chile in their eyes. They stumbled to their feet and began to stagger around the room. Just then, an earthquake opened up the floor, and they all fell into the crack that led straight to Xibalbaj.

With this story (considerably longer and more elaborate in the original), Don Lucas describes the creation of the moral universe, as light is separated from the dark, land from the sea, the good from the evil (with humankind between), and the temporal and spatial processes are begun. He is also describing the Easter passion, the re-creation of the agricultural year after the end of the dry season. This is also a "historical" explanation for the origin and condition of the saints. The good ones have ascended, so that there is a distinction between the cosmos, where the beings never die, and the earth surface, where the mortals dwell and pass away. The evil ones have fallen, to demarcate the domain of hell, the place for murderers and irresponsible clowns.[35] The story ultimately expresses a metaphor of the process of the dawning sun as well, as humankind moves out of the undifferentiated darkness and into the light of day, of corn, of procreative life.

The association of the benevolent saints with the solar realm is reflected in the house altar, again a spatial expression of a temporal theme. The saint, in this case San Juan, is celebrated once each solar year, around the time of the most northerly progression of the sun (June 24). For a week prior to this day, people from the neighborhood begin to frequent the altar room, leaving candles and their prayers. The family altar room becomes transformed at this time into a community church, as all the domestic possessions are removed and the floor is decorated with pine needles. By the time the saint day arrives, there are many offerings piled before the little "saint house." People arrive early in the day, to visit the outside and inside altars, to listen to the music provided, to eat, to drink, and to dance until dawn.

It is believed that on those days the saint "comes down" and is present, especially for the 24-hour period of the actual saint day. His or her sacred nature is periodic, increasing as the day of celebration draws near, waning as the dawn of the next day arrives. Saints are paternal (or maternal), like the sun ("our father"; the moon = *ratit*, "our grandmother"), and are thought to take care of the community in which they reside. They are like immortal elders, born like humans, with humanoid features, clothes, gender, and specific personalities, but never dying. They move above and beneath the cultural space of humanity, for they were born in a prior creation and will remain periodically visible into the future cycles of time.

In contrast to the "solar" saints is the Mundo, spiritual essence of the earth. While the saints address and are addressed by the public community, by the calculus of the Christian calendar and following the rhythms of the agricultural cycle, the Mundo as prior to creation and linked with the 260-day round is a deity of the private household and the rhythms of the human birth and growth cycle. Its spatial locus is fixed, in or on the ground, within certain indestructible stones, dwelling in significant topographical features, all of these either without specific gender or with both sexes present.[36] The *camahuil* stones are venerated on certain days determined by the divining calendar rather than the agricultural one, and these stones are considered to be the "eyes and ears" of the Mundo, informing the earth deity of the goings-on in the domestic sphere.

Don Lucas, indicting the religious reform groups for their lack of attention to the Mundo, explained that Jesus was all fine and good but of little use without the world for him to walk across. He asked me rhetorically, "Is it not the Mundo that sustains our lives, that provides the base for our corn, for our houses?" The Quiché also associate the dead with the Mundo, as I have previously indicated. They are the foundation from which grew the present generations, and moreover they are believed to sustain the existence of the living. At any time they can petition the withdrawal of their descendants' life from this world, convincing the Lord of Death that the people in question are not fulfilling their obligations of "feeding" and venerating the Mundo. The Quiché are not born with original sin but rather "original debt," a debt to their ancestors who made their own existence possible and who gave them their piece of the material world.[37]

This division between active-solar and fixed-earthly realms is apparent in the invisible world of the soul as it leaves the place of the living. As I mentioned earlier, there are two souls of the individual, the *jalajmac* and the *chijenel* "angels." The first, the "sinner," located on the front of the body, goes to the Mundo at death to be with the ancestors for all eternity. The second one, located on the back and called the "guardian," goes first to a place to atone for the sins of life.[38] When this is done, it ascends to *la gloria* ("heaven") to be placed again in a woman's womb by the grandmother saint of midwifery.

Don Lucas believes the guardian souls who serve as seeds for the newborn are limited in number, just as the seed corn is limited in each planting. He commented that people are not living as long as they once did because they must die sooner, in order to allow for enough seed for the next generation. This concept of cycling soul spirits seems to be yet another derivation of the solar metaphor. Just as the cycles of the sun and moon leave their effects upon the physical world, so the life of the individual leaves a contribution in the realm of the deceased. But while one spirit, the one that knew sin and temptation, becomes permanently interred in the spiritual graveyard, the other is recycled endlessly to watch over the course of the future generations. Like the daily return of the sun and the yearly return of the corn, the guardian soul returns at the dawn of a new life.

This resolves for the Pachaacs the difficult question of the afterlife of the soul, which must respond to both the unchanging domain of the earth (and the dead) and the dynamic and cyclic domain of the heavenly bodies. It also demonstrates how pervasive the dualistic sun-earth concept is. From the smallest unit of time and domestic space to the most abstract spatial, temporal, and conceptual domains the same structural principles are maintained. They are maintained through the power of the day metaphor, as it links the nested levels of time and space, encapsulating them within a concept that is intimately present in daily experience and infinitely repeated throughout the lives of the rural Quiché.

If life is like a day, the end of a lifetime must be like the sun setting. The shamans refer to one's fate as one's day, when they pray for a client's life, when they ask the judges and officers of justice in the world to not "cut short the day" of their patient. The shaman is one who is usually in the declining years, one who has retreated from the life of exclusively agricultural pursuits in order to count out the days of the calendar of human fate. By counting out the days into the future, Don Lucas, like the dreamer, leaves the present temporal chronology and goes outside of time. By calling up the spirits of the Mundo that exist in a multitude of locations and that reflect the diversity of the local ecosystem, Don Lucas moves beyond his particular space and enters a world that encompasses all space.

In this way the Quiché shaman becomes the mediator between the diverse elements of the Mundo and the celestial spirits. These latter have no space, only their earthly images represent them in the house, in the *cofradía*, or in the church. They are in a world above and beyond the reach of the farmer, just as the Mundo is outside of his time and beneath him. Only the shaman, as he approaches the world in the west where the sun and the earth come together, is capable of bringing together those juxtaposed forces and to mediate between them and the spiritual concerns of the community. Having passed through the cycles of solar time and having learned to become aware of the 260-day round of human time, he can truly be the "mother-father" one, the man of both celestial and earthly days. He is to the spiritual domain as the domestic unit is to the division of house and fields, as the house is to the division of earth and forest materials, as the household and its fields is to the environmental division of mountains and canyons.

This inquiry is only a beginning. The sun has just come up in our understanding of the relationships between the daily life of the rural Quiché and the central organizing principles that bind together their material and mental life. But progress has been made in providing the analytic framework that the structuralist ethnographer must have in order to discover the connections between the diverse classes of information encountered in the field. The temporal dimension of the day, year, and lifetime, and the spatial dimension of the body, house, domestic unit, and the conceptual universe have been my starting points for understanding the different permutations and transformations of the principle of the day. I maintain that every cultural expression, from the mundane chores of daily domestic life to the esoteric intricacies of calendric interpretation, respond to this same theme. Every cycle of life and every foundation of that cycle is expressed by the Quiché in terms of *u be k'ij*, "the path of the sun."

Notes

1. An unfortunate division of labor has developed in anthropology, whereby particularists tend to study surface structure and generalists deep structure. As a result, the generalist-structuralist is not interested in the content of the particular structural element under analysis as it relates to other structural dynamics within the culture, but rather only in the parallels across cultures, cultures between which little or no controlled comparison is possible. The cross-cultural framework of analysis is therefore necessarily external and an artifice of the structuralist without a uniform relationship to the conceptual categories of the cultures at hand. This has led many ethnographers who might have benefited from a structuralist approach away from this method, for they throw the structural baby out with the universalistic bathwater.

2. See, for example, David Hicks, *Tetum Ghosts and Kin* (1976).

3. A great amount of corroborative data are in these two works but space limitations do not allow me to discuss them. In the case of Bunzel's work, done in the 1930s, I believe the analysis presented here sheds a great deal of light on events recorded but not fully understood in Chichicastenango at that time.

4. Reform Catholicism, called *Acción Católica* (AC) in Spanish, is a reform movement started in the basin in the fifties. The history of the movement and a case study in the Quiché Basin are provided in Ricardo Falla's *Quiché Rebelde* (1979). The work presented here focuses exclusively on the traditionalists, who are the majority in most of the basin, but I have noted that many AC followers express beliefs very similar to the traditionalists when it does not directly conflict with doctrine. To understand the reform position, the social scientist must first have a working knowledge of the traditionalists, for change cannot be understood outside of the context of nonchange from which it departs.

5. The Tzotzil Maya of highland Chiapas have been studied by numerous scholars, mostly focusing upon the communities in close proximity to San Cristóbal de Las Casas. In Vogt's study of Zinacantan, he discovered that households were organized into groups he terms *snas* (patrilineal descent groups); *snas* into waterhole groups; and waterhole groups into barrios; finally yielding the maximal unit, the municipality. The units are symbolically analogous to one another in some important ways. For example, the house cross that each home maintains

is a miniature of, and a model for, the large crosses representing the barrio in the municipal center. Gossen's work at nearby San Juan Chamula reveals that this nesting of organization is not merely at the level of settlement pattern or social organization. He points out that the sun, as the "giver and maintainer of order" (1972b:149), is a symbol that provides a paradigm of spatial and temporal order that can apply to many smaller and larger domains, organizing them all within a fairly uniform conceptual pattern.

6. See Wallace and Carmack, *Archaeology and Ethnohistory of the Central Quiché* (1977), for the first use of this geographic name.

7. This study focuses exclusively upon the rural Quiché, which includes most of the population. The Quiché, like many other highland Maya groups, tend to have "abandoned" centers, towns which serve as market and sociopolitical centers, but which do not serve as the immediate model for the experienced world, a model that remains for the Quiché fundamentally rural and in touch with the local ecological circumstances and processes. Urban dwellers begin to lose this perspective, and I would assume (it would be worth testing) that their concept of the nonmaterial world would change accordingly.

8. See Robert Carmack, *The Quiché Mayas of Utatlán* (1981), for a detailed and accurate documentation of this continuous heritage.

9. This process, called *junba'* in Quiché, is reported in Falla (1979), Carmack (1981), and by other investigators. I have seen it in Zacualpa, where the off-season maize is raised to sell at times of great scarcity, when the price is unusually high.

10. Falla (1979) documents the westward movement of the Quiché Indian population, using land conflict documents from the last two centuries. Apparently, the Quiché Basin was far more decimated by the Conquest and early colonial period than the less accessible areas to the west.

11. The names given are all fictitious. The term "shaman-priest" is basically the same as used by B. Tedlock (1978), and for the same reasons. These spiritual practitioners serve the roles associated with that of a priest and also of a classic shaman. The *chuchkajauib* see the Catholic priests as shamans, in the same general category as themselves, and it is quite common for these shaman-priests to serve as religious officiators over marriage, birth, and death, as well as being diviners and spiritual curers.

12. The process of "weed management" is complex and well developed in the basin. Between the rows of maize wild plants are allowed to grow, but only those recognized as useful. These "semidomesticated" plants are a critical food source during the rainy season, for this is the time when corn supplies are shortest and the price of maize is at its highest. Those plants that are not useful for human or animal food are turned into the soil, providing organic material for the growing crops. The practice of planting corn closer together, much advocated by development agencies in the region, would destroy this food supplement and interrupt the process of soil regeneration.

13. There is more variation in temperature in a given single day between day and night than the difference in average or mean temperature between the warmest and coldest months.

14. Only a few people in this area are familiar with the year bearer, which currently occurs in early March. The Quiché town of Momostenango still holds this period to be of considerable importance (see B. Tedlock [1978] where this is described in some detail).

15. This is a critical time for the highland maize farmer, and the coming of the secure rains may vary as much as a month. Once there have been three or four heavy rains in succession, it is generally agreed that the rains are going to continue. To plant too soon or too late, even a few weeks out of schedule, could decrease considerably the yield of the *milpa*.

16. This seasonal migration pattern was first instituted in early colonial times, with the cacao boom (MacLeod 1973:80–95), and has continued right down to the present. When the colonial Spaniards found their early attempts at enslavement and forced permanent migration only caused a rapid decline in the Indian population, they gave much of it up for the seasonal system. It was probably employed in pre-Hispanic times as well, and it would not be surprising if much of the Post Classic warfare took place during the dry season. This compromise of partial employment and part-time autonomy of highland Indian communities may help to explain why these traditional groups have persisted for so many centuries without major changes in their belief system. Migrant labor forces "paid off" the outsiders by doing their work at circumscribed times in a place alien to the Quiché homeland, a homeland which was able to remain more intact and removed from the national economy because of this arrangement.

17. I tried an experiment with foreign corn types and found them unsuitable for the local environment. The Pachaacs know many of the other nearby seed varieties and are able to clearly explain what would happen if those types were planted in their own field. Some would grow tall and fall over, others would be short or without a developed ear, and still others would mature too rapidly or too slowly for their scheduling and rainfall patterns.

18. Leonhard Schultze Jena first noticed that the *tzolkin* was used by the Quiché for calculating gestation while doing fieldwork in Chichicastenango between 1929 and 1931. He says: "On various occasions I asked different diviners about the meaning of the period of the nine months (the 260 day count). . . . They told me with complete confidence on every occasion that it referred to the same period of time that elapses when a woman is pregnant" (1946:75; translation mine).

19. Don Lucas explained that poor and ignorant people rely upon the count of the moons to determine the time of birth, but those who know or have access to one who knows the ritual calendar can calculate with more accuracy. The day of birth, he said, is the same day as the day the moon does not produce the little blood (menstruation), only one "human year" later; it is significant that this same period is that used for the initiation process of a new *chuchkajau*, who is metaphorically reborn in the course of the initiation.

20. The 20 Day Lords cycle through the lifetime of each individual, 13 cycles for each 260-day "year," each of these years being related to the life fate cast in the first cycle, the gestation period. Within those 20 days dwell the determinants of future fate (20 in Quiché is *Jun winak*, literally 'one man'), and the diviner, by putting himself in contact with those day deities, is able to look at future cycles of time and advise his client as to how to respond to what is revealed.

21. The small bag or bundle that the diviner carries is often referred to as a *vara* or measuring stick.

22. The father cannot push his sons too hard, requiring excessive amounts of labor from them, because he knows that it may cause them to leave the family prematurely and endanger his chances for security as he becomes too old to maintain himself. Children who settle close by and who feel they have received a just inheritance, are likely to take good care of their aging parents.

23. Ruth Bunzel mentions this phrase being used in Chichicastenango in a number of transcribed prayers (1952).

24. The Pachaacs believe that the ultimate payment to the world spirit for the use of the land and the enjoyment of life is made with the physical body, which is said to "eat" the dead person, just as it eats offerings.

25. I surveyed many houses in the basin, visiting over 50 communities during my 13 months as assistant director of a housing development program after the 1976 earthquake. It was striking even at that time how consistent the house layout and orientation was.

26. It is of note that many oral traditions tell of women in prior positions that are later overcome by men. This is also found among the Tzotzil Maya (Gary Gossen, personal communication). This may relate to their daily role as rising before men to begin the domestic activities of the household, as well as to their role as engenderers of men.

27. The early colonial document called by most scholars the *Popul Vuh* is an account of the origin and development of the Quiché people. An elaborate analysis is inappropriate here, but it is notable that the day-night division presented here could be applied to the document. The first part, constantly referred to as the time "before the dawn," is the time of mythic heroes and villains in mortal combat, and is a series of tales without attention to chronology or reference to historical beings. Once the sun has risen, this all changes and history and temporal sequence take precedence over timeless and spaceless myth.

28. Barbara Tedlock (personal communication) translates the term in Momostenango as the foundation of the house.

29. If the rains are late, a small delegation of shamans will go to the two peaks that are thought to be where the water is loaded into the clouds that discharge in the local area, and perform rain requests at Mundo shrines there. Each town in the basin is said to have distinct mountains that provide them with rain, peaks always to the northeast.

30. This reduplication is reported for the towns of Momostenango, Chichicastenango, San Pedro Jocoopilas, Santa Cruz del Quiché, Zacualpa, Patzite, and Chiche.

31. Sakiribal, "the dawning place," is a religious site visited by traditionalists from all of the municipalities of the basin and even from beyond it. It has two major altar sites on top of the mountain plus a secretario or "companion altar" for one of the major ones, and two cave altars on the southwest escarpment.

32. I have not included a cosmological diagram in this work, although I have made a number of them, because I have wanted to avoid static models of dynamic processes.

33. I witnessed the actions of the *aj mes* many times, and as of my last field visit, Don Lucas was in apprenticeship. The *aj mes* falls into a kind of possession trance, where his own spirit is replaced by that of the earth. Through the earth spirit, clients can get in touch with their dead. This is often done in order to ask advice of the ancestors, and to present them with disputes in order that they resolve them.

34. The Stations of the Cross and the various distinct representations of Jesus are interpreted by Quichés like Don Lucas as different spirit manifestations of a single deity. Don Lucas tells of how the heart of Jesus was cut out and became its own spirit, Corazón de Jesús. The heart is supplicated to for ills of the heart.

35. Serious clowns (as opposed to ritual clowns) are considered the lowest of the low, for they have no sense of respect or morality, and take nothing, least of all God, seriously. This is the antithesis of righteousness for the Quiché, and those who appear to be clowns are sent straight to hell when they die, according to Don Lucas.

36. I asked whether specific Mundo shrines or mountains were male or female, and invariably the answer was that they are both.

37. The word *k'aslem* means "life" in Quiché, whereas the root *k'as* means "debt" or in some contexts "that which is borrowed." (Martin Pretchel first pointed out this connection to me, which was later confirmed by local Quiché speakers.) The language itself reflects the idea of life accruing debt and obligation.

38. Don Lucas says that the poor guardian hits the sinner soul four solid blows at the time of death, for making him suffer for the crimes of the other soul's errors. This is the twitching we sometimes see at the moment of death.

Sources

Bourdieu, Pierre. *Outline of a Theory of Practice.* Cambridge, MA: Harvard University Press, 1977.

Bunzel, Ruth. *Chichicastenango.* Locust Valley, NY: Augustin, 1952.

Carmack, Robert. *The Quiché Mayas of Utatlán.* Norman: University of Oklahoma Press, 1981.

Falla, Ricardo. *Quiché Rebelde.* Guatemala City: Universidad de San Carlos Press, 1979.

Gossen, Gary. "Temporal and Spatial Equivalents in Chamula Ritual Symbolism," in William A. Lessa and Evon Z. Vogt, eds., *Reader in Comparative Religion: An Anthropological Approach*, 3rd ed., 135–49. New York: Harper and Row, 1972.

———. *Chamulas in the World of the Sun: Time and Space in Maya Oral Tradition.* Cambridge, MA: Harvard University Press, 1974.

Hicks, David. *Tetum Ghosts and Kin.* Palo Alto, CA: Historia de los Mexicanos por sus Pinturas (HMP), 1976.

Kaufman, Terence S. *Idiomas de Mesoamerica.* Guatemala City: Seminario de Integración Social de Guatemala Pub. 33. 1974.

Leon-Portilla, Miguel. *Tiempo y realidad en le pensamiento Maya.* Mexico City: Instituto de Investigaciones Historicas, Universidad Nacional Autónoma de Mexico, 1968.

MacLeod, Murdo. *Spanish Central America: A Socio-Economic History, 1520–1720.* Berkeley: University of California Press, 1973.

Schultze Jena, Leonhard. *La vida e las creencias de los indígenas quichés de Guatemala.* Translated by Antonio Goubaud Carrera and Herbert D. Sapper. Guatemala City: Editorial del Ministerio de Educación Pública 49, 1946.

Tedlock, Barbara. *Quiché Maya Divination: A Theory of Practice.* Ph.D. diss., State University of New York, Albany, 1978.

Thompson, J. E. S. *Maya History and Religion*. Norman: University of
Oklahoma Press, 1970.

Vogt, Evon Z. *Zinacantan: A Maya Community in the Highlands of
Chiapas*. Cambridge, MA: Harvard University Press, 1969.

Wallace, Dwight, and Robert Carmack. *Archaeology and Ethnohistory of
the Central Quiché*. Albany: Institute for Mesoamerican Studies Publications 1, SUNY, 1977.

5

Pretos Velhos in Brazil: The Old Black Slaves of the Umbanda Religion

Lindsay Hale

Like those of indigenous America, the beliefs of Africa have also perme-ated popular religion in Latin America—particularly in that long cres-cent stretching south from Louisiana through the Caribbean and down the Atlantic coast, reaching deep into Brazil, where slavery once brought millions of Africans to the New World. The circumstances of their journey meant that Africans carried none of the material substance of their reli-gion to America, but they were nonetheless able to bring the metaphysics of African cosmology to the New World in their bodies and souls. While Spanish and Portuguese masters demanded that their slaves conform to the external rites of Catholicism, they generally did not put the kind of effort into converting or educating Africans that they did for Indians, on whom the religious rationale of the Conquest rested. Considered by Christendom to be the heretical Children of Cain, for Africans a superfi-cial conversion was enough. As a result, Africans were able to effectively shroud their beliefs within Catholicism. African gods and goddesses as-sumed the names and some of the attributes of Catholic saints, for ex-ample, while the sacred directional cycle of life came to be rendered in something that resembled the Celtic cross; and African cosmograms ap-peared as Christian symbols on walls and tombstones.

Slaves came to Latin America from all over sub-Saharan Africa, but the religion of the Yoruban people of West Africa bears the greatest influ-ence in the Americas, although a fair amount of Congolese belief is also apparent. This influence persisted not only because West Africans were the largest group sent to the Americas in the waning days of slavery in the nineteenth century, but also because Yoruban beliefs had just begun to

From "Embodied Ethnicity: Old Slaves and Indian Mermaids in Brazilian Spirit-Possession Religion" (unpublished paper, University of Texas at Austin, 1991). Reprinted by permission of Lindsay Hale.

spread across West and Central Africa to non-Yoruban peoples during the same period. As a result, paradoxically, one finds in African religion in the New World a cohesion and continuity that is not found in Africa itself. Many of the basic identities, characteristics, and iconography of deities are relatively standard throughout the Latin American regions of the African Diaspora, as are many of the ritual practices. Thus, Shango (Santa Barbara), the god (goddess) of iron, is evoked in much the same way in Cuba as in Brazil; and the essential rituals of animal sacrifice, drumming, and trance are found as readily in Haiti as in Bahia—or in Miami and New York.

Because African religion has such strong cultural resonance, it is enjoying a revival in parts of Latin America today—particularly in Brazil, where the faiths known as Candomblé and Umbanda derive in some measure from a fusion of African, Christian, and sometimes other—such as Indian or Spiritist—beliefs and practices. Candomblé is considered by its practitioners to be the "most African," Umbanda the "most Brazilian." As Lindsay Hale, an anthropologist and umbandista initiate, suggests here, Umbanda consciously fuses African references to folkloric figures and to archetypes that are distinct to Brazil, thus creating a corpus of belief that is uniquely Brazilian. In this text, the interview subjects are the archetype/spirits themselves who "mount" (or possess) the bodies of the Umbandista faithful, spirit possession being an essential element of West African ritual and belief.

Lindsay Hale is a Lecturer in the Department of Anthropology at the University of Texas, Austin. His dissertation is titled, "Hot Breath, Cold Spirit: Performance and Belief in a Brazilian Spirit Religion" (University of Texas, 1994).

O n my last night in Rio de Janeiro, Pai Joaquim gave me his pipe. I had come to say goodbye for awhile to this rugged old sorcerer from Angola, to drink a little sweet red wine and cinnamon from his battered old black bowl before I received his blessing. It was nearly midnight and I had been at the *terreiro*[1] since seven o'clock. I had already taken leave of several of my best spirit-friends. I had said goodbye to Maria Redonda and Maria Congo, the two old slave women who understood everyone's problems and made their own rustic wisdom and maternal love and painful memories understood despite the fact that their speech was peppered with Bantu words and confusing sound substitutions. Pai Benedito, as always, talked to me about my research and told me that as I entered the next phase, the writing, my path might sometimes be steep and rocky but it would always be open. I went to see Rei Congo, and he prayed over me and cleansed me, reciting an extemporaneous poem full of images of waterfalls and seashores and moonlight falling on the forest, the forces of nature that would protect me and make me wise. We said together the prayer that he had taught me almost a year earlier, when I had first come to sit with him in these slave quarters.

I was relieved that I would be leaving on a Tuesday and not a Thursday; that way, on my last night I could say goodbye to the old Black slave spirits and not to the cowboys and Indians, who work Wednesday nights. That would be better for everyone. Saying goodbye is a sentimental passage, and it would be better to negotiate those emotional moments with the talkative and gentle old slaves than with the taciturn and tough cowboys and Indians. The Cowboy of Time once told me that "this cowboy is not one for talking much; my herd is moving on and I need to be raising dust." And not one for mush and tears, either. Better not to see White Feather or Golden Mountain or the Cowboy of the Slave House or the Cowboy of Time or Seven Feathers with tears in their eyes, or for them to see me that way. No, better to think of them as they imagine themselves: strong and proud and forever young, roaming the moonlit forest and the blue sky where one star shines.

But it went easier than I expected. I kept my composure; I felt myself go misty no more than a half dozen times. One time was with the lady who ekes out a living selling coffee and snacks at the *terreiro*. She used to be a medium, but Seu Moura gave her permission to stop when her health deteriorated to the point that exertion became dangerous. She has diabetes and a weak heart, and sometimes her feet swell enormously because of her failing circulation. I would always buy a few cups of coffee from her and we would chat before the session started. Sometimes I would sit by her during the ritual because she sang the hymns, or *pontos cantados*, very clearly so that I could transcribe them. She always called me "O Senhor" (Sir). I gave up on trying to get her to address me less formally when I realized that it was important to her that the American friend who always asked her opinion and her explanation to be a *senhor*, and not *João Ninguém*, or "John Nobody," as they say in Brazil. We were talking about the fact that her home is three hours away by bus and train from the *terreiro*, and that she always spends the night there because it is impossible to return at all after nine at night. I tried to pay her for my coffee, but she informed me that my money was no longer any good. We sat on the rickety bench in silence for awhile. There was nothing more to be said.

And then there were a few moments with Maria Congo, when she was telling me how much her *cavalo* (horse; that is, the medium who receives Maria Congo) and her *cavalo*'s husband love me. I thought back to evenings we had spent sitting in their apartment, drinking beer and chatting; they reminded me so much of my parents, and I knew how much I would miss them. But that passed, and Maria Congo asked me something that had been on her mind for awhile. From what I had observed, did it seem that when spirits incorporate in persons of "this color"—holding her forearm to mine and pinching her dark skin—that they come with more force, with more grace, than when they work through mediums of "that color," pointing to my skin? I had to agree that of the mediums who impressed me the most, only one was white. And I knew more white mediums than Black, or mulatto. She giggled and told me that Umbanda is African; white people can be children of faith, bless their hearts, but their blood and their bodies do not remember African ways.

And then it was nearly midnight, and Pai Joaquim would soon be leaving Seu Moura's body. Most of the audience had left. Pai Joaquim had already gotten to his feet and was leaning on his cane when I reached him. He was on his way to the *fundamento* (foundation), the slab in the dirt floor under which are buried certain sacred objects. Pai Joaquim would kiss the *fundamento* before departing to Aruanda, the home of the Umbanda spirits. Pai Joaquim refers to this *fundamento* as the *raíz*, or root, meaning not only that structure beneath the floor but also the knowledge upon which everything at the *terreiro* is based. Many times I heard Seu Moura, or one of his spirits, address the audience and the personnel of the *terreiro* and explain that this root was planted by Pai Joaquim from Angola, and it is from this planting that the faith and truth of Pai Joaquim have taken root right here, in this holy house and in this slave quarters and in this dust where we walk. The *preto velho* (old Black) came from far away indeed, to save children of faith. Pai Joaquim repeated the story one more time, for everyone and no one in particular. He had his *ekedi* (ritual assistant) pour me some wine, and, stooped over his cane, sometimes with his free hand on my shoulder or on my neck, he described me to everyone as someone who came from far away, a man of learning and manners and intelligence, who had the humility to sit in the cold dirt at the feet of an old Black slave and learn the truth that Pai Joaquim had brought from Angola. To be humble, to pass in front of no one else, to not be grand because he who is grand is our father Oxalá, those are the virtues. He told the *ekedi* to bring him the case with his only pipe, and he gave it to me and blessed me and told me to follow my path. . . .

In Umbanda, a Brazilian spirit-possession religion, participants known as *mediuns* (mediums) incorporate spirits of various kinds. These include African deities, known as *Orixás*; colorful, more or less decadent, sometimes demonic spirits known as *Exus*; the spirits of Indians, called *caboclos*; and the category discussed here: the spirits of old Black slaves, known as *pretos velhos*. This article focuses on Umbanda as expression, as an active process in which participants utilize resources such as Orixás and spirits, myths, secrets, songs, gestures, and places to create spiritual meanings that speak to their circumstances and their selves. I focus on Umbanda not so much as an object or system of beliefs and practices, but rather as idioms, and poetic ones at that, used by people to mediate life and make it meaningful. These Umbanda idioms are means of engagement—engagement with self, situation, feelings, and the possibilities of being within the context of Brazilian culture.

A major concern of this meaning-making is ethnicity. This is not surprising. Perhaps in no other country are the issues of race, color, national identity, and self as thoroughly ambiguous as they are in Brazil. Historically, the issue has been framed in terms of the three "original" racial components of the Brazilian population: the European, the African, and the Indian. In contrast to the United States, where practice and discourse have constructed a problematic of separate and unequal ethnic groups, with national identity defined almost exclusively in terms of white culture—with "the other" safely distant, on the other side of the tracks or on a reservation on the other side of nowhere—in Brazil the key theme in racial discourse has been miscegenation, both cultural and biological. There is a sense in which "the other" is within; the standard belief is that even the "whitest" Brazilian has at least a drop of African blood as well as a drop of Indian blood, and in most Brazilians, far more. This belief has led to a recurrent occupation with one question: What does it mean to be a "mixture" of European, African, and Indian blood and culture? . . .

This question is especially poignant for two reasons. First, because it is a question with a rather unpleasant history. For many intellectuals of previous generations, the question has been posed as the answer to another question: Why does Brazil lag behind the civilized, that is, Euro-North American, world? To be part African and Indian, in race and culture, is to be inferior, the theories went; these writers saw the enemy, and it was their grandparents and lovers—and their own Brazilian culture, with its nonwhite traits, its African sensuality and fetishism, its indigenous acquiescence in the face of a deified natural world. On the other side of the coin, there were romantic novelists and poets who created counterimages of the noble savage and the wise, good African. But they were novelists, appealing to the heart and the senses. It was not until Gilberto Freyre, writing in the 1930s, that the non-European contributions were positively valued, at least by a social theorist who captured the interest of a large Brazilian audience. Despite the overwhelming acceptance of Freyre's position, ambivalence about, even opposition to, the African and the Indian remains a corrosive presence.[2]

The development of Umbanda from the 1920s has in large measure been a story of ambivalence concerning African blood and culture. One may argue that Umbanda is the product of a concerted effort at "whitening" African Brazilian religion by suppressing those aspects of ritual that referred to the "barbaric" African tradition. This argument is weakened by the fact that it ignores the strong presence and valorization of African elements by many *Umbandistas* (practitioners of Umbanda), such as those at Pai Joaquim's *terreiro*, but the basic tension that they identify is undeniable. This tension surfaces in Umbanda discourse, especially in the speech of, and about, the old slave spirits. What is said in regard to this varies greatly depending on the *terreiro*, the person, and his positioning vis-à-vis class structure and life experience.

Second, the question concerns the person at the level of self. Everyman's question, "Who am I?" always implies a certain play with alterity, with alternative models and versions of the self. In Brazil, the national myth of miscegenation and the fusion of three cultures provide a language for talking about the self in terms of ethnic others, both ancestral and within. In Umbanda, these issues are a constant presence. Roger Bastide and Diana Brown, in particular, have discussed Umbanda in terms of national identity.[3] They have argued that the old slaves and Indian spirits can be understood as rather thin metaphors of Brazilian identity. For them, the old slaves and Indian spirits are signs of Brazil, flat reproductions of racial stereotypes. I do not disagree with them entirely, but here I hope to build on their suggestion by demonstrating that these thin metaphors—ethnic spirits—are actually versatile sign vehicles that *Umbandistas* employ to link deep sentiments, the ineffable, personal history, and culture. These Indians and old slaves may indeed be based on stereotypes, but what emerges as Umbandistas develop these ethnic figures is at times an eloquent poetics of alterity.

This study takes a somewhat poetic look at old Black slaves and seeks to grasp the images and resonances that their speech and action evoke while focusing on what that speech and action do. While for some readers "poetics" may imply a loose and vague attempt at "interpretation," let me point out that the empirical data of ethnography are, for the most part, no more than what we see and hear people saying and doing. A poetic perspective is one that addresses this saying and doing in terms of its emotive effects and devices. My poetics, such as it is, looks at what Umbandistas say and do in terms of evocation and linkage: What do these spirits make present? What moods do they set? Where do they take the ritual moment? And what are their linkages to other realms of discourse, such as folktale, myth, literature, popular religion, and popular culture, that spirits refer to and resonate with?

~

Umbanda is largely concerned with constructing and managing different ways of being, both in the world and in the cosmos. What is most interesting about Umbanda, from a sociological perspective, is the way that this construction of otherness is utilized, by individuals and groups, to establish—and to comment upon—differences in terms of location and identity in social space. What old Black slaves say and do, and how they say and do it, and what people say about their saying and doing all express real differences among Umbandistas as to how the world is and was, and how it ought to be.

Before proceeding, a brief description of my sample is in order. I observed a number of *terreiros*, but I focused my investigation on four groups. I cannot say that the sample is exhaustively representative, but it does constitute an interesting range of variation, both in terms of positioning of participants, and the stylistic differences present in Umbanda.

1) Dona Zélia's. A seventy-six-year-old widow, Dona Zélia has been practicing Umbanda for nearly thirty years. She used to be the *mãe de santo* (literally mother of the saint, or religious leader) of a medium-sized Umbanda *terreiro*. Dona Zélia told me that the commitment of time and energy became too much for her. She now practices Umbanda in the bedroom of her apartment in Copacabana. Sessions are held weekly. Her nephew Arnaldo, who works for the navy, practices with her along with another medium, Dilza, a forty-five-year-old postal employee who is taking law courses at night, and Elis, a *cambône* (ritual assistant) in her twenties who works with Dilza. Dona Zélia comes from a traditional family that has seen its income diminish over the years. Her standard of living is comfortable, but by no means wealthy. The clients who consult spirits at Dona Zélia's are about equally divided between longtime friends and members of the family, and persons who have heard about her through mutual friends.

2) The Spiritual Center of Pai Joaquim from Angola. Pai Joaquim's *terreiro* is larger than the other three. Twenty mediums practice there on a fairly regular basis. The leader of the group, Seu Moura, comes from Pernambuco, in northeastern Brazil. He became seriously involved in Umbanda about thirty years ago, when he was an airline employee and Rio was his home base. He went through a period in which he would find himself, in the middle of the night, barefoot and shirtless, at the beach or in a cemetery, with no idea of how he got there. It turned out that his Exu spirit, Tranca Rua, was taking him on these excursions. Pai Joaquim then sought help from a *pai de santo* (father of the saint).

Pai Joaquim's attracts clients and mediums from all social classes, but the majority are not well off. In contrast to Dona Zélia's, the style of ritual at Pai Joaquim's is very "African." Many of the songs are in Nagô (Yoruban); the African deities known as Orixás are a major focus of ritual; animals are sacrificed to Exu and the Orixás; and the traditional African drums, the *atabaques*, are played.

3) The Tent of Tupinambá. This *terreiro* is directed by Dona Cesa, who also works with Seu Moura at Pai Joaquim's. It is located in Rocinha, the enormous slum on the other side of the hill from the wealthy Gávea district of Rio de Janeiro. The ritual at Tupinambá's is in many ways similar to that at Pai Joaquim's, but Dona Cesa distinguishes her practice as *Umbanda pura*, while characterizing Pai Joaquim's as *nação* (nation), which means more traditionally African.

Dona Cesa is presently training several young women and a young man to be mediums. She holds training sessions on Sundays, which I was privileged to attend, and public sessions on Thursday evenings. Her *terreiro* is a small room, indeed too small for the dozens of poor clients who come to Tupinambá's. Recently, the community council granted Dona Cesa a plot on the edge of Rocinha on which to construct a proper *terreiro*.

4) Casa São Benedito. Dona Linda, Casa São Benedito's leader, considers the ritual at her *terreiro* to be the epitome of *umbanda pura*. There are no drums, the African Orixás are interpreted as being "vibratory frequencies," and the *terreiro* itself is a monument to squeaky-clean middle-class aesthetics. Participants strongly contrast their Umbanda with African or African-Brazilian religion. Casa São Benedito is the oldest of the four *terreiros*; the present building was completed shortly after World War II but has seen several remodelings. Plans were first laid out in 1937, when Dona Linda, then twenty-three, was visited in the forest one day by an old Black slave by the name of Pai Joaquim.

In its heyday, Casa São Benedito was larger than Pai Joaquim's. There were as many as forty mediums on the membership list, and "charity" —that is, public sessions—were held three nights per week. That was in the days when Dona Linda's husband, an entrepreneur in the shoe industry, was the father of the saint. He died ten years ago. Now Dona Linda, who does not have the strength to carry on her husband's level of activity, works with five mediums, three of whom are in training. One of the mediums in training is married to a general. One of the full mediums is Dona Linda's daughter, who is married to a retired colonel; this daughter's son, an engineering student planning a military career, leads the singing in the *terreiro*. Some say that someday he will assume his grandfather's role as leader.

Pretos Velhos

> The Pretos Velhos present a striking contrast to the Caboclos. These
> "Old Blacks" are the spirits of Africans enslaved in Brazil, generally
> slaves from Bahia. All are elderly, and they are named and addressed
> familiarly and affectionately in kin terms: *Vovó* (Grandmother) or *Vovô*
> (Grandfather), *Tia* (Aunt) and *Tio* (Uncle), *Mãe* (Mother) and, less of-
> ten, *Pai*. They are characterized as humble, patient, long suffering, and
> good. Umbanda leaders repeatedly stressed to me their *humildade* (hu-
> mility), *bondade* (friendship), and *caridade* (charity) and tended to char-
> acterize them as subservient . . . more precisely, Uncle Tom.[4]

I must admit that I was feeling a little frustration in talking to the *preto
velho* Rei Congo (Congo King). I just could not get the kind of life history data, or the trenchant comments about race and slavery and ideology,
that I was after. During my previous fieldwork, in 1986, I had the good
fortune of working with Dona Zélia, a remarkable medium whose spirits
were very articulate and full of detailed stories of their experiences here
on Earth. But Rei Congo was simply impossible. His autobiography was
a closed book. All I could get out of him was that he was a tribal king
from the Congo (I gathered as much from his name) and that he was a
slave somewhere in Brazil. He told me that he knew very little, not as
much as the other *preto velhos*, but he would teach me what he could. He
told me about herbal remedies and different kinds of baths to cleanse
myself of the pollution of this world and of the envious, bitter thoughts of
others. He also told me about charity and not wanting anything in return
for helping others. Indeed, he became indignant at the thought of taking
money from clients, telling me that it was wrong to sell what God gives
freely, that is, mediumship. But that it warmed the heart of this *preto
velho* when a client would give him a twist of tobacco or a bottle of sweet
red wine to enjoy as he worked down in the old *senzala* (slave quarters;
the *pretos velhos* referred in this manner to the *terreiro*). In short, Rei
Congo was a wealth of information about everything but what it meant to
be a *preto velho*.

On top of that, Rei Congo was very difficult to understand. Like other
preto velho spirits, his vocabulary included a number of terms that are
not part of standard colloquial Portuguese. To drink, *beber*, became *plim
plim*, onomatopoeic perhaps for the sound of dripping water or the bob-
bing of the Adam's apple when swallowing; pipe, *cachimbo*, was *pito*, the
standard word for whistle, to give but two examples. It seemed as though
every other noun became either a "this," a "that," or a "that there." *Voce*
(you) was *sunce*; *eu* and *mim* (I and me) were both *eshe*, and so forth.
The sounds of standard Portuguese were regularly changed as well: *for*

became *fro*, *s* tended to lateralize out to *sh*, and final *r*s were dropped along with final syllables and definite articles. And he stuttered, although his medium, Seu Mané, spoke fluently. His language, his speech, his crippled body, his incessant spitting on the floor—Rei Congo was broken in body, humble in spirit, and rustic in manner. I stayed with Rei Congo and talked with him every week for three reasons: the other *pretos velhos* usually had so many clients that I felt uncomfortable about taking up too much of their time; I was learning a lot from him, most important the language of the *pretos velhos*, which would come in handy should I find a *preto velho* who was a better interview; and I liked Rei Congo a lot and he liked me. I just wished that he would talk more about himself.

I often talked to Rei Congo about my work and the difficulties it presented. We would sit on little low white benches (the same furniture that they used in the *senzala*, I was told) facing each other, legs apart, bending forward to better hear and maybe understand, Rei Congo smoking his pipe and sometimes looking into a little glass of water where he would "see" people and places. One afternoon I came to the *terreiro* with a specific problem. I would be giving a talk the next day about my research to an audience of professors and graduate students at the National Museum. I was nervous. I would have to speak in Portuguese for an hour to strangers, about a topic that I no longer felt like much of an authority on at all—Umbanda. I did not feel very confident or competent. In fact, I felt a little sick.

Rei Congo dealt with part of my problem in a rather perfunctory way. He reminded me that I already knew what steps to take. No sex until after the talk—I should go in *corpo limpo*, with a clean body; beforehand, in the morning, a regular shower followed by a purifying shower using *sabão de costa*, an oily black soap imported from West Africa that takes away impurity and negative energy. I should then dress in clean clothes and light a candle to my guardian angel while requesting protection and tranquility, seven times. During the talk I should visualize the *senzala* where we were sitting that afternoon, and everything would be fine. He was actually much more concerned about giving me some advice on what to say. I pricked up my ears when he said that if I really wanted my listeners to understand about the *pretos velhos* (ah! finally Rei Congo is going to address my Big Question!), I should tell them the story of the slave woman, Anastácia. He said he didn't tell stories very well, but he could relate the basic plot and I could buy a copy of the book about it to get it right for my audience.

I did not tell the story of Anastácia at the National Museum but kept to my original theme. However, I did buy a copy of the book. It was not hard to find: practically every bookstore in Rio devotes a shelf or two or more to books written by Spiritualists and followers of Umbanda and the other Afro-Brazilian religions. And Anastácia has become a popular legend. I remember seeing a full-color poster of Anastácia in a store near a metro station downtown that sells Umbanda materials—candles, cigars for the Indian spirits, beads, books, and professionally produced cassette tapes of Umbanda hymns. The poster depicted a young Black woman with close-cropped hair, very dark skin, and light blue eyes. She was wearing a muzzle that looked somewhat like a surgical mask, except that it was made of iron.

I confess that I did not read the book until months later, but I did not need to. One evening, while enjoying beer and conversation at the home of a couple of my informants, the subjects of Umbanda and the *pretos velhos* and African religion came up. My hosts—Maria Congo's *cavalo*, Deolinda, and her husband, Jorge—told me that I could learn a lot by watching some of his videotapes. Jorge turned on the VCR and we watched two episodes of a miniseries entitled "A Escrava Anastácia." They loaned me those episodes and the rest so I could make copies. The story goes like this:

In a village somewhere in some unspoiled part of Africa a blue-eyed baby girl is born of noble parents. Variously identified as a princess and as an emissary, she is chosen by the deities to bring the spiritual force of African religion to the New World. Africa, in the legend, is represented as a kind of utopia where there is plenty of food, time for dancing and sociability, and devotion to the deities. Anastácia's life as a child and then as a young woman is idyllic. But then, while dancing with her fellow villagers one night, Anastácia is ambushed by slave raiders. She is captured and sold to a plantation owner in Brazil. Extraordinarily beautiful—in some versions she is the daughter of Oxum, the seductive goddess of fertility and fresh water—she becomes the object of her master's lust. He brings her into domestic service, the better to seduce her. She steadfastly refuses his advances and is banished to the *senzala*. In one version, the rejected owner allows her to be raped repeatedly by his white visitors and sons, thus producing numerous blue-eyed offspring, symbolic, perhaps, of the miscegenized Brazilian people; in another, she somehow remains chaste. In both cases, her refusal to submit, combined with the jealous intrigues against her by the master's wife, leads the overseer to place an iron muzzle over the lips that refused to kiss those of her tormentors. She lives out her years in the *senzala*, constructing the moral community of the slave quarters and using the powers vested in her by the deities to cure illness. She contracts gangrene from the muzzle. As she lies dying, the master's child takes ill and, as a last resort, is brought to Anastácia. The parents beg her forgiveness. With her last strength, Anastácia cures the child. She gives up the ghost, and the master and his wife repent of their cruelty and seek redemption for their sins.

While there is no need to indulge in a thorough textual analysis for either version, it is important to note that my informants referred me to this legend as a way of making me understand about Umbanda in a way that they could not convey through words and explanations or questions and answers. They wanted me to feel as they feel in regard to *pretos velhos*, to share something of the emotional meaning of these spirits that they incorporate, these others that they embody. While the plot is itself moving and even emblematic—that is, if we drop our "sophisticated" and distanced stance, our discomfort in the face of a "naive," romantic, and perhaps hegemonic tearjerker, and enter into the story with the spirit that my informants exhibit—let me suggest that the significance of this legend lies more in the fact that it is densely packed with certain themes, images, and dispositions that occur over and over again in the construction of old Black slaves and that suffuse those constructions with feelings that are lived in the Umbanda experience. These images and themes and dispositions include torture, sexual violation, old age, crippling injury and disease, kindness, tragic love, Africa, Brazil, plantation houses, slave quarters, guilt, and forgiveness. These concerns emerge as *pretos velhos* reminisce about the way things were.

Beginnings

Umbandista writers and many of my informants stress that Umbanda is a Brazilian religion; for instance, a *preto velho* once told me that Brazil is the New Israel because it was in Brazil that Umbanda, the religion of the next millennium, was rediscovered and resynthesized. Nonetheless, Umbandistas inevitably locate the origins of their religion in some remote idealized past, usually on the other side of the Atlantic. The vision of this past is always of a place where culture, social justice, morality, and spirituality achieved superior levels. Before the Fall, Umbanda; and now it is Umbanda that will restore utopia.

The book that Rei Congo had me read and the miniseries that I copied from Jorge and Deolinda's video collection place this utopia in Africa. That setting is not a unanimous point of view. Pai Benedito, a *preto velho* at the Casa São Benedito, told a very different story. One evening, as I sat at his feet on the polished linoleum floor in the unearthly blue glow that lit his *terreiro*, he told me that the word "Umbanda" comes from two words originating thousands of miles apart. *Um* is actually the root of the Sanskrit *om*, but infinitely older, while *banda* is a Bantu word. *Om*, according to Pai Benedito, is sacred to the Hindus because it signifies the totality of all vibrations; and indeed, he said, if I were to sit cross-legged on the floor in front of a candle in a darkened room and clear my mind and hum *om* I would feel, though weakly, the resonance of the infinite. The Hindus, he continued, learned this word and this technique from extraterrestrials. These visitors were from a planet whose inhabitants had evolved so far beyond us that they no longer had material bodies. They were pure spirit. But over the millennia, the density of the spirit population became so great that it overwhelmed the gravitational force of the planet, and untold numbers of spirits were flung away by the centrifugal forces generated by the planet's rotation. They wandered in space until they encountered other planets, including Earth. What they found on Earth were, for the most part, terribly backward people, lacking technology and culture, living in caves, and using crude stone tools and communicating by grunts and gestures. The most advanced earthlings, living in India and Mesopotamia and along the Nile, had agriculture and the rudiments of writing and culture, but even they were little more than tribesmen.

The new arrivals set about promoting the cultural and spiritual evolution of humanity. They did so because they recognized that they and the Earth people were fundamentally the same, because they too had spirits. (At this point, Pai Benedito asked me a question: "Do you know about this Charles Darwin? What do you think of his ideas?" I replied that his theory seemed to me to be fairly plausible. Pai Benedito told me that Darwin was precisely right about Evolution, except for one crucial detail: monkeys evolved into animals that look just like human beings, but those animals were not human beings. They became human beings only when God gave them something no animal has. "Do you know what that something is?" "A soul?" I ventured. "No! Monkeys have souls, dogs have souls, all the animals have souls! They suffer and feel happiness just like us. The thing that only humans have is a spirit, and that is why no other animal ever evolved into a human being.") The visitors took material form and set out to teach the most advanced tribes. They taught them architecture and mathematics and writing (as evidenced by the Pyramids and other monumental structures, hieroglyphics, etc.) and, most important, religion. The civilizations that they planted thrived. Law, science, medicine, the arts, philosophy, all the cultural pursuits flourished—in fact, our accomplishments in those areas are child's play in comparison. Pai

Benedito's eyes shone as he recounted the glories of the past. Thinking that their work was done, the travelers left to find new worlds.

Pai Benedito paused in his narrative. If he were like most other *pretos velhos*, at this moment he might have relit his pipe and taken a long, nostalgic draw, looking far off into the past before continuing with his story. But Pai Benedito, according to his medium, is so spiritually evolved that he no longer craves tobacco and wine and other material things. He limits his sensual indulgences to the fragrance of rose water and lavender, and to the touch of leaves and flowers on his fingertips. His eyes became wistful and sad, as *preto velho* eyes so often do when their thoughts linger over the end of the Golden Age.

The travelers, he continued, left too early. Earth people were not ready to govern themselves without their guidance. They had learned much, but spiritually they were not ready to use their new knowledge. Babylon, seduced by luxury and sensuality, fell into wickedness. The Egyptians used their knowledge of government to enslave the Israelites, and their engineers and architects built monuments to Pharaoh and ignored the welfare of the people. Incompetent scientists, experimenting with nuclear power, blew up Atlantis. And religion was almost forgotten. Only a small number of Israelites—the Lost Tribe—kept the faith. Fleeing the chaos, they wandered into Africa, teaching what they could to the primitive peoples. But so much was lost, so much was distorted and degraded; the sublime truths were mixed with the grossest forms of materiality, with the blood sacrifice, fetishism, and orgiastic celebration of savages. Only a few rudiments survived of the Umbanda that once was, mangled almost beyond recognition. The forces of history brought the bits and pieces (including the other half of the name, the *banda*) to Brazil on slave ships, where the philosophers of Umbanda, using the Kabala, the techniques of Allen Kardec (the founder of the Spiritism movement), the principles of charity, and with the help of the enlightened spirits from Aruanda, are now resynthesizing the religion that will set the world right.

Pai Benedito's story may seem fantastic and fanciful; and, indeed, the idea of an old plantation slave holding forth on extraterrestrials, Charles Darwin, nuclear power, and the Lost Tribe of Israel must seem astonishing to anyone unacquainted with Umbanda. Pai Benedito exhibits none of the overt ethnic markers that would identify him as a plantation slave. But, at least from the point of view of one major current in Umbanda, Pai Benedito is no less a *preto velho* than Rei Congo. That point of view holds that *preto velho*-ness is not an ethnic definition, but rather a functional category that includes spirits that have achieved a certain level of evolution (not the lowest, but not the highest; in fact, some Umbandistas claim that they are "inferior" to the Indians). They are referred to as "workers" and are generally humble, simple, and kind. In one important re-spect, Pai Benedito is more typical because Rei Congo is neither loqua-cious nor a good storyteller. *Preto velho* sessions always run late because, as everyone says, "*Pretos velhos* love to talk!" Oh, how they love to talk!

What Pai Benedito's story represents is an ideological current that strongly shaped the development of Umbanda and continues to flow in much Umbanda discourse. Several researchers have traced the origins of Umbanda as a distinct religion back to the first decades of this century. They maintain that Umbanda began as an attempt to purge the existing Afro-Brazilian religion known as Macumba of its African flavor. Diana Brown and Renato Ortiz, in particular, attribute this "whitening" to middle-class white practitioners who wished to bring spirit possession in line with their ethnic and class ethos, but it would not be too much to say that at the time, Africa was a symbol of backwardness, savagery, and supersti-tion for much of the Black community as well. Certainly that prejudice is well documented by the research of Florestan Fernandes and Roger Bastide on the Black press during the first half of the century. So, we find numer-ous Umbandistas tracing the religion to the "civilized" utopias of ancient Egypt and Atlantis while denying or attenuating connections to "savage" Africa.[5]

This rejection of Africa never achieved complete hegemony, and the entire current of which it is a part has weakened considerably in recent years. Black awareness, Black pride, an increasingly critical perspective on Eurocentric versions of the Diaspora and the colonial enterprise have strengthened voices, already there, that proclaim Umbanda as the fruit of African roots. For most of my informants, Africa is a sign of authenticity. Recall Maria Conga's question—it was really an assertion—about medi-ums with African blood. Pai Joaquim's *terreiro* is a powerful place, par-ticipants assert, because its foundation, its root, was planted by an African from Angola. Seu Moura attributes his abilities, in part, to having an Af-rican great-grandmother. Even at Casa São Benedito, where the mediums concur with the story about space travelers and the Lost Tribe, most all of the *pretos velhos* remember their Africa with nostalgia. At Pai Joaquim's and Tupinambá's, certainly, the paradise lost was along the Congo or the Niger and not the Nile.

Casa Grande

Between the auction block and the whipping post where so many died in legend and fact, most *pretos velhos* passed their time of earthly purgatory on sugar plantations. The plantation was not a homogeneous social space. Gilberto Freyre, the anthropologist *cum* social historian whose works have most strongly influenced popular conceptions of Brazilian slavery, wrote a book whose title, *Casa Grande e Senzala*, neatly divides the plantation into two domains: Big House and slave quarters. Both figure in the Anastácia myth, and both are prominent in the construction of *pretos velhos*. The *senzala* was the place where the slaves lived, where African rituals were secretly performed, where slaves tended to their sick and dying, and where the human community affirmed itself in the shared suffering of the oppressed. The *senzala* is the space that is re-created in Umbanda when the *pretos velhos* incorporate . . . The history as told by the *pretos velhos*, however, seems to deal as much or more with the Big House as with the *senzala*. The Big House was the plantation manor, center of white power and culture and the focus of a bundle of conflicting emotions. It could be a way out of the *senzala* for the slave who found entry into the capricious domestic world of the master's family; but, in the end, the Big House was the arbitrary source of all suffering and death. *Preto velho* biographies very often turn around the consequences of being caught between these two domains. These stories are laden with themes of guilt, sex, privilege, and betrayal. The Anastácia legend is a case in point, but there are other biographies, other tragic tales, that illuminate this structural asymmetry and bring forth different constellations of sentiment and scene.

One such tale was told to me by Pai Gerônimo, the *preto velho* of Dona Zélia, the old *mãe de santo* whose *terreiro* is the bedroom of her tiny apartment in Copacabana. Pai Gerônimo is one of a number of *pretos velhos* I know who do not fit the stereotype of the broken-down, humble, slightly scatterbrained old slave, the "Uncle Tom" of Diana Brown's unfortunate characterization. Pai Gerônimo is a big, strong man in his forties. He is kind, but his voice is firm, his mind is very quick and focused, and he is not overly patient. He has a younger brother, Pai Joaquim, a cowboy who lived on another plantation, who walks with a limp because a bull gored his knee. I know this because one night, Pai Gerônimo told me that someday soon he would incorporate in me, and then the brothers would be together again, working in the *senzala*, I with my right pant leg cut off to accommodate Pai Joaquim's swollen knee, clutching three of the large, smooth brown seeds known as *olho de boi* (bull's eye) that are the sign and the tools of Pai Gerônimo's brother. Pai Gerônimo could see Pai Joaquim leaning on me, and he told me that I was feeling Pai Joaquim as a stiffness in my knee, as the pressure of his muscles under my skin, a restlessness in a body that yearned to ride and work cattle. . . .

Pai Gerônimo was not old because he died during the prime of his life, on the whipping post. Pai Gerônimo told me the following story. He lived on a big plantation in Bahia, the northeastern state whose principal city and port, Salvador, was once the colonial capital, and a focal point for the slave-driven sugar economy. Pai Gerônimo lived in the *senzala* along with the other slaves, but he did not have to labor in the fields and he was well fed. He lived a relatively privileged life because, due to his remarkable size, physical strength, and good appearance, the plantation master—who had always liked Gerônimo, the faithful boy who took care of the young master's horse and accompanied him on his childhood expeditions—had chosen him to serve as a breeding slave, a *reprodutor*. He fathered many children. (How many? Pai Gerônimo could not say because he could not count, but he warmly assured me that it was "many, many." He was always sad when a child was sold off to another plantation, but that was the way it was.) All in all, life was good and his master denied him only one thing. And what was that? Pai Gerônimo sighed, and his laughing eyes turned sweet and sad. There was a beautiful servant woman, a creole slave, who worked in the Big House. Her name was Catarina. Her body was firm and graceful, her skin dark brown and smooth, her eyes a shade lighter. She had been brought up in the Big House and knew how to read, play music, converse, and behave as a white lady would, but with infinitely more charm, of course. It was the master's plan to win her love, willingly, and enjoy his waning years in her company. Pai Gerônimo, therefore, was not to have Catarina. But Catarina loved Gerônimo and Gerônimo loved Catarina. Although they were discreet, they were caught. The master, who until then had always shown deep affection for his *reprodutor*, had his rival whipped to death on the *tronco*. Pai Gerônimo does not know what happened to Catarina, and he longs for the day when he can sit in the *senzala* with Joaquim, who perhaps can tell him what happened to his love.

I met a Catarina at Dona Zélia's *terreiro*, but this one was not Gerônimo's fatal lover. *Vovó* Catarina was not actually a grandmother at all, because she had no children. Vovó Catarina was born in the *senzala*, but at an early age her good appearance and charm brought her a place in the Big House as the maidservant and companion of the *sinha moça*, that is, the young lady of the house, the daughter of the master. Like Gerônimo's Catarina, she learned all the social skills. However, she was not protected by her master's sexual jealousy, and from adolescence onward she was the target of the lascivious pursuits of the men of the household as well as of the visiting and local gentry. Her feelings about this situation were ambivalent. On the one hand, the young Vovó Catarina was vain; she enjoyed luxury, and it pleased her to know that her beauty and manners were affording her a comfortable and amusing lifestyle. On the other hand, her deepest wish was to be the mother of children begotten from virtuous and true love with one man. The moral education given to the *sinha moça* had rubbed off on the servant, for whom such scruples were never intended. Tortured by desire and guilt, Vovó Catarina increasingly smothered her feelings in licentiousness and the ease it brought. One day, the years and use wore on her too heavily, and she was sent back to the *senzala* to live out her days. It seemed at first a fate worse than death to live without her parties and presents and aristocratic young suitors. But she adjusted. She learned to live among the poor, suffering people from whom she came. The selfish Catarina learned to give of herself; she doctored, she taught, she intervened with the Big House on behalf of her fellow slaves. They became the children she never had. She found grace and lived two years in the *senzala* doing her charity work for every year that she had spent in luxurious dissipation.

Senzala

Rei Congo referred to the place where we would sit and chat as the *senzala*, the slave quarters. They tell me at Pai Joaquim's that their *terreiro* is actually constructed on the site of an old *senzala*. They have found artifacts—tools and nails and bottles, mostly. There is a grotto that they built as a shrine for Iemanjá, the goddess of the sea, and Oxum, the mother of fresh water; it contains a little spring that used to fill a tank where the slaves drew their water and did their washing. Seu Moura says that Pai Joaquim is buried in the cold, red clay that used to be the floor of the *senzala* and is now the floor of the *terreiro*.

Not all *terreiros* are built on the site of a *senzala*, but every Umbanda *terreiro* becomes a *senzala* from time to time. The *senzala* is the place where the broken in body and humble of spirit perform acts of charity and where mediums embody the Black grandfathers and grandmothers and great-uncles and great-aunts and mothers and fathers of Umbanda. The *senzala* is constructed within the ritual space of the *terreiro* by virtue of signs generated in performance. Special songs, accoutrements, furnishings, ways of speaking, and modes of moving the body re-create the *terreiro* and its members as elsewhere and as other, as scene and actors in a play of imagined reliving. But it is more than a site for nostalgia. The *senzala* is a space fraught with certain kinds of meanings and peculiar tones of feelings, where the contemporary world—in the form of problems brought by clients to the *pretos velhos* in consultation—is recast and re-viewed from the moral perspective of humility, charity, love, and patience. Those are the spiritual qualities embodied by the *pretos velhos*.

Preto velho sessions are regularly scheduled events. Dona Zélia and the Casa São Benedito, which meet once per week, both receive the old

Black slaves on the second Monday of the month. At Pai Joaquim's, where Rei Congo works, these sessions are every Monday night, except for the last Monday of the month, which is devoted to Exu. During the daytime sessions at Pai Joaquim's (twice per week, on Mondays and Wednesdays), which have a much lower attendance of mediums because most of the younger ones work during the day, the *pretos velhos* share their *senzala* with two, sometimes three Exu spirits. Several Umbandistas from other centers have questioned the wisdom of having Exus and *pretos velhos* in the *terreiro* at the same time—the Exus are carnal, clever, aggressive, sometimes malicious representatives of a different constellation of values. As Dona Zélia put it, the two together create the potential for a *choque*, a shock or collision, and she would not bring the two together under any circumstances. How could one subject those good-hearted but simple old characters to the tricks and schemes and mockery of the Exus? Of course, her Pai Gerônimo could hold his own; but, generally speaking, it would be like putting wolves in among the lambs. But somehow, the mediums at Pai Joaquim are able to mitigate the inherent moral contradiction between the people of the *senzala* and the people of the street, as the Exus are often called. Perhaps it is because at Pai Joaquim's (and at Tupinambá's) the *pretos velhos* are strong and do not need protection. And so during the afternoons, the *pretos velhos* sit along the walls of the *senzala* while the Gypsies and *malandros* (scoundrels) drink and cackle and work their magic at the threshold of the ritual space.

A *terreiro* is not a *senzala* simply because the clock and the calender say that it is time for the *pretos velhos* to come visiting from Aruanda. The *senzala* is brought into existence; it is a temporary state of being, a phase in a cycle of the ritual transformation of Umbanda space. A *preto velho* session never begins in the *senzala*; rather, the *terreiro* becomes a *senzala* for awhile through the performances that take place during a *preto velho* session.

The construction of this space begins in earnest as hymns are sung to the African deities known as Orixás. At evening sessions for *pretos velhos* at Pai Joaquim's, the homage to the Orixás is usually marked by a special emphasis on Omolu, the old but physically powerful god of sickness and curing. There are affinities and resemblances linking Omolu and the old Blacks since both carry in their bodies the marks of age and physical suffering. When Omolu descends, his mediums often adopt the crippled, shuffling gait common to *pretos velhos*. Omolu is ravaged by smallpox and running sores; while the *pretos velhos* tell of the beatings, brandings, and accidents inscribed upon their flesh and in their bones. As is the case with many of the *pretos velhos*, Omolu's body is ruined and wracked, but somehow it retains a great, vital force. Omolu and the *pretos velhos* are wanderers: in the myths, Omolu travels from village to village in Africa, spreading death and smallpox.

A recurrent theme in the imagery of *pretos velhos* is perambulation, a slow meandering along the twilight paths. At Pai Joaquim's, Omolu sets the stage, with the deity foreshadowing the arrival of the human spirits who most closely embody his character. Sometimes the connection between Omolu and the *pretos velhos* approaches identity. Several times, I observed mediums who received *pretos velhos* during hymns to Omolu. On those occasions, the *pretos velhos* formed a line and hobble-danced out to the Omolu shrine, in time with the lyric *O to to ba lu a ei, o to to ba ba*, their canes tapping the ground hard on the *to*. Participants referred to those in the procession as Omolu, *pretos velhos*, and *almas*, or souls.

Not all Umbandistas emphasize Omolu, nor do all bring him into close ritual proximity to the *pretos velhos*. Omolu is an Orixá, and the Orixás are African; therefore, Omolu's presence in ritual varies in proportion to the *terreiro*'s orientation toward Africa. For both Dona Zélia and the Casa São Benedito, the celebration of Africa by way of the Orixás is strongly muted. At Casa São Benedito, on most occasions the Orixás are saluted by hymns and do not appear. Only once did I see mediums incorporate Orixás there. Dona Zélia gives a thorough homage to the Orixás on special occasions, singing for each one seven verses of a song, but for most sessions they are merely mentioned in an opening prayer. I asked Dona Zélia about the role of Omolu in Umbanda. She told me that the old one is not a major Orixá, like Iemanjá or Oxossi or Ogum, mainly because Omolu is a very material deity—indeed, he is often referred to as the Orixá of the Earth—and in her style of Umbanda (like that of Casa São Benedito), materiality is a highly negative value. She said that Omolu is very important in the Candomblé, which she described as African. For her style of Umbanda, Omolu is marginal. But at Pai Joaquim's and Tupinambá's, Omolu is as central as he is in Candomblé, and the *pretos velhos* there are imbued with a certain intensity and depth that comes from association with this virile and threatening symbol of Africa.

But Omolu is an Orixá, magnificent, a force of nature, and the *senzala* is a space for the spirits of the most humble of men and women, not gods. The transformation begins with songs that call the *pretos velhos*. These are typically vignettes that capture the *preto velho*'s qualities and experiences of simplicity, faith, patience, and suffering.

eu andava perambulando	I was going around perambulating
sem ter nada pra comer	without a thing to eat,
foi pedi as santas almas	went and asked the holy souls
para vir me me socorrer	to come and help me out.
(bis)	(repeat)

> *foi as almas me ajudou*   It was the souls [that] helped me,
> *foi as almas me ajudou*   it was the souls [that] helped me,
> *meu divino espírito santo*   my divine Holy Ghost.
> *viva deus, nosso senhor*   Long live God, Our Lord.
> *(bis)*   (repeat)

I heard this ballad in every *terreiro* I visited. People truly enjoy singing this song; it is a pleasure to draw out and overnasalize the penultimate syllable of *perambulando* before attacking the next three lines of clipped syllables, mapped onto a joyful, easy-to-sing melody of rising and descending scales, and then turning to the final four lines where syllables again reaggregate into words and not primarily sounds. Dona Zélia, who as a child in private school studied Latin and voice, pointed out to me that the lyrics are one grammatical error after another. "It should be *fui pedir* or, better yet, *eu pedi*; and *foram as almas que me ajudaram* would be correct; *foi as almas me ajudou*, my God!" But, as she said, the *pretos velhos* might not have mastered grammar, but they learned a lot of wisdom in the school of life, and to her the song is beautiful just as it is.

The theme of wandering hungry in the world, forsaken but for the good souls (another way of referring to *pretos velhos*) and the Father, Son, and Holy Ghost, speaks for itself. It speaks to the faith of the *preto velho*. But there is something about this song that puts the singer into the shoes of the perambulator, and vice versa. The song is a double narrative. The *eu*, the "I," here has a double reference. At one level, the "I" is a *preto velho* telling his or her story of receiving help from the spirits along the road; at another level, the "I" can be the singer, acknowledging the help that he or she has received from the *pretos velhos* in the *terreiro*. The two narratives run parallel, bleeding into each other, shifting signifiers in a play of identity: "I," the real I, and "I," the *preto velho* in the song; *preto velho*, good souls, me, nothing to eat, a metaphor of the lack in my life, the good souls helped me (which me?), the *pretos velhos* helped the me who is really me, the wandering *preto velho*, me finding my way: *meu divino espírito santo/ viva deus, nosso senhor!* The song is a kind of rehearsal and diagram for the deeper play of self/other that occurs with spirit possession.

It is surprising that the musical construction of the *senzala*, the slave quarters, includes relatively few songs that speak of captivity. There is a song for Pai Benedito that recalls that were it not for the old sorcerer, the singer would have ended up captured by slave hunters—but that is a song of relief, which contributes to the ambiance of gratitude by referring to what did *not* happen, the fate that was avoided. One of the few songs that does recall captivity in a direct way suggests that the memory may be too painful:

vovó não quer cáscara de	Grandmother doesn't like
coco no terreiro	coconut shells in the *terreiro*
(bis)	(repeat)
porque faz lembrar	because it reminds her
o tempo no cativeiro	of the time in captivity.

It would seem that neither coconut shells nor narrative song should bring back the painful memories. And indeed, the purpose of these songs is to invite the *pretos velhos* to sit in a *senzala* that is as it should be: happy, without fear, a place of caring and refuge from the cruel world outside. A song from the Casa São Benedito suggests another motive: that *pretos velhos* are persons averse to confrontation and anger, to which they might be moved were they to dwell on injustice:

Lá, no cruzeiro divino	There, in the divine *cruzeiro*
é onde as almas vão passear	is where the souls go passing by.
eles estão felizes	They are happy
quando as pessoas combinam	when people get along
e choram quando eles discordam	and cry when they disagree.

But this image of the *preto velho* comes from a stereotype that is not universally shared in Umbanda. There are strong *pretos velhos* who do not cry and shy away from controversy. Generally speaking, my informants at Pai Joaquim's and Tupinambá's, many of whom identify themselves as Black and/or victims of Brazil's extreme social inequality historically exemplified by slavery, see different qualities embodied in their *pretos velhos*.

There was a time, for example, at Pai Joaquim's when personality clashes among certain members had reached the boiling point. The tension was unbearable when, one Monday night, the *preto velho* session began with Seu Moura receiving the spirit of Pai Sebastião. Instead of crying over the discord in his *terreiro*, he stomped and pounded with his cane and spat out the following warning to anyone who would challenge the order in his *senzala*:

> *Olha bem: comigo ninguem pode! Se você não respeita a lei desse nego velho vai embora, vai a rua; ou ficar para eu quebrar! Brigar com este negão não é brincadeira não; sou machão da senzala, estou no caminho, estou na poeira da estrada.* (Look here: No one messes with me! If you don't respect the law of this old *nego* [a colloquial term for Black, with no acceptable English gloss], leave, hit the road, or stay so I can break you. To fight with this *negão* [a big *nego*] is no joke; I am real *macho*, I am in the path, I am in the dust of the road.)

Pai Sebastião exemplifies that type of *preto velho* whom Renato Ortiz lamented as a vanished species in "O Morte Branco do Feiticeiro Negro."

Pai Sebastião is a sorcerer, or *feiticeiro*, a potentially dangerous character whose magical abilities and capacity for fighting and vengeance pose a threat. He appears when Pai Joaquim's kindness and patience are abused. Pai Sebastião may be the epitome, but there is at least a little of him in many, if not all, *pretos velhos*. Many a *preto velho* has that other side, as we hear in a song from Tupinambá's, which hearkens back to a time when sorcery was a weapon of the enslaved:

O Bahiana, O Bahiana,	Oh! Bahian woman, Oh! Bahian woman,
ela é velha feiticeira	she is an old sorceress
(bis)	(repeat)
com sua toalha de lã,	with her wool towel,
dela sorriam;	they made fun of her;
com sua pemba na mão	[but] with her chalk in her hand
ela lhes desafiam	she defied them.

The towel, according to one informant, is the old woman's woolly white hair; the chalk is an instrument of *preto velho* magic.

The presence of the *feiticeiro* in the *senzala*, or of the *feiticeiro* in the *preto velho*, shifts the tone far away from the kind of warm, sentimental, nonthreatening constellation of feelings that we might expect in encounters with Diana Brown's Brazilian Uncle Toms. Chill drafts of fear and consequence filter in through the night. Sometimes those sad twinkling eyes see too much; in another song from Tupinambá's, a client admits to a *vovó* that she is afraid that the smoke from the sorceress's pipe will uncover her secrets. And sometimes the *preto velho* will play hardball. A woman came to Dona Zélia's Pai Gerônimo several times because of her brother, an alcoholic whose all-night carousing and brawling had become unbearable. Pai Gerônimo's initial approaches—advising her on how to deal with her brother, making offerings, saying prayers—were not working. The woman was beginning to have doubts about Pai Gerônimo. Finally, one night Pai Gerônimo asked her what she really wanted done. She replied that she just wanted her brother to stay at home so she would not have to worry about what might be happening to him at all hours of the night; she wanted him off the street before something really awful happened. Pai Gerônimo promised her that he would arrange things. The next week, the woman told Dona Zélia's Indian spirit, Jurema, that her brother had gone out drinking and, staggering around in the street, met with some kind of accident. His leg was smashed, and he now would have to recuperate in bed, at home, for several months. Jurema remarked that the *feiticeiro* Pai Gerônimo was no joke.

While the *pretos velhos* may resonate with Omolu, with undertones of sorcery and black magic, they always strike a Christian chord. They suffer at the hands of those who know not (or worse, *do* know) what they do. Jesus is their Savior, they revere the Virgin, and they place their faith in the saints. They are imbedded in folk Catholicism.

Cajoeiro bento	Blessed cashew tree
onde nasceu Jesus	where Jesus was born.
(bis)	(repeat)
O! Virgem imaculada	Oh! Immaculate Virgin
reza no pé da cruz	prays at the foot of the cross.
(bis)	(repeat)
Abre a porta do céu São Pedro	Open Heaven's door, Saint Peter,
deixe almas trabalhar	Let the souls work.
(bis)	(repeat)
O! Virgem imaculada	Oh! Immaculate Virgin
reza no pé da cruz	prays at the foot of the cross.

With this song, another ode to joy sung with the spirit of "Eu Andava Perambulando," participants at Tupinambá call down the *pretos velhos*. Saint Peter releases them from an Aruanda that is Heaven, to return to an Earth where Jesus is born under a cashew tree (a symbol of Brazil) and agonizes on the cross, where Mary prays.

The decisive moment in the construction of the *senzala* is when the *pretos velhos* arrive. They come one by one, the first arrival being the *preto velho* of the leader of the *terreiro*. In a small *terreiro*, where only a few *pretos velhos* appear, it is usually the case that each will be welcomed by his or her own song. That is not possible in a large *terreiro*, but, at the very least, the *preto velho* of the leader will be honored in this way. The songs are often simple greetings that tell a little about the spirit in question—for example, Pai Joaquim is greeted with a ditty that merely gives his name and tells us that he is from Angola—but others are more complex. The song for the Bahiana (given above) is a tense sketch of duality and conflict, while the following hymn to Pai Gerônimo summarizes both the ritual moment and the supplicatory relationship of person to spirit:

está iluminada nossa banda	Our "line" is illuminated,
está cheia de flor nossa gongá	our altar is full of flowers.
(bis)	(repeat)
o pai Geronimo	Oh, Father Geromino,
é tudo que o peço	this is all I ask you!
meu pai Geronimo	My Father Geronimo,
amena caminhos	smooth the roads
por onde que passo	over which I pass.
(bis)	(repeat)

The *preto velho* comes with suffering inscribed on his body. As Pai Joaquim arrives, Seu Moura's powerful body doubles; he is given his cane and hobbles over to the spot where he planted the root of the *terreiro*. His back is stiff and his knee is ruined, but somehow he bends his forehead down to the spot. He struggles to his feet, salutes the drums, and sits down on his stump to smoke his pipe and sip wine from his bowl and rest awhile before he starts his work. When Vovô Catarina comes to Dona Zélia's, she arrives in a heap on the floor; I help her to her feet and sit her down on her little white bench along the wall of the *senzala*. *Pretos Velhos* are in almost every case broken in body, or otherwise marked by pain or abuse. Most have difficulty in walking; the cane joins the pipe, the bowl of sweet red wine, and the little white bench as metonymical signs of the *preto velho*. Some can barely see; others suffer from tremors. We know that Rei Congo stutters (his medium does not), while another Rei Congo at the same *terreiro* suffers brief seizures and convulsions as he prays with his clients. Occasionally, Dona Zélia receives a *preta velha* by the name of Gertrude, an old woman from India, not Black. Gertrude's limbs are twisted and she cannot walk at all. Her arthritis is so bad that Dona Zélia is stiff and sore for days after her fortunately infrequent visits.

As they arrive, the *pretos velhos* are helped to the little white benches. Ritual assistants, such as I was at Dona Zélia's, bring them their equipment. They need a glass of water (some of them look into the water to see things—persons who have something to do with their clients' problems, places and diseases and subtle signs that guide them as they do their work). They need a candle; nothing can be done without a candle. They need chalk. There are other items: a rosary; a bag of the round, dried seeds known as Our Lady's Tears; a few old coins; some little cowry shells; perhaps an *olho de boi* like those that Pai Gerônimo tells me that my Pai Joaquim will work with. The *preto velho* takes the chalk and draws his identifying emblem. Then he places his candle by the glass of water and lights it, lights a pipe, and indicates to the assistant that it is time to begin. The *senzala* is ready.

Notes

1. *Terreiro*: literally, earth, although in this context it refers to the sanctified places where Umbanda rituals occur. Umbanda meeting places take their name from the fact that slave religion in Brazil was usually practiced outside and at night out of concern for secrecy. Today, an Umbanda *terreiro* may recall that history by having an earthen floor that is open on three sides, with the back wall against a mountain.

2. Gilberto Freyre, the noted Brazilian historian and author of *Casa Grande e Senzala*, was the first to reinterpret the role that Africans have played in his country's history and national culture.

3. Roger Bastide, *The African Religions of Brazil* (Baltimore: Johns Hopkins University Press, 1978); Diana Brown, *Umbanda: Religion and Politics in Brazil* (Ann Arbor: UMI Research Press, 1986).

4. Brown, *Umbanda*, 67–68.

5. Renato Ortiz, *O moderna tradição brasileira* (São Paulo: Brasiliense, 1988).

III

The Catholic Church in Transition:
Liberation Theology and Beyond

6

Brazil: The Catholic Church and the Popular Movement in Nova Iguaçu, 1974–1985

Scott Mainwaring

*Brazil is the biggest country in Latin America and has the largest popula-
tion of Roman Catholics in the world. It is also the first place where Christian base communities (CEBs) became widespread and where the ideas of
Liberation Theology were embraced by the institutional Catholic Church.
The first CEBs began in Brazil around 1962, thus predating both Vatican
II (1962–1965) and the Episcopal conference at Medellín, Colombia
(1968), where the Latin American bishops articulated the "preferential
option for the poor." The CEBs then, as now, were a way of extending the
Church's active presence to the poor, an issue that is particularly urgent
in Brazil, where the chronic shortage of priests is especially acute and
where religious competition from Protestantism, African religions, and
Spiritism is strong.*

*In the mid-1960s a bishop from Brazil's impoverished northeast, Dom
Helder Cámara, emerged as one of Liberation Theology's first and most
outspoken proponents. In 1967, Cámara denounced the military government that controlled Brazil from 1964 to 1986 for human rights viola-
tions, and he continued to oppose the regime despite threats against him
and the assassination of some of his associates. Although all of the Brazilian Catholic hierarchy did not share Cámara's vision, Liberation Theology spread rapidly through the lower clergy and, even more significantly,
among the vast sea of the urban and rural poor. The role of Catholic activism became even more crucial as Brazil underwent its "economic
miracle" in the 1960s and 1970s, a process that dramatically increased*

From *Religion and Political Conflict in Latin America*, ed. Daniel H. Levine
(Chapel Hill: University of North Carolina Press, 1986), 124–55. © 1986 by the
University of North Carolina Press. Reprinted by permission of the University of
North Carolina Press.

migration into the shantytowns (favelas) *of the cities, opened new areas of the country for exploitation, and brought new stresses to traditional family structures and means of subsistence.*

Although the military government did repress some Church activists, participation in CEBs provided many poor Brazilians in the 1960s and 1970s with a political and social cohesion and a voice that many could not have found in any other forum. As the following article suggests, for poor, disenfranchised Brazilians, Church activism paved the way for their overt participation in the political opening and return to democracy, known as abertura, *which, for Catholic activists at least, carried implicitly Christian overtones.*

Scott Mainwaring is Eugene Conley Professor of Government and International Studies and director of the Kellogg Institute of International Studies at the University of Notre Dame. He is the author of several books and many articles on Brazil and on South American social movements. His most recent publication is Politics, Society, and Democracy in Latin America *(1998), coedited with Arturo Valenzuela.*

This chapter examines the relationship between the Catholic church and the neighborhood movement of Nova Iguaçu, a large (more than 1 million inhabitants) working-class city thirty kilometers to the north of Rio de Janeiro. This case is interesting because of the importance and dynamic growth of the movement and its strong ties to the church. After 1974, the limited and dipersed efforts of the local population to obtain better urban services were gradually transformed into one of the best-known and organized movements in the state of Rio de Janeiro, and the Catholic church played an important role in the movement. The case is also highly suggestive about the way the church's role has changed during the process of political liberalization, which began around 1974—the same year the work that led to Nova Iguaçu's neighborhood movement began—and about the way the church contributed to the democratization process. Finally, the example of Nova Iguaçu illustrates some dilemmas confronting both the popular church and the popular movements and the alliances and tensions that exist between the church and these movements.

During the past decade, as the Latin American church has become a more vital force within the international church and within the political debates in many countries, the number of studies on the church has proliferated.[1] Until recently, however, the great majority of studies have focused almost exclusively on the hierarchy and on church-state relationships. This essay breaks from this perspective and insists upon the need to pay more attention to grassroots organizations and to church-civil society relationships. The church's political significance in Nova Iguaçu—

and more generally, throughout Latin America—cannot be comprehended through an exclusive focus on the hierarchy and on church-state relations. In Nova Iguaçu, although the bishop's support for progressive grassroots experiences has been critical, it is the grassroots organizations rather than the bishop that have been most important in supporting the popular movements. Furthermore, it has been the church's role in empowering civil society (especially the popular movements) rather than its negotiations with the local political elite that has been most significant.

The Church, Ecclesial Base Communities, and Politics

During the early part of the twentieth century, after undergoing a lengthy period of institutional decline, the Brazilian Catholic church began to express concern about its weak linkages to the popular masses. In a famous pastoral letter written in 1916, Dom Sebastião Leme, the outstanding leader of the Brazilian church until his death in 1942, called attention to the weakness of the institutional church, the deficiencies of popular religious practices, the shortage of priests, the poor religious education, and the church's limited presence among the masses. Leme argued that the church needed to develop a stronger presence in the society and encourage more orthodox and acceptable popular religious practices.[2]

Despite marked institutional renovation in other areas, for several decades the church was only moderately successful in developing stronger linkages with the popular sectors. The real breakthrough did not occur until the emergence of the ecclesial base communities.[3] The CEBs seem to have originated in Brazil, where the first ones were created around 1962 or 1963. In some rural areas, progressive priests who were unable to say mass in a given area every Sunday because of the vast territories they had to cover decided to encourage the local people to meet for a Sunday service. This was not only a way of answering Dom Leme's old appeal for developing a deeper understanding of principles of Catholic faith and strengthening the church's ties to the popular classes, it also coincided with the trend to encourage greater lay participation and responsibility.[4] The base communities were originally intended as a means of strengthening the church, not, as they would become, a new form of the church.

The 1964 coup marked a watershed, both in Brazilian politics and for the Catholic church. Responding to fears of social chaos and economic crisis, the military overthrew the progressive populist government of João Goulart, beginning a period of twenty-one years of uninterrupted military rule. The military government represssed popular movements and initiated ambitious growth projects. Especially during the presidency of

General Emilio Garrastazu Médici (1969–74), it silenced the most significant opposition forces. Partially in response to the repression, the Catholic church changed in a more progressive direction. Progressive grassroots innovations such as the CEBs became a more central part of pastoral initiatives.[5]

A major turning point in the discussion about and role of CEBs came at the Medellín meeting of the Latin American Bishops' Conference in 1968, which encouraged the creation of base communities, now recognized as structures that could have some political significance.[6] By the early 1970s the number of CEBs started to grow rapidly. In their short history, the base communities have become a defining feature of the Latin American church; Brazil's most renowned theologian speaks of them as "reinventing the church."[7] New approaches to liturgy, catechism, community building, and theology have emerged within the communities.[8] The CEBs are known for encouraging both participation in religious life and a context that allows the members (mostly poor people) to take active responsibility for running group life: setting the agenda, making key decisions, and organizing for a variety of religious, social, and political activities. These innovations have profoundly affected the church in many Latin American countries; in this sense, the Brazilian church has exported aspects of its transformation to other Latin American nations. At the Puebla gathering of the Latin American Bishops' Conference in 1979, the bishops recognized that the base communities "create better interpersonal relationships, acceptance of God's Word, reflection about life and reality in light of the Bible; in the communities, the commitment to family, work, the neighborhood, and the local community are strengthened."[9] From modest beginnings, the CEBs in Brazil have grown to embrace an estimated eighty thousand groups with 2 million participants.

The proper role of the CEBs has become one of the major debates in the Latin American church. Conservative church leaders claim that the base communities are excessively involved in politics and threaten the church's specifically religious identity. They see the base communities as a threat to traditional hierarchical lines of ecclesiastical authority. Conservative hierarchies, such as the Colombian, have essentially renamed extant groups and called them base communities and have exerted strong pressures against the more popular and politically involved CEBs. While co-opting the name, they have fought for tighter clerical control over grassroots ecclesial groups.[10]

The impact of the CEBs and the debate about them does not derive exclusively from their religious role. Based on their reading of the Bible, many CEB participants have become involved in popular movements, though their political activity has been characterized by a remarkable and generally understated heterogeneity. The case of Nova Iguaçu suggests that although Brazilian CEBs are not particularly politically sophisticated or even active, they can help strengthen popular movements that are working toward progressive social change. Furthermore, despite their political limitations, Brazilian CEBs have been significant in providing a basically democratic, participatory space in a generally elitist society.[11] The CEBs' political significance has been particularly great in Brazil, Chile, and Central America, where many CEB members have participated in revolutionary struggles.[12] Thus these grassroots organizations have become an essential element of the religious and political future of several Latin American nations. It is within this general context that the significance of the case of Nova Iguaçu must be analyzed.

The Socioeconomic, Political, and Ecclesial Context in Nova Iguaçu

Located in the Baixada Fluminense, a large lowlands which has a hot climate, Nova Iguaçu became one of the most important orange-producing regions in the country around the turn of the century. Orange production entered a decline in 1926, when diseases started to kill the trees in some parts of the Baixada. The municipality's population grew from 33,396 in 1920 to 105,809 in 1940,[13] but the area was still predominantly rural. By the end of World War II, orange production had dropped off dramatically.[14]

After 1945, Nova Iguaçu began a new phase characterized by being a distant periphery of Greater Rio. As Greater Rio grew and as real estate prices pushed the popular classes into the favelas or the periphery, the city itself grew rapidly.[15] From 145,649 inhabitants in 1950, the population increased to 359,364 in 1960 and 727,140 in 1970, making Nova Iguaçu the fastest-growing major city in the country. In 1950, 46.60 percent of the municipality's population still resided in rural areas, but by 1970 this figure had dropped to 0.39 percent. This growth slowed during the 1970s, but the population still increased to 1,094,805. It is predominantly a working-class (generally unskilled labor) city with a high percentage of migrants. In 1980, 55.59 percent of the total population were migrants. Of 374,000 people in the workforce, 76,000 were involved in industry, 155,000 in services, 54,000 in construction, 48,000 in commerce, and 19,000 in public sector jobs (see Table).[16]

The expansion of social services lagged far behind the city's growth. In 1980, only 37.7 percent of the municipality's population had running water. Only 30.3 percent had sewers; sewage is disposed through open canals and rivers, which is severely damaging to the local ecology and helps account for the bad health conditions. The city had only 265 doctors, 27 dentists, and 961 hospital beds, in all cases approximately one-

Population of the Municipality of Nova Iguaçu

Year	Population	Percent in rural areas
1920	33,396	
1940	105,809	
1950	145,649	46.60
1960	359,364	28.34
1970	727,140	0.39
1980	1,094,805	0.29

Source: Instituto Brasileiro de Geografia e Estatística, *Censo*, various years.

eighth Rio's per capita level.[17] Between 1968 and 1972, the mortality rate for children in their first four years of life was 39 percent.[18] Partially because of a shortage of schools, in 1978, according to the mayor's estimate, 150,000 school-aged children were not enrolled, and most schools were in poor condition and seriously deficient in supplies. The illiteracy rate for people over ten years old was 17 percent in 1980, and only 39 percent of the population had completed high school. As of 1978, only about 15 percent of the municipality's garbage was collected, leaving some five hundred tons of garbage per day in open sewers and unoccupied land. Inadequate police facilities have led to one of the highest crime rates in the country. Less than 10 percent of the municipality's roads are paved, and the dirt roads create major transportation problems in rainy weather. A 1980 estimate showed that if the city administration continued to pave roads at the same pace as in the preceding decade, it would take 250 years to pave the streets that already existed.[19] The intermunicipality buses are in poor condition, overcrowded, and insufficient in number, and buses to Rio are very expensive relative to local income. The train takes two hours to cover thirty kilometers, is badly overcrowded, and has a high accident rate because of poor track conditions.[20]

The population of Nova Iguaçu has some tradition of battling to obtain better social services.[21] At least as early as 1945, there were isolated attempts to organize the population for this purpose. In 1950, the first neighborhood associations were formed. As the national and local climate of the late populist years (1958–64) stimulated a rich political debate throughout the society, the neighborhood movement expanded rapidly. In 1960, leaders of the neighborhood movement organized the first Congress of the Commissions for Urban Improvements of the Neighborhoods of Nova Iguaçu, mobilizing many neighborhood associations and obtaining some concrete concessions from the city administration. The precoup years saw other experiences of popular mobilization in the Baixada

Fluminense, including a significant labor movement and occasional movements among peasants and rural workers. After 1974 the movements would draw upon this history of popular mobilization, in which several leaders had actively participated.

The coup wiped out the most important popular movements. Key leaders of the neighborhood movement were imprisoned, and the repression prevented efforts to coordinate the movement between different neighborhoods, reducing it to isolated efforts. The associations that survived articulated their demands individually, and there was little public sensitivity to them. The high levels of repression against the popular sectors and the disarticulation of local opposition forces made any popular organizing outside the church almost impossible.

The years following the coup were difficult for much of the local population. The city continued to grow at a rapid pace, bringing new social tensions. Real wages declined for most workers until around 1976, and the city's urban services failed to keep pace with the population growth. In addition to the official repressive apparatus, the infamous Death Squad was very active in the Baixada. By 1979 the Death Squad had executed 2,000 people in Nova Iguaçu, and another paramilitary organization executed 764 in the first half of 1980 alone.[22] The progressive local opposition leaders were imprisoned, and by 1970 the opposition party, the Brazilian Democratic Movement (MDB) entered a deep crisis. Statewide, the MDB fell into the hands of a conservative group closely linked to the federal government and known for being corrupt.[23] The local government party, National Renovative Alliance (ARENA), was conservative even compared with its counterpart in other major cities. It was notorious for corruption and was largely uninterested in resolving the urban problems confronting the population. Despite the local MDB's problems, ARENA was defeated in 1974 and subsequent elections.[24]

Meanwhile, the church of Nova Iguaçu was undergoing the changes that would make it the bulwark of popular movements. The diocese of Nova Iguaçu was created in 1960, and until 1966 its orientation was relatively conservative. That year, Dom Adriano Hypólito was named bishop and began to encourage the changes that led the church to become closely identified with the popular sectors.[25] At the first Diocesan Assembly, held in 1968, the diocese voted to establish base communities as one of its principal priorities.[26] Coincident with the constriction of civil society after 1964, the church began to create community groups—Bible circles, mothers' clubs, youth groups, catechism clubs—which reflected on faith and social reality. During the most repressive years, the base communities, which started to flourish during the early 1970s, were virtually the only popular organizations to promote critical political perspectives.

Although these communities were involved only in rudimentary political actions such as signing petitions for urban services, their existence would prove important for the development of the Baixada's popular movements. Between 1964 and 1974, the only attempt to organize the local popula-tion in a more continuous fashion was the Movement of Community Inte-gration, created by the diocese in 1968. This movement hoped to organize Catholics to get better urban services, but in 1970 it was dissolved by the repressive apparatus.

This picture began to change around 1974, when the military regime began to promote a "slow and gradual" liberalization process within the context of increasing divisions in the armed forces, the annihilation of the left, increasing opposition in civil society, and the "economic miracle." The *abertura* ("opening") profoundly affected the political process, in-cluding the church's role and relationship to popular movements. The lib-eralization coexisted with attempts to continue many key elements in the system of domination, with limited popular participation, tight control over major economic decisions, a strong executive, and an unegalitarian economic model. In this sense, the *abertura* was initially more an elite attempt to secure a continuation of important features of the system than a fundamental alteration in the regime.[27] During the early phases of po-litical liberalization (1974–78), the liberal sectors of society benefited the most, but by 1978 popular movements were in a period of growth. In 1978, the first major strike in a decade occurred among the auto workers in the greater São Paulo region, and the Cost of Living Movement grew to national proportions.[28]

Political liberalization followed the same general contours in Nova Iguaçu as nationally, with a gradual easing of repression, especially after 1978. But the process in Nova Iguaçu had some distinctive features. The city administration and local government party were particularly discred-ited, especially by the late 1970s, remaining unresponsive to popular de-mands even though the repression was easing. The MDB in the state of Rio de Janeiro also remained discredited because of its close linkages to the military government. The Nova Iguaçu MDB entered a deep crisis that began around 1970 and lasted through the 1982 elections. Conse-quently, in contrast to other cities, where some MDB politicians supported the popular movements, the neighborhood movement remained politically isolated, with the church as its most significant ally. Finally, although the official repression eased up, the paramilitary Right remained active. The systematic repression of the Médici years (1969–74) disappeared, but the far right continued terrorist practices, including many incidents of re-pression against the Nova Iguaçu church and members of the neighbor-hood movement. The most spectacular incidents involved the kidnapping and torturing of Dom Adriano Hypólito in 1976 and the bombing of the cathedral in 1979.[29] The specter of repression was therefore one of the factors that conditioned the development of the neighborhood movement after 1974.

The Emergence and Growth of MAB:
The Neighborhood Movement, 1974–1985

In the second half of the 1970s, there was an unprecedented growth of and interest in popular neighborhood movements.[30] The seeds of the Nova Iguaçu movement go back to 1974, when two young doctors committed to working with the poor began to practice in one of Nova Iguaçu's outlying neighborhoods.[31] Initially, they attended the population almost gratuitously and offered courses on health, but they gradually became aware of the limitations of this work. Medical treatment had only palliative effects on a region with widespread malnutrition, open sewers, no garbage collection, and other health problems, so they began to think about organizing the population to help change those living conditions.[32]

In 1975, the diocese's branch of Cáritas, an international organ of the Catholic church for serving the poor, hired these doctors and two others to start a health program. These four doctors would be responsible for transforming the previously isolated neighborhood efforts into a coherent popular movement. Committed to working with and attempting to mobilize the poor, the doctors made it clear from the beginning that they were not Catholics and that their contributions would be medical and political, not religious. This frankness led to good relations with Dom Adriano and the progressive clergy, including the Cáritas director, but the conservative clergy had reservations about their work.

In November 1975, the diocese began to hold health discussions led by the four doctors. Beginning the second meeting, in March 1976, Cáritas issued a report as a means of publicizing the meetings and disseminating ideas. At the second meeting the group's fundamental orientation was articulated: "The solution of health problems depends more on the population's unity and action than on the presence of a doctor. Having a health post is important, but it does not resolve health problems. Therefore, all the forms the population has of uniting to reflect on its problems and develop its consciousness and unity are important. Actions which are purely palliative, which are not concerned with the population's conscientization, discourage true learning and do not resolve health problems."[33]

In this early phase, the majority of people attending the courses worked at health posts. The doctors were satisfied with these courses, but they also wanted to reach a different public, the poor themselves. In 1976, they held health courses in six different neighborhoods throughout the municipality, usually visiting already established groups, most of which were connected to the diocese: Bible groups, mothers' clubs, baptism clubs, youth groups. These visits often strengthened the extant organizations or led to new embryonic organizations. The doctors emphasized awareness about the causes of health problems rather than medical treatment and encouraged the population to organize to get better urban services as a way of dealing with the problems.

The immersion in the neighborhoods represented an important step in the young movement. The clientele began to change, with fewer people who worked in health care but more people from a working-class background participating. All problems faced by the population, not just health issues, began to be discussed. Simultaneously, the population began to organize neighborhood associations to address these needs. From the beginning, these efforts emphasized the concrete needs of the local population rather than the more theoretical discussions characteristic of the church's conscientization work.

In May 1977, the movement began to call itself Amigos do Bairro (Friends of the Neighborhood) and assumed responsibility for putting out the newspaper that disseminated information. At the eleventh health encounter, in November 1977, the movement's objectives were stated explicitly: "Friends of the Neighborhood is a movement concerned with the good of all people, with a better and more dignified existence." At this same meeting, the concern was expressed that "Friends of the Neighborhood cannot be closed, it must communicate with all people and encourage all to participate."[34] This was a call to expand beyond church horizons and become a mass movement. Around this time, the movement began to define one of its principal strategies, direct confrontation with the city administration in fighting for urban services.

The movement continued to expand, involving a growing number of neighborhoods. This expansion dictated the need for more formal leadership structures, and at the thirteenth meeting, in March 1978, the movement voted to create a coordinating commission whose functions would be to "orient the movement, attempting to encourage the groups, but without dominating them; encourage the exchange of experiences; visit the neighborhoods; do a summary of the meetings; encourage the formation of new neighborhood associations; represent the movement whenever necessary; publish a newspaper about the problems and struggles of the neighborhoods; organize a central archive which includes the experiences of all the groups, important addresses, and other information for whomever needs it; offer mini-courses."[35] This leadership structure was an important step in expanding beyond isolated material needs to developing a mass movement with broad political horizons. Other steps in this direction occurred around the same time, including turning the health newspaper into a newspaper for the movement. A period of consolidation and rapid expansion was under way.

By May 1978, the bimonthly meetings involved people from eighteen different neighborhoods of Nova Iguaçu. At that time, the movement adopted the name Movimento de Amigos de Bairro, MAB (Friends of the Neighborhood Movement). The local associations continued to be the primary instrument for organizing the neighborhoods, and MAB became the means of coordinating the efforts of different associations and turning them into a cohesive project, capable of pressuring the state into becoming more responsive to local needs.

Two issues that arose in May 1978 had a major impact on the movement's development. One of the most active associations took a petition with fifteen hundred signatures to the city administration, but the administration refused to receive it, stating that it would accept demands only from people who had paid their building tax. The residents wrote to several council members (*vereadores*) protesting this policy, and the movement brought the issue to the attention of the local press. These pressures from different segments of the society forced the mayor to modify his initial statement on 25 July. MAB had achieved its first major victory in pressuring the city administration to reevaluate its policies toward the popular sectors and for the first time had received considerable press attention and won allies among local politicians.

Around the same time, another serious conflict between MAB and the city administration occurred. The mayor agreed to attend a meeting with residents from one neighborhood, but he sent a representative instead. The residents were angry about his failure to come or to notify them beforehand. In protest to the initial decision to refuse to receive petitions and to the mayor's failure to listen to the demands of the local population, MAB decided to hold an assembly to discuss the administration's irresponsibility and what the residents could do about it. The assembly was held on 14 October 1978, with seven hundred participants representing thirty-eight neighborhoods, of which thirty-four had signed a letter to the mayor protesting the administration's lack of responsiveness. The assembly began a new period in MAB's development, marked by stronger linkages to local politicians and the press and by more extensive participation. The development of local allies would give the movement greater impact than it previously had.[36]

Until late 1978 and early 1979, even though MAB was becoming a mass movement, it was still almost exclusively concerned with immediate material needs of the local population. This focus began to change in

late 1978 and early 1979 as the leadership became more interested in local and national politics. MAB participated in the solidarity movement
with the 1979 auto workers' strike and with a teachers' strike in Rio and
sent representatives to local demonstrations. The leaders began to support issues related to the democratization of the society such as party
reform, political amnesty, and reform of local government. Organizational
and political changes accompanied the movement's expansion and the
parallel changes in the national political situation. In January 1979, MAB
elected its first formal Coordinating Council, which met every week rather
than every two months. The movement divided into five regional groups
to attempt to ensure better sensitivity to grassroots needs.

MAB's dynamism created a new problem for the city administration,
which was accustomed to ignoring popular demands. During MAB's early
phases, 1975–78, the administration, headed by a notoriously conservative and corrupt branch of the government party, consistently showed disrespect for MAB leaders. MAB participants were frequently told to meet
with a city representative at a given time and place, only to arrive and
find that the official was engaged elsewhere. After agreeing to hold bimonthly hearings to listen to the population's demands, the administration attempted to renege on the commitment.

MAB used this unresponsiveness as a means of further delegitimizing
the city government. The movement publicized the government's repeated
failures to meet promises, the disrespect it had shown for MAB participants, the financial scandals that surrounded the administration, and its
failure to attend to the needs of the local population. Largely in response
to the administration's repeated failures to meet promises and provide
urban services, MAB decided to hold a second major assembly on 15 July
1979, again leading to an increase in the number of participating neighborhoods. It had three thousand participants, representing sixty neighborhoods of Nova Iguaçu. The importance the movement had acquired
was evident in the publicity the assembly received and in the presence of
important political figures, including federal senator Roberto Saturnino.
The meeting was also successful in forcing the administration to agree to
meet weekly with representatives from different neighborhoods of Nova
Iguaçu. MAB, by now the most important popular movement in Nova
Iguaçu, was in a new, more mature phase.

The party reform initiated in January 1979 was one of the most important steps in the *abertura*. The government dissolved the biparty system it had created in 1965 and established regulations for the creation of
new parties. The party reform has deeply affected the entire subsequent
political struggle, including the evolution of popular movements and the
church and in this specific case, MAB. Although party reform had been a

fundamental demand of the opposition, the government skillfully managed the reform to maximize divisions within the opposition, which split into five parties.[37] MAB's leaders had always experienced some internal divisions, but the party reform accentuated these divisions. Some MAB leaders opted for the largest opposition party, the PMDB (Party of the Brazilian Democratic Movement); others joined the Workers party (PT) or the Democratic Labor party (PDT). These party divisions reflected differences in basic philosophy about what should be done at that political juncture and how popular movements should be led. Some MAB leaders (mostly PT) were most concerned about grassroots discussions and about making sure the common people led the process, and others (mostly PMDB) emphasized the importance of creating a mass movement that would participate in the redemocratization process. Ironically, then, the *abertura*, which facilitated the growth of the movement, also created conditions for internal competition and division.

Despite tensions between PT, PDT, and PMDB leaders, until December 1981 the existence of competing conceptions about how to run the movement probably helped MAB to articulate a careful balance between grassroots work and broader political issues that made it one of the more successful neighborhood movements in the country. By late 1981, almost one hundred neighborhood associations were participating. The demonstration at the Government Palace in Rio on 13 June 1980, with seven hundred participants, was the first time MAB had gone to the state government rather than to Nova Iguaçu's government to demand urban improvements. This approach to the state government marked an important step in MAB's visibility and capacity to negotiate with the state. It meant dealing with a higher level of government and initiated a strategy of forcing the government party, the Social Democratic party (PDS), and the now extinct Popular party (PP), which controlled the state government, to compete in providing services.

MAB's successes have not made its tasks any easier; indeed, they have become more complicated as the movement has gained maturity. Mobilizing the local population remains difficult because of the region's security problems, the poor and (relatively) expensive transportation, and the limited time so many people have. Financial problems continue to plague the movement. Until the November 1982 elections, the city administration remained fairly unresponsive to MAB and to popular demands; the normally cautious *Jornal do Brasil* reported that "nowhere in the state of Rio is the Government party so discredited as in Nova Iguaçu."[38]

In December 1981, a period of greater internal conflict at the leadership level and some demobilization of the grass roots began. The most important problem was the accentuation of internal tensions in the movement, principally stemming from partisan disputes. In December 1981, MAB held the second Congress of Neighborhood Associations of Nova Iguaçu (the first had been held in 1960), became a federation, and held elections for a new Coordinating Council. The elections for the Coordinating Council led to sharp and unforeseen disputes. Many of the original leaders, including the four doctors, were not elected. Twelve of the nineteen original members remained, but the overall composition of the council changed. There were tensions between the new leaders and some of those who left, and charges of manipulation were made on both sides. Never before had MAB experienced such deep internal disputes. These tensions played into the government's hands. The regime fared relatively well until 1982 at institutionalizing an elitist system within the bounds of electoral politics because the opposition was somewhat disarticulated. Popular movements no longer had the dynamic growth that had characterized the 1974–80 period.

The 1982 elections for governor, federal and state congress, and local government stimulated many debates and conflicts within the movement. Officially, MAB adopted a position of autonomy vis-à-vis political parties. This meant that as a movement, MAB did not opt for any particular party and that it was open to all individuals, regardless of party affiliation. At the same time, however, many MAB leaders recognized the importance of electing individuals more sympathetic to the movement, so approximately a dozen MAB leaders ran for office, all in the PMDB or the PT.

The election results proved a major disappointment to the movement's leaders, most of whom had worked for the PMDB and the PT. None of the popular candidates of Nova Iguaçu were elected. Leonel Brizola won by a large plurality in Nova Iguaçu, and the PDT easily won the municipal elections. In the dispute for mayor, the election yielded the following results:[39] PDT, 129,789; PDS, 67,484; PMDB, 66,252; PTB, 20,084; PT, 7,262.

In Nova Iguaçu, a relatively conservative faction of the PDT came to power. Although less repressive and more open than past local governments, it also faced problems of corruption and lack of responsiveness. Throughout the state, Brizola implemented populist practices aimed at developing popular support. Faced with the severe economic crisis, the federal government's strategy of reducing resources to opposition governors, and a PDT minority in the state parliament, Brizola had difficulties in effecting major changes. At both the municipal and state levels, the opposition's winning of free, competitive elections but inability to introduce substantial improvements in popular living conditions created new problems for MAB. As one movement leader stated, "When the PDS was in power, everyone knew that the government was against the people. With Brizola, with the PDT, it is harder. Brizola says he is your friend, but in practice he is not much better than the PDS. But most people don't see this."[40]

Despite these new challenges and a temporary demobilization of the grass roots, MAB continued to be one of the most important popular movements in the state. In December 1983, the movement held new elections for the Coordinating Council, and the different factions once again improved their relations, beginning another phase of growth. In early 1984, the movement participated extensively in the campaign for direct elections. In November 1984, it held its largest demonstration ever, attended by about four thousand people, around issues of public health. By January 1985, when Tancredo Neves was elected president, MAB represented 120 neighborhood associations in the Baixada Fluminense.

The Church and MAB

During the MAB's early development, the movement was highly dependent on the church. As the regime began to permit a limited liberalization, the popular movements gained more autonomy from the church for two principal reasons. First, the dynamics of the social process pushed them into a more autonomous position. Whereas earlier the popular classes could not organize outside the church, as the regime opened up, they gained more space for mobilizing and had less need to organize within the church. The church's politically limited organizations became somewhat inadequate as the strategic, organizational, and financial demands on popular movements became more complex. Conflicting ideas emerged regarding how the movements should be led as political organizations became reactivated and started to challenge the church's hegemony of the popular movements. The church often lagged behind in its political formulations, strengthening the tendency for other groups to assume the leadership of the most important movements. This nonchurch leadership was materialized in Nova Iguaçu through the role played by the four medical doctors and a number of other individuals associated with the Left.

Second, Dom Adriano and most other church leaders made a conscious effort to encourage the autonomy of popular movements, which they perceived as a means of strengthening the movements and opening them to non-Catholics. The diocese recognized that it did not have any special competence in the political decisions facing popular movements. It also perceived this option as a means of reaffirming its identity as a religious institution. Thus, in Dom Adriano's words, "It is advantageous for pastoral work that the movement be autonomous. That way, pastoral work can concentrate on the religious sphere, on the Bible Circles, religious ceremonies, base communities. The communities can continue focusing on the Bible and the social concerns which emerge from their faith."[41]

More Catholic activists assumed leadership positions, but the dependence on the church diminished as MAB focused more on popular mobilization and less on medical work. As the movement became better known, it relied less on support from local parishes. Even though it continued to encounter financial difficulties, it became more autonomous in this sphere, too. An important step in this regard was Cáritas's decision in 1978 that it would no longer finance the work of the four doctors on the grounds that in the new political climate it should use its limited financial resources to support work with the Catholic population. At the same time, the base gradually became less Catholic. As MAB became a mass movement and did less medical work, many CEB participants stopped attending the health seminars. People from other religious groups or who did not actively participate in any church joined the movement. Individuals with a history of leadership in the region's popular struggles started to participate, further diversifying the movement.

Nevertheless, the autonomy of the popular movements with respect to the church should not be overstated. In Nova Iguaçu, as in many parts of the country, a strong connection between the popular movements and the church continues to exist. It would be more accurate to say that the church and the movement have sought a relationship of autonomy than to assert that this autonomy exists in an absolute form.[42] The institutional church has continued to play an important role in MAB's development through several means:

1. Until November 1982, it helped protect the movement from the repressive apparatus. At critical periods, the diocese still can speak out against authoritarianism. When the church was attacked in the late 1970s, it was Dom Adriano and the Justice and Peace Commission that responded. When some urban squatters were involved in a difficult struggle for land in 1981 and 1982, it was the church that defended them. MAB lacked the resources to handle such a difficult case.

2. Many neighborhood associations hold their meetings in churches, which not only resolves the space problem but also serves as a visible sign of ecclesial support. The diocese provides space for MAB's office at the Formation Center, where the Coordinating Council meets weekly. Because one of MAB's major problems has been lack of financial resources, it has been important that the movement does not have to rent an

office. The use of a diocesan building is also a source of legitimation, both in the population's eyes and in avoiding repression.

3. The diocese provides limited financial support, usually indirectly, as through helping to finance the health program. The diocese has loaned MAB a mimeograph machine, does not charge the movement for the use of electricity or water, and occasionally gives MAB small financial donations for its work toward social justice.

4. The diocese provides a moral legitimacy that encourages grassroots Catholics to participate. The church enjoys greater legitimacy than other institutions in Nova Iguaçu. Much of the population views the church as the one institution it can count on and as the only institution that will not act in pursuit of its own self-interests. The clergy are usually the only educated people who have ongoing contact with the population, so their credibility is unparalleled. Consequently, the support of most clergy has been very helpful to the movement.

The outstanding key to the close connection between MAB and the diocese has been Dom Adriano, who gave his full support to MAB from the beginning. In an interview, he stated, "We have an evangelical commitment to make a preferential option for the poor. So how are we going to realize this option? It's not enough just to talk and pray. As a Christian and as a pastor, I feel I have the duty to support the movements which work for the good of the people."[43]

The diocese's most important organizations have also supported MAB. Cáritas, for example, made possible the health work that led to MAB's creation, provides space for MAB's office, lets MAB use a mimeograph machine, and has hired two MAB leaders. The Justice and Peace Commission and the Pastoral Workers Commission (CPO) have generally backed MAB, although there have been some tensions between the CPO and MAB.

Most of the clergy have supported MAB, principally through developing a vision of faith that emphasizes social justice and political participation. Some priests have encouraged people to participate in MAB or to form neighborhood associations, and many let the associations use the churches for meetings. Characteristic of the support from progressive clergy for the popular movement was one foreign priest who arrived in a neighborhood of Nova Iguaçu in 1978. From the beginning his attitude was that the church should back the popular movements while respecting their autonomy: "The church has the grass roots, but it doesn't have many people who know what to do politically. It doesn't have people who can lead the grass roots. Therefore we must support the people who can. Also, it is not the church's role to lead the movement. What projects should be undertaken? How should the struggle be concretized? These questions go beyond the church's domain."[44]

When the priest arrived in 1978, he began to encourage the creation of more base communities and to promote a vision of faith linked to social justice. A few months later, several lay people and he prepared and distributed a questionnaire on the neighborhood's major problems. They invited all the residents—not just Catholics—to participate in the survey. At this point, a man who had participated actively in the region's popular struggles until the early 1970s and who had been jailed thirty-two times for political reasons under the military regime became involved. He had long ceased being active in the church, but the priest's orientation and willingness to work with non-Catholics encouraged him to attend the meetings. He spoke of how the church's transformation affected him: "For many years, even though I am a Catholic, I didn't have much to do with the church. The church felt it didn't need the poor. The priests didn't baptize our children, they didn't say funeral masses for peasants, they didn't give us any support. This bothered me. . . . The Church was against the common people and for the wealthy. . . . In '78, seeing that the church was helping the people, I began to participate again. It wasn't that I stayed away from the church for all those years, but rather the church that was removed from the people."[45]

After organizing the assembly and helping initiate a neighborhood association, the church changed its role. The population assumed control of the association, and the old activist became the outstanding leader. This association quickly became one of the best organized in all of Nova Iguaçu. Even though the movement had become autonomous, the church's support did not cease. The priest continued to encourage CEB participants to act in the association by stressing the value of political participation, and the meetings are still held in the church.

In addition to the support the bishop, many priests, and diocesan organizations have provided, grassroots church movements have contributed to MAB's growth even though the base communities in Nova Iguaçu are primarily dedicated to religious reflection and are not politically sophisticated.[46] MAB and other movements do the political organizing, and the diocese focuses on evangelization, which includes encouraging people to live the social and political dimensions of faith. Yet by encouraging a large number of people to think more critically about politics, CEBs have helped create a willingness to particpate in politics. The existence of CEBs meant that there was a large number of people with some prior experience of organization and participation, disposed to fight for urban improvements. Significantly, the neighborhood associations are generally strongest in areas where the church has encouraged the creation of CEBs.

An MAB leader who was a longtime activist in the area's popular struggles reflected on how the grassroots church work has strengthened the popular struggles:

> The people who participated before '64 were directed from above, by the parties and politicians of the period. The movement grew a lot but didn't have much substance. It made a lot of noise but lacked continuity. Before elections, it grew rapidly, but after the elections, it gradually faded. Today's movements are different. Today, the work is more politically conscious. The participants know why they are there, they discuss more, participate more actively. Today they aren't just dragged along. That's what the difference is, that today the movement has a firm base. This difference is largely because of the church's work.[47]

In addition to helping create a grassroots constituency that has bolstered the base of the popular movements, the diocese has encouraged the formation of popular leaders. Eight of the nineteen members of the initial Coordinating Council acquired their political education principally through the church, and six more had strong ties to the church. Nine members of the second Coordinating Committee had developed their political consciousness through the church, and at the neighborhood level, the predominance of Catholic activists is greater. A woman who first participated in the local CEB, later in the Pastoral Workers Commission and her local neighborhood association, and was eventually part of MAB's first Coordinating Council explained her own political evolution: "My political consciousness grew through the church. I was always a very religious person and was active in the church. But before coming to Nova Iguaçu, I had experienced only the closed church of Rio. It didn't get involved in politics, or if it did, it was on the government's side. Seven years ago, we moved to Nova Iguaçu. That's when I started to develop a political consciousness. I participated in the base community and learned a different understanding of the Bible, committed to the poor and to social justice."[48]

MAB, the Left, and the Church: Alliances and Tensions

Between the early 1970s and about 1978, there was a historically unprecedented alliance between the popular church and the left, which had traditionally seen the church as one of its principal enemies. After the total defeat suffered between 1968 and 1974, significant sectors of the left rejected vanguard approaches and became more concerned about basic human rights, more willing to work with democratic opposition forces, and more interested in doing grassroots work with the popular classes. And even though they diverged with many political conceptions of the left, some popular dioceses opened a space for people committed to social transformation to work with the popular classes. In Nova Iguaçu, the diocese created the space that enabled the politically committed doctors to begin their work. Without the diocese's financial support, legitimation, and help in creating contacts with the already organized Catholic groups, it would have been almost impossible to do anything more than palliative medical work.

This alliance between the left and the church was important in the development of the neighborhood movement in Nova Iguaçu. Even though the population of Nova Iguaçu has a history of different forms of popular resistance and organization, it was not until a stable, politically aware leadership emerged that these efforts transcended immediate material perspectives. Before 1975, Catholics were organized in local ecclesial communities concerned with social reality, but there were no efforts to articulate a broad social movement that could change the way local government was run. It would take the active involvement of the four doctors committed to working with the popular classes to transform the isolated petitions into a significant popular movement. The presence of the doctors played a significant role in helping the local population to organize. One person who became a leader in the movement stated,

> The population was still completely passive, and there was almost no organization. Then the doctor arrived and everyone woke up. It encourages the people to have a doctor who shows some interest in their problems. He encouraged the people to reflect about the causes of the problems in the neighborhood. He asked, why do these problems exist? Then the people started to say that it was because of the miserable wage levels, because the city administration never does anything it promises, and so forth. Some people started to see that things weren't going the way they should, that it is better for us to demand our rights than to pay for medications.[49]

The four doctors and other individuals from the left helped raise broader political issues and actively worked to coordinate efforts between neighborhoods. The step from a movement concerned solely with the population's immediate needs to one whose leaders attempted to relate these needs to broader political issues was important. Popular movements can create pressures that cause authoritarian regimes to open up, but to do so, they must work beyond immediate material benefits toward issues related to democratization. Excessive focus on the broader issues easily leads to gaps between the leaders, who in a movement like MAB are politically sophisticated, and the rank and file, who generally are not very aware of the linkages between broader political issues and their immediate material needs. Yet exclusive concern with immediate material needs prevents a movement from contributing to broader social change and makes the movement susceptible to internal crisis once it has obtained the benefits it initially sought or, conversely, once it becomes frustrated from repeated failure.

The efforts to coordinate work between neighborhoods also gave a new character to the movement. From a relatively early time, the movement was concerned about articulation between the participating neighborhoods. This attitude was in marked contrast to previous neighborhood movements in Nova Iguaçu because only during the brief period before and after the 1960 congress had there been serious efforts to coordinate work between neighborhoods. It is also one of the characteristics that made MAB an unusually well-articulated movement. Coordinating work between neighborhoods created the possibility of a mass movement, with greater chances of pressuring the state. The new movement consequently provided different political experiences, which more local movements do not afford. Visitation between neighborhoods proved to be a source of encouraging other neighborhoods, expanding the movement, and exchanging ideas about how to work.

The role the doctors played in helping organize the local population is common to most popular movements in Brazil. The popular sectors have always expressed some resistance to domination, but without the input of leadership generally drawn from outside circles, these expressions have not led to political movements that could change the society. Even the post-1974 movements, which have been more autonomous with respect to political parties and intellectuals, have generally relied on outside support, especially in the early phases.[50]

Despite the strong presence of the Catholic left in the movement and despite the predominance of Catholics participating at the neighborhood level, the four medical doctors who began the movement retained the hegemonic orientation until December 1981. This phenomenon of a predominantly Catholic base and hegemonic non-Catholic leadership is common, but it has generated some tensions. Earlier I noted that Dom Adriano has fully supported MAB and its autonomy, but this perspective is not uniformly shared in the diocese. In contrast to some popular dioceses, where overwhelming numbers of the clergy are committed to the popular cause, the Nova Iguaçu diocese is somewhat divided, with a number of moderates and even some traditional conservative priests, some of whom openly and sharply disagree with Dom Adriano. Within the diocese there are many competing conceptions of the church's role, its relationship to politics, and consequently its relationship to popular movements. Although the predominant tendency has been to support MAB, some clergy have opposed the movement, and even some progressive Catholics have viewed it ambivalently.

Among progressive Catholics, the criticisms derive from the feeling of many priests that the left has done little grassroots organizing and therefore should not lead the movement. They feel that MAB is controlled by intellectuals and that popular movements must be led by people from the popular classes. They argue that MAB's leadership is an elite with limited understanding of popular needs and values and that the movement has worked toward broader political issues at the expense of grassroots work. Even though most of the diocese's priests and religious verbally eschew organizing the population for political purposes, some clergy delegitimize the efforts of "outsiders" in doing so. Finally, others criticize MAB for not developing more effective participation.

In MAB's case it is not clear that these criticisms are justified. More than half of the members of both of the Coordinating Councils have been workers, and the others live in simple conditions in Nova Iguaçu and have shown a long-term commitment to working with the popular classes. Furthermore, the movement's success in mobilizing the local population, contributing toward obtaining material improvements, and fighting for a more responsive local government suggests that it has captured popular needs and channeled them in an effective way. These positive attributes, however, do not eliminate tensions between some church people and MAB.

More important than the occasional tensions between progressive Catholics and MAB have been the conflicts between conservative clergy and the movement. One example of how the conservative clergy view MAB and especially the four doctors and other leftists in the movement will suffice to indicate the criticism they voice. One priest who has a moderate discourse but authoritarian practices and paternalistic attitudes openly discouraged people in his parish and in the mothers' clubs from participating in MAB:

> MAB was started by outsiders. It started here, in my parish, but escaped from my hands. They were doctors from Rio who wanted to do something about the misery of the Baixada. We didn't support them because they were outsiders. I didn't know why they were here. They were taking advantage of the grassroots work I had done. . . . I feel suspicious about MAB. I see in it an ideology which I don't completely share, and the workers don't have a means of defending themselves against this ideology. MAB takes church people and makes them think things they might not want to. . . . It is impossible to defend the workers against this ideology.[51]

These criticisms reflect the tensions and debates found in the Brazilian and Latin American church in general. The priest's views about avoiding church participation in politics and encouraging clerical control of the popular sectors are common among conservatives. His discourse indicates a competition for popular sympathies and control that is also common. His opposition to MAB shows that even in progressive dioceses, the church often has a contradictory political impact. Equally striking is the priest's attitude that MAB could make people believe things that "they might not want to." His attitude that the popular classes can easily be manipulated into participating in movements whose objectives they do not understand is questionable. The popular classes may not understand the political debates that take place at the leadership level of popular movements, and they can undoubtedly be manipulated in some ways, as the lengthy history of authoritarian populism suggests, but far from being easily manipulated into participating, they are usually suspicious of external agents who try to organize the population. There has been a generalized experience of needing to offer concrete benefits to be successful in political work with the popular classes; they participate only if they gain some benefit.[52]

The left is also sometimes critical of the church. Although the doctors who helped start MAB appreciate the support they have received from Dom Adriano, Cáritas, and other progressive clergy, their vision of how to lead the popular movement differs from that of most progressive Catholics. One of them said, "The church has the idiosyncracy, the internal contradiction, of not admitting how it works. It leads the popular process, but then it claims that this process is spontaneous, that it is the popular classes who are directing their own process. It delegitimizes the kind of leadership, of vanguard, needed to develop effective popular movements. For us, the leaders must elaborate a project that indicates their ability to understand popular demands. The challenge is in being able to capture and channel those demands. The church delegitimizes that step."[53]

Notwithstanding the tensions between some MAB leaders and the diocese, one of the reasons MAB has been such a dynamic movement is the combination of the leadership of the left and the strength of the popular church. Whether MAB's relationship with the diocese will remain harmonious will be a key factor in the movement's future.

At the beginning of this study I noted the importance of paying more attention to grassroots Catholic organizations, especially the ecclesial base communities. The analysis should make clear that these communities are a significant force, both in the Catholic church and in Brazilian politics. Although Brazilian CEBs are distinctive of their number, age, and close linkages to the hierarchy, base communities have also become an important source of change within the church in many Latin American countries. Not without reason have all sides of the ecclesiastical spectrum shown a keen interest in or concern about the CEBs.

In their political consciousness, action, and impact, Brazilian CEBs are remarkably heterogeneous. As we have seen, the linkages between CEBs, popular movements, and political parties are very complex, far more so than most analyses have suggested. CEBs of the major industrialized areas such as São Paulo and Nova Iguaçu have the most sophisticated political consciousness, yet even in these cases this consciousness is rudimentary among the majority of participants. Furthermore, despite the presence of some leaders who are on the left and despite being one of the most successful neighborhood movements in the country, MAB's objectives and capacity to effect political change are relatively limited in the short run. In fact, by 1982, MAB faced serious difficulties, showing that even well-organized movements can be fragile and cyclical.[54] On the other hand, CEBs have helped introduce new social practices with an emphasis on participation and democratic methods and have strengthened popular movements throughout many parts of the country. Although the charge of the conservatives that the CEBs are deeply political has little to do with the reality of the vast majority of base communities in Brazil, their perception that CEBs affect political life is clearly correct. As Berryman and Dodson show elsewhere, this impact is even greater in Central America, where many CEB members have actively participated in the revolutionary process.

The chapter calls attention to the importance of not restricting analysis of the church's political impact to church-state relations. Political life includes a vast network of nonstate activities that can bolster different sectors of civil society. Despite infrequent interactions with or criticisms of the political elite, the Nova Iguaçu church has been one of the most important political forces in the region and has helped empower local popular movements. The analysis has also called attention to the limits to the church's involvement in popular movements; the competition among the church, political parties, and popular movements that frequently exists at the grassroots level; the tensions and debates within the church concerning its proper linkages to politics; and the dilemmas the popular movements have faced. It is also important to emphasize that the relationship between the church and popular movements varies markedly from region to region and diocese to diocese.[55]

Finally, the chapter provides many suggestions about the way the church's political role has changed during the process of political liberalization. Even progressive church leaders feel that the church's work must change as civil society develops the capacity to articulate its own political mechanisms. One of the outstanding intellectuals of the popular church, Frei Betto, captured this new relationship between politics and religion in an important essay:

> The church cannot attempt to substitute political parties, unions, neighborhood associations, the mechanisms specific to the political struggle. . . . Asking the base communities to also become the union movement, a grassroots organization, or a social center is a mistake. . . . The specificity of the base communities lies in their religious character. The people who participate in these communities are not motivated by professional, educational, or political interests. They are there because of their faith. This faith in Jesus Christ, lived and made explicit in communion with the church, impels the simple people to participate in the base communities.[56]

During the period under consideration, the Nova Iguaçu church changed from being the only institution capable of defending human rights to one among many forces interested in promoting social change. But though no longer alone, the church retains an important political function through developing a vision of faith that encourages people to participate politically.

Curiously, in the Brazilian case it has been precisely during this period of decreasing church involvement in the political sphere that the conservatives have most attacked the progressives for being too deeply involved in politics.[57] The explanation is not hard to find. On the one hand, the liberalization process has enabled the conservative sectors to claim that there is no longer any need for the church to intervene in politics and that the church should be apolitical.[58] Ultimately, of course, all conceptions of faith have political consequences; the question is really the nature of those consequences. On the other hand, the turn toward the right of the international church has strengthened the conservative sectors, even in Brazil, which probably has the most progressive Catholic church in the world. Thus the struggle for hegemony in the church goes on, and the grassroots organizations and political involvement that have been at the center of this chapter remain central issues in the debates.

Notes

1. Among the best studies are Brian H. Smith, *The Church and Politics in Chile: Challenges to Modern Catholicism* (Princeton: Princeton University Press, 1982); Daniel Levine, *Religion and Politics in Latin America: The Catholic Church in Venezuela and Colombia* (Princeton: Princeton University Press, 1981); Thomas C. Bruneau, *The Political Transformation of the Brazilian Catholic Church* (New York: Cambridge University Press, 1974); and Bruneau, *The Church in Brazil: The Politics of Religion* (Austin: University of Texas Press, 1982).

2. D. Sebastião Leme, *Carta Pastoral a Olinda* (Petrópolis: Vozes, 1916).

3. Among other discussions on the CEBs, see Thomas C. Bruneau, "Basic Christian Communities in Latin America: Their Nature and Significance (Especially in Brazil)," in Daniel Levine, ed., *Churches and Politics in Latin America* (Beverly Hills: Sage, 1980), pp. 111–34; Frei Betto, *O que é comunidade eclesial de base*

(São Paulo: Brasiliense, 1981); Clodovis Boff, *Comunidade eclesial, comunidade política* (Petrópolis: Vozes, 1979); Cândido Procópio Ferreira de Camargo et al., "Comunidades eclesiais de base," in Paul Singer and Vinicius Caldeira Brant, eds., *São Paulo: O povo em movimento* (Petrópolis: Vozes/CEBRAP, 1980); Alfonso Felippe Gregory and Maria Ghisleni, *Chances e desafios das comunidades eclesiais de base* (Petrópolis: Vozes, 1979); Sergio Torres and John Eagleson, eds., *The Challenge of Basic Christian Communities* (Maryknoll: Orbis Books, 1981); Faustino Luiz Coutro Teixeira, "Comunidade eclesial de base: Elementos explicativos de sua gênese" (M.A. thesis, Pontifícia Universidade Católica of Rio de Janeiro, 1982). Despite the importance of the base communities, reflections on their significance by social scientists have been limited.

4. Among the earliest discussions of base communities are Bernardo Leers, "A Estrutura do Culto Dominical na Zona Rural," *Revista da Conferência dos Religiosos do Brasil* 99 (September 1963): 521–34; Antônio Rolim, "O Culto Dominical e os Religiosos," *Revista da Conferência dos Religiosos do Brasil* 100 (October 1963): 631–36; Raimundo Caramuru de Barros, *Comunidade eclesial de base: Uma Opção pastoral decisiva* (Petrópolis: Vozes, 1968); José Marins, *A comunidade eclesial de base* (São Paulo: N.p., n.d., ca. 1968); José Comblin, "Comunidades eclesiais e pastoral urbana," *Revista Eclesiástica Brasileira* 30 (December 1970): 783–828.

5. I discuss the church's transformation at length in *The Catholic Church and Politics in Brazil, 1916–1985* (Stanford: Stanford University Press, 1985).

6. Conselho Episcopal Latinoamericano, *A Igreja na atual transformação da América Latina* (Petrópolis: Vozes, 1969), C. 15, para. 10–12.

7. Leonardo Boff, *Eclesiogênese: As comunidades eclesiais de base reinventam a igreja* (Petrópolis: Vozes, 1977).

8. On the theology and religious practices emerging from the CEBs, see Leonardo Boff, "As eclesiologias presentes nas comunidades eclesiais de base," in *Uma Igreja que Nasce do Povo* (Petrópolis: Vozes, 1977), pp. 201–9; Carlos Mesters, "A Brisa Leve, uma nova leitura da Bíblia," *SEDOC* 11 (January–February 1979): 733–65; Leonardo Boff, *Igreja: Carisma e poder* (Petrópolis: Vozes, 1981), pp. 196–212; Carlos Mesters, "Interpretação da Bíblia em algumas comunidades eclesiais de base no Brasil," *Concilium* 158 (1980); Marie-Dominique Chenu, "A nova consciência do fundamento trinitário da igreja," *Concilium* 166 (1981): 21–31; Almir Ribeiro Guimarães, *Comunidades de base no Brasil* (Petrópolis: Vozes, 1978), pp. 34–39, 117–215.

9. Conselho Episcopal Latinoamericano, *Puebla: A Evangelizacão no presente e no futuro da America Latina* (Petrópolis: Vozes, 1980), para. 629.

10. On this point, see Daniel Levine's article on Colombia in Levine, ed., *Religion and Political Conflict in Latin America* (Chapel Hill: University of North Carolina Press, 1986).

11. I discuss the contributions and limitations of Brazilian CEBs in creating a more democratic political order in "The Catholic Church, Popular Education, and Political Change in Brazil," *Journal of Inter-American Studies and World Affairs* 26 (February 1984): 97–124. See also the commentaries on this article by Daniel Levine, Philip Berryman, and Michael Dodson.

12. On Chile, see the article by Brian Smith in Levine, *Religion and Political Conflict*. On Central America, in addition to the articles in Levine, *Religious and Political Conflict*, by Michael Dodson and Philip Berryman, see Jorge Cáceres et al., *Iglesia, política y profecia* (San Jose: Editorial Universitaria Centroamericana,

1983). On the role of the churches in the Nicaraguan revolution, see Michael Dodson and Tommie Sue Montgomery, "The Churches in the Nicaraguan Revolution," in Thomas W. Walker, ed., *Nicaragua in Revolution* (New York: Praeger, 1982), 161–80. On the church's role in El Salvador, see Tommie Sue Montgomery, *Revolution in El Salvador* (Boulder, Colo.: Westview Press, 1982), pp. 97–118; and Jorge Cáceres Prendes, "Radicalización política y pastoral popular en El Salvador, 1969–1979," *Revista ECSA* 33 (1983): 93–153.

13. Data are from the official census.

14. On the development of Nova Iguaçu, see Leda Lúcia Queiroz, "Movimentos sociais urbanos: O Movimento Amigos de Bairros de Nova Iguaçu" (M.A. thesis, COPPE, 1981), chap. 2.

15. The population of Rio grew from 1,157,873 in 1920 to 1,764,141 in 1940; 3,281,908 in 1960; 4,251,918 in 1970; and 5,183,992 in 1980. Real estate prices in Rio increased 3.76 times in real terms between 1957 and 1976 (Conferência Nacional dos Bispos do Brasil, "Solo Urbano e Ação Pastoral," *Documentos da CNBB* 23 [São Paulo: Paulinas, 1982], p. 8). The expansion of the favela population outstripped the overall population growth, increasing, according to one estimate, from 57,889 in 1933 to 965,000 in 1961 (Fundação Leão XIII, *Favelas: Um Compromisso que Vamos Resgatar* [Rio de Janeiro: Estado da Guanabara, 1962]). Today there are about 1.8 million favela dwellers according to estimates of the archdiocese of Rio. The figures can be debated, but the trend they suggest is clear.

16. Instituto Brasileiro de Geografia e Estatística, *Censo 1970.* For a socioeconomic profile of the Baixada Fluminense's population, see Christina Saliby et al., "A política de habitação popular: Suas consequências sobre a população proletária do Grande Rio" (manuscript, Rio de Janeiro, 1977). The urban problems of Nova Iguaçu are not totally unlike those of the peripheral areas of greater São Paulo. For a discussion of São Paulo's recent development and urban problems, see Cândido Procópio Ferreira de Camargo et al., *São Paulo 1975: Crescimento e pobreza* (São Paulo: Loyola, 1976); Lúcio Kowarick, *A Espoliação urbana* (Rio de Janeiro: Paz e Terra, 1980); and Manoel Tosta Berlinck, *Marginalidade social e relações de classe em São Paulo* (Petrópolis: Vozes, 1975).

17. Movimento Amigos do Bairro, "Primeiro ciclo de debates populares do MAB" (mimeo, November 1980); 1980 census.

18. Queiroz, "Movimentos sociais urbanos," p. 79.

19. Movimento Amigos do Bairro, "Primeiro ciclo de debates populares" (mimeo, 1980).

20. On the transportation situation, see Pastoral Operária de Nova Iguaçu, "A Condução do Trabalhador," in Carlos Rodrigues Brandão, ed., *A Pesquisa Participante* (São Paulo: Brasiliense, 1982), pp. 63–85. In the late 1970s, workers destroyed several trains in their rage over the constant delays and the maimings and deaths resulting from accidents. See José Alvaro Moisés and Verena Martinez Alier, "A revolta dos suburbanos ou 'Patrão, O Trem Atrasou,' " in José Alvaro Moisés et al., *Contradições urbanas e movimentos sociais* (Rio de Janeiro: Paz e Terra/CEDEC, 1978), pp. 13–64.

21. See Queiroz, "Movimentos sociais urbanos," chap. 2, on the pre-1974 popular mobilizations.

22. Maria Helena Moreira Alves, "The Formation of the National Security State: The State and the Opposition in Military Brazil" (Ph.D. dissertation, Massachusetts Institute of Technology, 1982), p. 500.

23. On the MDB in Rio de Janeiro after 1964, see Eli Diniz, *Voto e máquina política: Patronagem e clientelismo no Rio de Janeiro* (Rio de Janeiro: Paz e Terra, 1982).

24. In 1974, the top MDB candidate for federal deputy had 47,929 votes compared to 22,862 for the top ARENA candidate; the top MDB candidate for state deputy had 19,917 votes, compared to 9,974 for the top ARENA candidate; and the MDB candidate for federal senator outpolled the ARENA candidate by 99,628 to 43,352. Election coverage and data are found in *Correio da Lavoura* no. 2299 (November 16–17, 1974). In 1978, the MDB won 118,774 votes for federal senator and ARENA got 72,942 (*Jornal do Brasil*, 16 May 1982).

25. See the "Entrevista com D. Adriano," *Revista de Cultura Vozes* 75 (January–February 1981), for an introduction to Dom Adriano's perception of the church and politics. See also the interview with Dom Adriano in *SEDOC* 11 (November 1978): 496–511.

26. Information on the diocese's development came from interviews and from diocesan publications such as the annual *Plano Pastoral da Diocese de Nova Iguaçu* and *O Povo de Deus Assume a Caminhada* (Petrópolis: Vozes/IDAC, 1983). Interviews with Dom Adriano Hypólito, the director of Cáritas Diocesana, a member of the Peace and Justice Commission, one of the founders of the Pastoral Workers Commission, and an adviser to the Pastoral Workers Commission, were especially helpful on this subject. Also see Ivo Lesbaupin, "Direitos humanos e classes populares" (M.A. thesis, IUPERJ, 1982), pp. 16–19, on the Nova Iguaçu church.

27. An abundant literature is emerging on the liberalization process. My own views of the *abertura* are developed in two articles, both of which make reference to most of the literature. See Eduardo Viola and Scott Mainwaring, "Transitions to Democracy: Brazil and Argentina in the 1980s," *Journal of International Affairs* 38 (Winter 1985): 193–219; and Donald Share and Scott Mainwaring, "Transitions through Transaction: Democratization in Brazil and Spain," in Wayne Selcher, ed., *Political Liberalization in Brazil: Dynamics, Dilemmas, and Prospects* (Boulder, Colo.: Westview Press, forthcoming).

28. On the Cost of Living Movement, see Tilman Evers, "Os movimentos sociais urbanos: O caso do 'Movimento Custo de Vida,' " in José Alvaro Moisés et al., *Alternativas populares da democracia* (Petrópolis: Vozes/CEDEC, 1982), pp. 73–98. On the new labor movement, see José Alvaro Moisés, "Current Issues in the Labor Movement in Brazil," *Latin American Perspectives* 6 (Fall 1979): 71–89; John Humphrey, *Capitalist Control and Workers' Struggle in the Brazilian Auto Industry* (Princeton: Princeton University Press, 1982); Maria Hermínia Tavares de Almeida, "Tendências recentes de negociação coletiva no Brasil," *Dados* 24 (1981): 161–89; Ronaldo Munck, "The Labor Movement and the Crisis of the Dictatorship," in Thomas Bruneau and Philippe Faucher, eds., *Authoritarian Capitalism: Brazil's Contemporary Economic and Political Development* (Boulder, Colo.: Westview Press, 1981), pp. 219–38. A fine overview of a number of social movements in São Paulo is Singer and Brant, eds., *São Paulo*.

29. Some of these incidents are discussed in the introduction to the "Entrevista com D. Adriano," *Revista de Cultura Vozes* 75 (January–February 1981). See also *Revista Eclesiástica Brasileira* 40 (March 1980): 177–82.

30. I use the term "popular neighborhood movements" rather than the more common "urban social movements" because it is more specific. Urban social movements encompass a wide range of middle-class activities, such as ecologi-

cal movements, efforts to obtain better facilities from the state, and attempts to develop community resources such as athletic facilities. Some intellectuals who have studied urban social movements (Manuel Castells, Jordi Borja) have emphasized the transformation potential of all these movements. Although there is some possibility that the demands of the middle and popular sectors will lead them to join together to confront the state, in the Third World context it is equally likely that the middle strata and popular classes will desire different urban services.

In the past few years urban social movements have received significant attention. The works of Europeans Manuel Castells, Jean Lojkine, and Jordi Borja were seminal in reassessing these movements. By Castells, see *Movimientos sociales urbanos* (Mexico City: Siglo XXI, 1974) and *Cidade, democracia e socialismo* (Rio de Janeiro: Paz e Terra, 1980). Borja's most influential work is *Movimientos sociales urbanos* (Buenos Aires: Siap, 1975). By Lojkine, see *Le Marxisme, l'état et la question urbaine* (Paris: Presses Universitaires de France, 1977) and *La politique urbaine dans la région parisienne, 1945–1971* (Paris: Mouton, 1972). A fine critique of Castell's work is Paul Singer, "Urbanizacão, dependência e marginalização na América Latina," in Singer, *Economia política da urbanização* (São Paulo: Brasiliense, 1977). In this vein, see also Luiz Antônio Machado da Silva and Alícia Ziccardi, "Notas para uma discussão sobre movimentos socialis urbanos," *Cadernos do Centro de Estudos Rurais e Urbanos* 1st ser., 13 (1980): 79–95. Much of the Brazilian discussion has suffered from the same theoretical problems. Important critical contributions are Renato Boschi, "Movimentos sociais e a institucionalização de uma ordem" (Rio de Janeiro: IUPERJ, 1983); Renato Boschi, ed., *Movimentos coletivos no Brasil urbano* (Rio de Janeiro: Zahar, 1983); José Alvaro Moisés, "Classes populares e protesto urbano" (Ph.D. dissertation, Universidade de São Paulo, 1978); José Alvaro Moisés, "Experiências de mobilização popular em São Paulo," *Contraponto* 3, no. 3 (1978): 69–86; Paul Singer, "Movimentos de bairro," and "Movimentos sociais em São Paulo: Traços comuns e perspectivas," in Singer and Brant, eds., *São Paulo*, pp. 83–108 and 207–30; Anna Luiza Souto, "Movimentos populares urbanos e suas formas de organização ligadas à igreja" (paper, Rio de Janeiro, 1979); Ruth Cardoso, "Movimentos sociais urbanos: Balanco critico," in Sebastião Velasco e Cruz et al., *Sociedade e política no Brasil Pos-64* (São Paulo: Brasiliense, 1983), pp. 215–39.

31. The history of the neighborhood movement presented in this section draws extensively on Queiroz, "Movimentos sociais urbanos," even though my interpretation of the movement differs significantly from hers. Other information comes from extensive interviews with movement and church leaders; the movement's newspaper, *Encontro*; and the Nova Iguaçu newspaper, *O Correio da Lavoura*.

32. On the connection between this health work and the early development of the neighborhood movement, see Estrella Bohadana, "Experiências de participação popular em Ações de Saúde," in IBASE, *Saúde e Trabalho no Brasil* (Petrópolis: Vozes/IBASE, 1982), pp. 107–28.

33. *Encontro* 2 (March 1976).

34. *Encontro* 11 (November 1977).

35. *Encontro* 12 (January 1978).

36. On this phase of MAB's development, with more detailed information on the assembly, see *Encontro* 15 (July 1978) and 16 (October 1978).

37. On the party reform, see Thomas Sanders, "Brazil in 1980: The Emerging Political Model," in Bruneau and Faucher, eds., *Authoritarian Capitalism*,

pp. 193–218; Robert Wesson and David Fleischer, *Brazil in Transition* (New York: Praeger, 1983), pp. 108–20. There is an extensive body of literature on parties and elections in the post-1974 period. See, among others, Bolivar Lamounier and Fernando Henrique Cardoso, eds., *Os partidos e as eleições no Brasil* (Rio de Janeiro: Paz e Terra, 1978); and Bolivar Lamounier, ed., *Voto de Desconfiança: Eleições e Mudança Política no Brasil, 1970–1979* (Petrópolis: Vozes/CEBRAP, 1980).

38. 27 September 1981.

39. *Correio da Lavoura*, 24 December 1982.

40. Interview, 21 January 1985.

41. Interview, 3 July 1981.

42. One of the strongest statements that the popular movements are still dependent on church support is Luiz Gonzaga Souza Lima, "Notas sobre as comunidades eclesiais de base e a organização política," in Moisés et al., *Alternativas populares da democracia*, pp. 41–73.

43. Interview, 3 July 1981.

44. Interview, 1 June 1981.

45. Interview, 2 June 1981. He refers to peasants because he lived in a rural part of the municipality until 1974.

46. On the political limitations and religious primacy of Brazilian CEBs, see J. B. Libânio, "Uma comunidade que se redefine," *SEDOC* 9 (October 1976): 295–326; Leonardo Boff, "Teologia à escuta do povo," *Revista Eclesiástica Brasileira* 41 (March 1981): 55–119; Frei Betto, *O que é comunidade eclesial de base*; J. B. Libânio, "Igreja—povo oprimido que se organiza para a libertação," *Revista Eclesiástica Brasileira* 41 (June 1981): 279–311; Paulo Cézar Loureiro Botas, "Aí! Que Saudades do Tempo em que o Terço Resolvia Tudo," *Tempe e Presença* 26 (March 1980): 3–10.

47. Interview, 26 June 1981.

48. Interview, 27 March 1981.

49. Interview, 18 May 1981.

50. The leadership of most popular movements has been closely linked to one political current or another, so the political conceptions of the parties, the left, and the ecclesial sectors involved in working with the popular classes have a major impact on the direction of these movements. It is impossible fully to understand the popular movements or the left without analyzing the linkages between them.

51. Interview, 12 September 1981.

52. On this point, see Antônio Ivo de Carvalho, "Saúde e Educação de Base: Algumas notas," *Proposta* 3 (December 1976): 19–33; Cristiano Camerman and Estrella Bohadana, "O Agente Externo na Favela" (paper, Rio de Janeiro, 1981); and Anthony and Elizabeth Leeds, *A Sociologia do Brasil Urbano* (Rio de Janeiro: Zahar, 1978), esp. pp. 26–52, 264–88. This observation is not unique to the popular classes in Brazil. A classic tenet of some strains of liberal political theory is the difficulty of getting people to participate in collective movements. See Mancur Olson, *The Logic of Collective Action* (Cambridge, Mass.: Harvard University Press, 1965).

53. Interview, 19 September 1981. For written criticisms of the church by different sectors of the left, see Queiroz, "Movimentos sociais urbanos"; Roberto Romano, *Brasil: Igreja contra Estado (Crítica ao Populismo Católico)* (São Paulo: Kairos, 1979); Ricardo Abramovay, "Marxistas e Cristãos: Pontos para um

Diálogo," *Proposta* 16 (March 1981): 11–20; Vanilda Paiva, "Anotações para um Estudo sobre Populismo Católico e Educação Popular," in Vanilda Paiva, ed., *Perspectivas y dilemas da educação popular* (Rio de Janeiro: Graal, 1984), pp. 227–66; Octávio Guilherme Velho, "A Propósito de Terra e Igreja," *Encontros com a Civilização Brasileira* 22 (April 1980): 157–68.

54. Much of the literature on the urban social movements has been excessively optimistic about their capacity to promote social change. Recently a more critical literature has emphasized the limited nature and cyclical character of these movements. See Boschi, "Movimentos sociais e a institucionalização de uma Ordem"; Cardoso, "Movimentos sociais urbanos"; Renato Raul Boschi and Lícia do Prado Valladares, "Movimentos Associativos de Camadas Populares Urbanas: Análise comparativa de seis casos," in Boschi, ed., *Movimentos colectivos no Brasil urbano*, pp. 103–43; Singer, "Movimentos de bairros" and "Movimentos sociais em São Paulo"; Fernando Henrique Cardoso, "Regime político e mudança social," *Revista de Cultura e Política* 3 (November 1980–January 1981): 7–25. On a more theoretical level, see Albert Hirschman, *Shifting Involvements: Private Interest and Public Action* (Princeton: Princeton University Press, 1982); and Frances Fox Piven and Richard Cloward, *Poor People's Movements: Why They Succeed, How They Fail* (New York: Pantheon, 1977).

55. Some of this diversity in the relationship between the church and popular movements is apparent in the different studies in Boschi, ed., *Movimentos coletivos no Brasil urbano.*

56. Frei Betto, "Da prática da pastoral popular," *Encontros com a Civilização Brasileira* 2 (1978): 104, 95. On this point, see also Frei Betto, "Prática pastoral e prática política," *Tempo e Presença* 26 (March 1980): 11–29; Clodovis Boff, *Teologia e prática* (Petrópolis: Vozes, 1978).

57. See Herbert Lepargneur, *Teologia da libertação: Uma Avaliação* (São Paulo: Convívio, 1979); Bonaventura Kloppenburg, *A igreja popular* (Rio de Janeiro: Agir, 1983); D. Eugênio Sales, "Comunidades eclesiais de base," *Boletim da Revista do Clero* 19 (September 1982): 20–33; D. Karl Josef Romer, "Por que o Livro de L. Boff, *Igreja: Carisma e Poder*, não é Aceitável," *Boletim da Revista do Clero* 19 (April 1982): 30–36.

58. This situation was anticipated in the prescient article by Ralph Della Cava, "Política a Curto Prazo e Religião a Longo Prazo," *Encontros com a Civilização Brasileira* 1 (July 1978): 242–58.

7

The Limits of Religious Influence: The Progressive Church in Nicaragua

Philip Williams

In the first heady months after the Sandinista victory in 1979, Nicaragua seemed to represent the promise of Liberation Theology fulfilled. The Catholic Theology of Liberation had taken root early in Nicaragua and had spread rapidly, thanks to an influential group of activist clergy who determinedly applied the Church's "preferential option for the poor" to a population who, under the Somoza family dictatorship, was one of the poorest, worst educated, and least helped by basic services in all of Latin America. In the mid-1960s a handful of progressive Nicaraguan priests established some small but influential Christian base communities (CEBs) in the barrios of the capital city, Managua, and somewhat later in rural areas of the western and northern parts of the country. One of the most notable of these was the CEB located on Solentiname, a small island in Lake Nicaragua, established in 1966 by Ernesto Cardenal, a priest and poet who later was Minister of Culture under the Sandinistas. In the early 1970s, Cardenal published The Gospel in Solentiname, *an account of the process of discussion,* concientización, *and praxis (action) among the campesinos on the island. The book (published in English in 1976) introduced Liberation Theology to popular audiences across Latin America beyond Nicaragua (where at first it was available only clandestinely) as well as to sympathetic readers in the United States and Europe.*

In 1972, Nicaragua was stricken by a devastating earthquake that killed tens of thousands of people, nearly destroyed Managua, and exposed in the recovery efforts the corruption rampant in the authoritarian regime of Anastasio Somoza Debayle, whose family had ruled the country

From *Conflict and Competition: The Latin American Church in a Changing Environment*, ed. Edward L. Cleary and Hannah Stewart-Gambino (Boulder, CO: Lynne Rienner Publishers, 1992), 129–46. © 1992 by Lynne Rienner Publishers. Reprinted by permission of Lynne Rienner Publishers.

either in fact or by proxy since 1934. In the wake of the earthquake, oppo-
sition to the regime arose from nearly every sector of society, finally forc-
ing Somoza to relinquish power in July 1979. It was during the insurrection
that Christian activists, whose political consciousness had been raised in
the CEBs, began to join the opposition, which ranged from coalitions of
businessmen to the Sandinista Front, an armed, Marxist-influenced popu-
lar movement that had been active in the country since the early 1960s.
When the Sandinistas took power in 1979, they rewarded Catholic activ-
ists for their role in the insurrection by naming several priests to the rul-
ing Sandinista Directorate and by adopting the popular slogan: "There is
no contradiction between Christianity and revolution."

This congenial relationship between the Sandinista government and
the Catholic Church was short-lived, however, due largely to what many
Church people and orthodox Sandinistas alike believed to be incontro-
vertible ideological differences between Christianity and Marxism. None-
theless, even as the institutional Church moved in the opposite direction,
many Christian activists remained loyal to the revolution, producing a
grassroots, laity-driven sector known as the iglesia popular *(popular*
church), or, here, the "progressive church." As the following article indi-
cates, the influence of the progressive church within institutional Catholi-
cism declined dramatically over the course of the 1980s, along with that
of the Sandinista movement itself. The author, writing in the early 1990s,
makes some accurate predictions about the directions that the Nicara-
guan Church took during that decade.

Philip Williams is associate professor of political science at the Uni-
versity of Florida, Gainesville. His most recent book is Militarization and
Demilitarization in El Salvador *(1997).*

The historical significance of the Nicaraguan revolution cannot be overstated. It represented the first time that a Marxist-inspired revolutionary movement had come to power with the support of significant sectors of the Catholic church. The revolution was heralded as a major breakthrough by Marxists and Christians alike, a unique opportunity to join together believers and nonbelievers in a project of national reconstruction.

In this chapter I focus on the progressive church in Nicagarua, arguing that since July 1979 its influence within the institutional church has declined significantly. The reasons for this decline are several. Besides the counteroffensive launched against it by the Catholic hierarchy and the Vatican, the progressive church had difficulty finding its role within the revolutionary process after Anastasio Somoza was overthrown. This "identity crisis," in addition to fueling disillusionment within the base community movement, sometimes led the progressive church to pursue strategies that were counterproductive to its development and consolidation. The extent to which each of these various factors limited the construction of a grassroots church is discussed in the first part of the chapter. In the second part I assess the future prospects for the progressive church, especially in the wake of the opposition victory in the February 1990 elections. On the one hand, the changed political landscape will present new challenges for the progressive church, but on the other hand, it may bring a new sense of purpose and dynamism lacking in recent years.

The term *progressive church* refers to that sector of the institutional church dedicated to building a grassroots church in Nicaragua.[1] In contrast to the traditional hierarchical notion of ecclesiastical authority, the grassroots model advocates the decentralization of church decisionmaking and authority, with *comunidades eclesiaies de base* (CEBs) serving as the fundamental organizational units in the church. According to this communitarian notion, clergy in the grassroots church exercise their functions as copartners within the CEBs, rather than simply presiding over the CEBs.

Besides restructuring ecclesiastical authority within the church, this alternative grassroots model also seeks to transform the church's traditional relationship with civil society. Rather than seeking its "social insertion" by way of alliances with dominant economic groups, the grassroots church seeks its place amid the dominated and oppressed classes in society. This "preferential option for the poor" is seen as necessarily having political implications. In the context of revolutionary Nicaragua, the church's option for the poor translated into supporting government programs that benefited the poor and encouraging Christians to participate in them. Such collaboration with the government was rooted in an interpretation of the gospel message that equates serving the poor with organizing people for their own benefit. Accordingly, it was only natural to support those government projects that advanced the cooperation and organization of the people. Simply put, by giving the revolutionary process its critical support, the church was fulfilling its mission of serving the poor.

The progressive church in Nicaragua is not an entity separate from the institutional church, and few progressives would advocate such a formal separation. Nevertheless, many of its activities take place "at the margin" of the institutional church (i.e., without the hierarchy's explicit approval). Finding it increasingly difficult to promote change from within the official structures of the church, the progressives have sought to provide an alternative Christian discourse to compensate for the hierarchy's silence on a number of issues. Not surprisingly, some of the bishops have viewed these activities as an attempt to form a breakaway church.

The Crisis in the Progressive Church

After Somoza's overthrow, the progressive church was confronted with several challenges. One of the most serious of these was the radically different political context after July 1979. Before Somoza's fall, the burning issue within the Nicaraguan church was its relationship vis-à-vis the dictatorship. During the late 1960s, progressives began pressuring the hierarchy to break its silence concerning government human rights abuses and socioeconomic injustices. As the brutal nature of the Somoza regime became increasingly apparent during the 1970s, a consensus emerged within the church on the need to speak out publicly against the dictatorship. With Somoza's overthrow in 1979, the question was no longer whether to speak out but to what end. Should the church become the "moral conscience" of the revolution, pointing out deviations from the revolution's original goals and criticizing government abuses of power? Or should it be more concerned with awakening people to the benefits of the revolution and encouraging their active participation? Related to this was the question of whether the church should actively collaborate with the Sandinista-led government in the tasks of the revolution or whether it should assume a less activist role so as not to jeopardize its political autonomy.

Progressives were inclined to collaborate with the new government in some form, but even so, their responses varied. Elsewhere, I have identified three distinct positions within the progressive sector of the church: direct participation, active collaboration, and passive collaboration.[2] Here, I will only summarize.

The first group included those priests and religious who took up positions in the government.[3] They considered their participation in the government a manifestation of their obedience to God, viewing the project of the revolution as consistent with the gospel message. As long as the revolution was under threat from external aggression, they saw their presence in the government as a necessary sacrifice to defend the revolution. Moreover, this presence ensured the church an active role within the revolutionary process, which could prevent it from becoming antireligious. In response to the bishops' ultimatums that they leave the government, these priests and religious adopted a position of "conscientious objection," insisting upon their loyalty to the church hierarchy, but affirming that their duty to serve the poor was more important than retaining their ecclesiastical status. If anything, over time they became more determined than ever to continue in their posts, despite being sanctioned by the bishops in late 1984 and early 1985.[4]

The second group, of which the majority were foreign religious, corresponded to priests and religious actively collaborating in the tasks of the revolution. Their support for the revolutionary process was based on the belief that its objectives were in basic agreement with the gospel message. Their activities included assisting in various government programs, especially health and education, encouraging Christian participation in mass organizations, and providing an alternative Christian discourse supportive of the revolutionary process. Although their activities were criticized as being overly politicized, these priests and religious maintained that the church cannot and should not divorce itself from politics. They argued that Christ's own option for the poor had political implications, and that the church, as follower of Christ, should carry out his project regardless of the political repercussions.

After 1982, because of confrontations with the hierarchy, this second group undertook a reevaluation of its objectives and strategies. Recognizing the futility of conflict with the bishops (which led to the removal of a number of priests and religious from their parishes), some members of this group became more prudent in their criticisms of the hierarchy and went out of their way to demonstrate their loyalty to the church. They no longer referred to themselves as the Popular Church because this term was exploited by conservative sectors of the church to accuse progressive clergy of attempting to form a breakaway church.

The third group was characterized by a posture of passive collaboration. Although generally in agreement with the revolution's objectives and fairly supportive of government programs, priests and religious within this group tended to be more critical of what they considered unnecessary government abuses and less inclined to participate directly in government projects. Although respecting those priests and religious who collaborated actively in the revolution, this group was more wary of such political identification. Drawing a distinction between politics in the general sense of the word and partisan politics, priests and religious in this group argued that the church can never divorce itself from the former, but that it should try not to involve itself in the latter.

Within this group, in addition to a handful of Nicaraguan secular priests, were several foreign religious who served as parish priests. After initially assuming a posture of active collaboration, they had to curtail their public identification with the revolution because of tensions with their bishops.[5] With the hierarchy's growing opposition to the revolutionary process, many found it impossible to sustain a position of active collaboration.

From this brief discussion, it is clear that a key issue distinguishing these three groups from one another was that of partisan politics. There was some disagreement as to whether the progressive church, by identifying with the Sandinista National Liberation Front (FSLN), was pinning its future to a political party and thereby endangering its influence in civil society. What happened, for example, if the FSLN's popularity began to wane; would this damage the progressive sector's credibility among the populace? The concerns over the church's partisan identification reflected the subtle differences within the progressive church.

There are some interesting parallels with the progressive church in Brazil. There, the changing political landscape during the 1980s presented the church with a whole new set of issues. After years of struggling against government abuses and repression, the church was suddenly faced with a process of political liberalization. The most pressing issue became the progressive church's relationship with opposition political parties, which had been strengthened by the political *abertura* (opening). Whereas some grassroots activists were highly suspicious of traditional political parties and shunned any formal contact, others "devoted themselves principally to partisan politics."[6] For those who chose greater political involvement, the issue of which party to support also became important.

Although there are many parallels between the two cases, it is important to point out some differences. In the Nicaraguan context, it was in a sense logical for progressives to identify with the FSLN after 1979. During the insurrections of 1978 and 1979, the urgency of the situation brought many church activists into close collaboration with the Sandinistas, whom they saw as the only real alternative to Somoza. The FSLN's credentials to speak on behalf of poor Nicaraguans undoubtedly were enhanced by the presence of a handful of Catholic priests within its ranks. In short, strong links already were forged and a pattern of collaboration established before the Sandinistas assumed power. This contrasts with the Brazilian case in which formal contacts between Catholic grassroots groups and political parties before the *abertura* were minimal. Until the creation of the Workers' Party (PT) in 1980, most Brazilian parties were viewed as essentially elitist and not representative of popular interests. Consequently, partisan political involvement was a much less obvious choice than in the Nicaraguan case.

A good example of how the issue of partisan politics affected the progressive church was the decline of the CEB movement. The crisis became so serious that in 1987 a progressive Christian magazine asserted:

> In fact, currently in the cities there are not many dynamic or creative CEBs, but rather only some groups or remnants of groups. . . . There scarcely exist CEBs that include men and women who live out their faith within the revolutionary process. . . . Instead what one sees are groups of men and women who come together because of their traditional religious sentiment.[7]

The reasons behind the CEBs' decline were several. On one level, CEBs had difficulty in redefining their evangelizing role. Unfortunately, before the revolution, CEBs did not focus on their future role within a revolutionary Nicaragua. Instead, the emphasis was on more immediate concerns such as denouncing human rights abuses and political repression. Before the triumph, the CEBs served as the only channels for political expression and grassroots organization. With Somoza's fall, however, the possibilities for political participation were greatly expanded, as people could take part in popular organizations, trade unions, and political parties. In some neighborhoods, CEBs became almost redundant, because their composition and activities differed little from that of the *comités de defensa Sandinista* (CDSs).[8] To avoid becoming merely another mass organization, the CEB movement needed to develop its own separate identity within the revolutionary process.

Efforts by the base community movement to carve out a space for revolutionary Christians were not very successful. Because of the lack of coordination at the national level, CEB members tended to participate in the revolutionary process in a personal capacity, not as part of an organized movement that could serve as an effective interlocutor for its rank and file. Given the CEB movement's dispersed nature, the FSLN made little effort to incorporate it into the revolution in a more organic manner. Consequently, instead of advocating the interests of revolutionary Christians in a programmatic fashion, CEBs acted in a more conjunctural manner, responding to periodic crises that threatened the revolution. The lack of coordination also complicated the efforts to develop a national plan for the training of new pastoral agents and for the reactivation of idle CEBs, goals fundamental to the movement's growth and consolidation.[9]

The identity crisis also manifested itself in the efforts of some CEB members to rediscover the spiritual dimension of their faith. During the insurrection, the urgent tasks of the armed struggle permitted very little time for any serious theological reflection; as a result, CEBs came to function more like political action groups than Bible reflection groups.[10] Even after 1979, many CEBs continued to focus primarily on sociopolitical issues. This led some CEB members to turn to such movements as the *catecumenado* (intense religious instruction), in hopes of rediscovering the spiritual element that seemed to be lacking in their base communities.[11]

Reintroducing this spiritual element was essential if the CEB movement was to maintain its identity within the revolutionary process. As [Daniel] Levine points out in his paper, "the most durable and successful" grassroots groups tend to be those that "have a vital and continuing religious message, and manage to keep religious practice and discussion at the core of their activities."[12] The Brazilian case would seem to confirm this. In Brazil, CEBs have been relatively successful in maintaining their religious character and avoiding explicit partisan involvement. Instead of focusing primarily on issues of national political import, Brazilian CEBs have tended to concentrate on local issues. Also contributing to their vitality has been their enduring linkage with the institutional church. Support from the hierarchy, though possibly limiting the autonomy of CEBs, has been essential to their growth.[13]

In contrast, CEBs in Nicaragua maintained a highly tenuous relationship with the institutional church. Even before 1979, CEBs, particularly in the archdiocese, had weak ties to the hierarchy. Rather than constituting a key component of the archdiocese's pastoral strategies, they were regarded as isolated pilot projects, tolerated by the archbishop. After 1979, when the hierarchy became preoccupied with asserting its authority over the institution of the church, CEBs increasingly were seen as being overly politicized and a threat to the bishops' authority.

The hierarchy's less tolerant attitude toward the CEB movement fueled tension. In some parishes, CEB members occupied churches to protest the hierarchy's removal of priests and religious supportive of the revolution and publicly criticized the bishops' more controversial pastoral letters. Instead of focusing on redefining their role within the revolutionary process, the CEBs devoted much of their energy to an ideological struggle against the hierarchy. Because of their criticisms of the hierarchy, some of the bishops no longer considered CEBs to be in communion with the institutional church. Although CEBs insisted on their loyalty to the bishops, some found it difficult, if not impossible, to maintain their ecclesial identity. On an individual level, this led to a feeling of isolation and confusion on the part of some members. Consequently, many CEB members no longer felt themselves accepted as part of the church.[14]

Because most of the bishops refused to support the CEB movement, its activities took place largely on the fringe of the institutional church. This, of course, presented it with a number of problems. First of all, the CEB movement lacked access to the resources that the institutional church could obtain. Also, without the official blessing of the hierarchy, its credibility was questioned by some of the faithful. And finally, the potential for conflict with the hierarchy was great, with serious repercussions for the progressive church. Tension escalated during 1981 and 1982, when criticisms of the hierarchy were converted into a personal struggle against the archbishop. As a result, the progressive church lost sight of its primary objectives and instead devoted much energy to its conflict with archbishop Miguel Obando y Bravo. This was at a time when it should have been consolidating its accomplishments and elaborating its new role within the revolutionary process.

Another challenge facing the progressive church was the problem of "membership drain." After the triumph, many of the best lay leaders who were involved in the armed struggle gave up their pastoral duties to become local leaders in the FSLN or to take up positions in the government. In fact, there was a much diminished participation in pastoral activities in general, as many Catholic were involved full-time in other activities (e.g., popular organizations, adult education programs, militia duties, and production brigades). This was especially true in the case of CEBs, which lost many of their most dynamic members. After 1984, the situation was compounded by the deepening economic crisis. In a typical Nicaraguan family, family members had to work two or three jobs simply to make ends meet, which left little time for other activities.

Catholic youth groups also were hard hit because many of the most capable student leaders were involved in Sandinista youth organizations and were constantly being mobilized for militia training or crop harvesting. Large numbers (of young males) were called up for their two-year military service. The war greatly exacerbated the membership drain. In northern departments, many lay leaders were kidnapped or assassinated by the *contras*, and those working in conflictive zones were in constant danger.[15] They were targeted by the *contras* because of their participation in the struggle to overthrow Somoza and their support of the revolution.

The membership drain presented the progressive church with a curious dilemma. On the one hand, it welcomed the participation of Catholics in the government and mass organizations, because this involvement guaranteed the church a Christian presence within the revolutionary process.[16] On the other hand, the loss of such dynamic pastoral agents was a setback to the efforts to build a grassroots church in Nicaragua. The question, then, was whether the institutional interests of the church should be put before the interests of the revolution. Most progressives were inclined to point to the positive aspects of the phenomenon, but it served as an important limitation on their influence.

Undoubtedly the most serious challenge for the progressive sector was the neoconservative offensive launched by members of the Nicaraguan hierarchy and the Vatican, who blamed progressive clergy and religious for the divisions within the church and for attempting to create a popular church outside the authority of the bishops. According to the church hierarchy, internal unity and stability were threatened by the political activities of priests and religious in support of the revolution. One of the clearest statements of this view was contained in the bishops'

April 6, 1986, pastoral letter entitled "The Eucharist: Source of Unity and Reconciliation."[17] In it, the bishops denounced a "belligerent group" of progressive priests and religious for trying to undermine the unity of the church "with acts and postures of open rebellion" against the hierarchy. They also accused the group of attempting to damage the hierarchy's credibility by linking the bishops with the "imperialist plans of the United States" and portraying the pope as "*ejecutor* of said plans." Resting total responsibility for the church's divisions with this group of priests and religious, the bishops called on them "to reconsider their errors" and rectify their situation with the church hierarchy. The bishops did not mention dialogue or a healthy diversity of views as facilitating unity. Rather, uniformity—"one single mentality and one single judgment"—was considered the best guarantor of unity.

One example of the hierarchy's efforts to undermine the progressive sector was the removal of several priests and religious from their parishes. The archbishop of Managua, Cardinal Obando y Bravo, pursued a strategy aimed at purging the archdiocese of progressive clergy. Between 1980 and 1982, fourteen priests and twenty-two sisters supportive of the revolution were transferred from their parishes or had their official pastoral authorization suspended.[18] Although a large number of progressive priests and religious still remained, only a handful were authorized to engage in pastoral work. Generally, the replacements were priests loyal to Obando, who attempted to undo the pastoral strategies of their predecessors. This fueled tensions in a number of parishes, particularly those where the CEB movement was strongest.

The removals were not confined to the archdiocese. In the diocese of Estelí, for example, twenty-eight priests and religious (of a total of sixty-six) were removed from their parishes between 1983 and 1987. The majority of these did not even receive an official explanation from the bishop.[19] Furthermore, the purges extended beyond the clergy to lay leaders. For example, in September 1984 the bishop of Estelí, Monsignor Rubén López, sent out a circular informing priests that any Delegates of the Word not trained in courses expressly authorized by the bishop no longer had the authority to carry out pastoral work.[20] The bottom line was that hundreds of Delegates of the Word were no longer recognized by the bishop as legitimate lay leaders. Such strategies no doubt were aimed at undermining the pastoral work of priests no longer considered to be in communion with their bishops.

The Vatican also publicly expressed its support for the bishops and its distaste for the progressive sector of the church. For example, during his March 1983 visit to Nicaragua, the pope blamed progressive clergy and religious for divisions within the church and ordered them to respect the doctrinal and pastoral directives of their bishops, so as to preserve the church's internal unity. Likewise, in a December 1985 letter to the Nicaraguan bishops, the pope applauded the hierarchy's efforts to achieve national reconciliation, alluding to the bishops' April 1984 pastoral letter that called on the government to begin talks with the *contras*. The pope also lamented recent "difficulties in pastoral work," implying that the church was being persecuted by the government.[21] An even more significant affirmation of support for the Nicaraguan episcopate was the pope's appointment of Obando y Bravo as cardinal in April 1985, the only one in Central America.

Besides public expressions of support for the bishops, the Vatican adopted other more subtle strategies in its offensive against priests and religious who identified with the Sandinistas. One such strategy was to modify the statutes of the Association of Nicaraguan Clergy (ACLEN) and the National Conference of Religious (CONFER), both of which were known to take a line independent of the bishops with regard to the revolution. By revising these organizations' statutes, the Vatican was able to alter significantly their political configuration and to bring them under control of the local hierarchy and regional superiors.[22]

Another strategy was the appointment of bishops who were loyal to the Vatican line. Besides having ultimate authority over these appointments, the Vatican, through its papal nuncios, ensured that nominees were properly conservative and noncontroversial. Although such a strategy can never be foolproof (as the case of Archbishop Oscar Romero would indicate), recent appointments in Nicaragua should not alter the increasingly conservative nature of the bishops' conference. In 1988 two new auxiliary bishops were named for the archdiocese. Both are conservative and have close ties to Obando. In the case of Monsignor Abelardo Mata, his relationship with Obando seems to have been more important than his pastoral experience in Nicaragua, where he has spent very little time during the past twenty years. In fact, one of the bishops confided that before seeing the list of nominees, he had never heard of Mata.[23] Such strategies may serve the short-term interests of the Vatican in its offensive against the progressive sector, but in the long run they may weaken the church's ability to respond dynamically to social change.

Undoubtedly, the influence of the progressive sector within the institutional church has been greatly weakened since 1979. This does not mean, however, that its influence among the faithful is no longer significant. Opinion surveys, in fact, demonstrate quite the opposite. For example, an August 1988 poll taken among Managua's youth (ages 16–24) revealed that 44 percent identified with the "popular" current of the church as opposed to 31 percent who identified with the "traditional" current.[24]

Although its influence among younger Nicaraguans does not carry over to the population as a whole—a June 1988 opinion poll revealed that 18 percent of Managuans identified with the popular current versus 47 percent with the traditional—the figures are nonetheless significant.[25] According to Roger Lancaster's study of popular religion in working-class barrios of Managua:

> A substantial majority of the population in Managua's popular barrios affiliates with, identifies with, or supports the activities of the Popular Church to one degree or another. Various observers . . . have commented on the "weak social base" of the Popular Church. . . . But in fact the strength lies less in its activism at the base community level and more in its relative hegemony over popular religious ideology.[26]

Thus, although the progressive sector may no longer hold much sway over the institutional church, it still maintains a considerable degree of influence within civil society as a whole. It is this continuing influence, in addition to its relationship with the Sandinistas, that so much concerns the church hierarchy. The question is whether the new political landscape in Nicaragua will serve to limit yet further the religious influence of the progressive church.

New Challenges in the 1990s

The National Opposition Union (UNO) victory in the February 1990 elections has presented the progressive church with a whole new set of challenges. On the one hand, these challenges may reduce even further the influence of the progressive church; on the other, they may bring a new sense of purpose and dynamism that was lacking in recent years. The future of the progressive church will depend largely on (1) the extent to which the elections contribute to the emergence of a consensus within Nicaraguan society; (2) the way in which the progressive church defines its role within the new political context; and (3) its relationship with the institutional church. These three factors are, of course, closely related to one another. For example, the progressive sector's vision of the church's mission in society will be affected by the particular political context within which it must operate. Similarly, their relationship with the institutional church will depend in part on how they define their mission and the strategies they adopt. Finally, the degree of consensus in society will be influenced to some extent by the church's efforts at internal reconciliation.

One factor that will be important in determining the future of the progressive church is the extent to which the February 1990 elections contribute to the emergence of a consensus among the key political actors in the country. For this to happen, however, there needs to be an agreement as to the ground rules of the political game. The prospects for such a consensus emerging are mixed. On the positive side, the Sandinistas carried through with their commitment to administer a democratic electoral process and to respect the results. This, in addition to Daniel Ortega's conciliatory gestures immediately after the elections, paved the way for a transition agreement between the FSLN and the government-elect of Violeta Barrios de Chamorro in March 1990.

Although the transition agreement may have contributed positively to the emergence of a consensus, several caveats are worth mentioning. First of all, the agreement was very exclusive in nature. Only the FSLN leadership and Chamorro's personal advisers participated in the discussions. Neither UNO political leadership nor COSEP (Superior Council for Private Enterprise) was consulted during any stage of the process. The danger of marginalizing such groups was illustrated during the July 1990 general strike, when leaders from UNO and COSEP displayed an unwillingness to play by the agreed-upon "rules of the game."[27] Rejecting accommodation with the Sandinistas, these groups have tried to cultivate support among demobilized *contras*—another group marginalized from the transition negotiations—by supporting their demands for land, credit, and technical assistance. The Chamorro government's failure to deliver on its promises has led to widespread disaffection among former *contra* soldiers. In the months after the elections, bands of ex-*contras* staged land invasions, often with the support of right-wing UNO politicians. Beginning in January 1991, a number of former *contras* took up arms against the government because of the slow pace of the proposed land distribution program. Sporadic violence, involving both ex-*contras* and former members of the Sandinista military, continued throughout 1991.[28]

Maintaining a consensus depends not only on the willingness of leaders to abide by the terms of agreements but also on their ability to control the demands of party faithful. Given the deteriorating economic situation, it is uncertain whether the FSLN can or will enforce discipline over its mass organizations. The FSLN's support for the workers' demands during the strikes of May and July 1990 reflected its unwillingness to cooperate with the government's stabilization and structural adjustment program, especially given the program's impact on living conditions of lower-class Nicaraguans. Furthermore, without access to state resources, the FSLN's ability to restrain the demands of Sandinista-affiliated mass organizations has declined. This no doubt has been compounded by the party's internal crisis, which has resulted in a less coherent leadership and a generalized sense of disorientation among the rank-and-file.

Despite these setbacks, during the first two years of the Chamorro government there has been a growing degree of collaboration between it and the FSLN leadership. Lacking a cohesive political party with links to organized interests in civil society, the Chamorro government increasingly has looked to Sandinista leaders to play an intermediary role that would facilitate implementation of its stabilization and structural adjustment program. For example, in October 1990 talks were held to hammer out a socioeconomic pact between the government, labor, and employers. At the same time, the FSLN leadership engaged in behind-the-scenes lobbying to persuade the government to abandon the more "explosive" elements of its program. These parallel conversations, which produced compromises on both sides, removed important obstacles that otherwise may have precluded an agreement in the public negotiations.[29] Since then, despite outbreaks of violence and disaffection among more-radical elements of the UNO coalition and the FSLN, Sandinista leaders have maintained a working relationship with the Chamorro government.

A second factor which will shape the future of the progressive church is the way in which it views its mission within the new political landscape. During the two years since the elections, progressives have dedicated their efforts to defending the "social conquests" of the revolution and searching for new strategies to improve the conditions of poor Nicaraguans. This commitment to defend the accomplishments of the revolution in the areas of agrarian reform, education, health care, and women's rights probably has led to tensions with the Chamorro government and continuing tension with the hierarchy. The level of conflict has been limited somewhat by the FSLN leadership's success in moderating the government's structural adjustment program. Nonetheless, the deepening economic crisis has led to growing demands by mass organizations, at a time when the government's capacity to respond to these demands has diminished. In the future, the majority of progressive clergy and religious can be expected to continue to support the demands of mass organizations. Whether this will lead to an increase in tensions with the government ultimately will depend on the government's success in improving the conditions of poor Nicaraguans.

The last factor is the progressive sector's relationship with the institutional church. This relationship will be influenced both by the new political context and the way in which each side defines the church's mission. As mentioned above, as long as progressives view the church's role as that of defending the accomplishments of the revolution on behalf of Nicaraguans, conflict with the more conservative bishops will be likely, given their contrasting vision of the church. These bishops see the church's mission as mediating between God and humankind—personal salvation must be mediated through the church—and this view, of course, connotes a hierarchical conception of decisionmaking and authority, with the bishops as the ultimate authority. Not surprisingly, efforts by progressive clergy and religious to decentralize the church, are seen as an obstacle to the church's completion of its mission. Furthermore, in line with established church tradition, the conservative bishops oppose revolutionary political change and favor a "third way" between communism on the left and capitalism on the right. They object to progressives' partisan identification with the FSLN, viewing it as a threat to the church's political autonomy. According to these bishops, the church should foster reconciliation between conflicting interests rather than taking sides.

Immediately following the elections, the conservative bishops, including Cardinal Obando y Bravo, sought a relationship of active collaboration with the new government. Although the hierarchy adopted a formally "neutral" position during the electoral process, it was no secret where Obando's political sympathies lay. The coincidence of political positions between the most conservative sector of the church and political opposition groups before the February 1990 elections has been well documented.[30]

A clear indication of the hierarchy's identification with the new government was its June 1990 pastoral letter calling on Nicaraguans to close ranks behind the government in support of its economic recovery plan.[31] This was followed by another letter in August, in which the bishops warned workers against staging politically motivated strikes that could lead to "the paralyzing of all socioeconomic life"—an obvious reference to the July general strike.[32]

On a symbolic level, church leaders, particularly Obando y Bravo, have been present at state occasions, as have government officials at important religious ceremonies. This public support for the new government has not gone unrewarded. For example, soon after her inauguration, President Chamorro promised to assist the archdiocese with the construction of a new cathedral, a long-held dream of the cardinal. Even more significant was the appointment of Sofonías Cisneros, member of the archdiocesan secretariat and a close associate of the cardinal, as minister of education, thereby guaranteeing the church hierarchy considerable influence over the planned reform of school curriculum. In an interview in July 1990, Vice Minister of Education Humberto Belli (another Obando confidant) stated that the government intended to introduce an "education with Christian values," echoing similar statements made by Cardinal Obando.[33] Finally, the government has provided the church with free space on the state television station to broadcast Obando's regular Sunday mass.

Since the summer of 1990, the more conservative bishops have become increasingly critical of the Chamorro government, adopting public positions similar to those of UNO's right wing. In November 1991, for example, the Bishops' Conference issued a pastoral letter criticizing the government's failure to take a hard line against Sandinista militants implicated in violent disturbances that same month. According to the bishops, instead of bringing those responsible to justice the government continues to justify its inaction in the name of peace and reconciliation. Echoing the demands of UNO's right wing, the bishops also called on the government to sharply reduce the defense budget, given that the country is no longer involved in a military conflict.[34]

The degree of identification between the conservative sector of the church and the right wing of UNO will have an important impact on the bishops' strategies toward the progressive church. Refusal to accept a relationship of peaceful coexistence with the Sandinistas can only complicate efforts to reconcile divisions within the church. Consequently, it is doubtful that the conservative bishops will tolerate the pastoral initiatives of the progressive clergy and religious. Rather, they will continue to view such initiatives as politicized and as a threat to their authority within the church.

There are, of course, limits to how far the conservative bishops can go in their efforts to undermine the progressive church. Given the relative scarcity of pastoral agents in the country, a continued offensive against progressive clergy and religious could lock the hierarchy into a dangerous conflict which ultimately will be counterproductive to the institutional church. Over the years, progressive clergy and religious have been effective in training lay leaders, especially in rural parishes where the ratio of parishioners to priests can reach as high s 20,000 to 1. Their removal would further weaken the church's presence in such areas. Even in urban parishes, the church has been stretched thin of late—partly the result of the numerous removals discussed above and the massive influx of war refugees. For example, in the urban parish of Matagalpa current levels of church personnel are insufficient to attend the thousands of new parishioners that have flooded into squatter settlements in recent years.[35] The problem of insufficient personnel has been compounded by the bishop of Matagalpa's refusal to implement pastoral strategies, such as the promotion of CEBs, that might otherwise have strengthened the church's presence in marginal towns. However, the success of evangelical sects in winning hundreds of new converts in squatter settlements may have tempered Bishop Santi's fear about CEBs becoming excessively politicized. Recently, the bishop has been considering the adoption of new pastoral strategies, including the formation of CEBs, to check the influence of evangelical sects in these areas.[36]

The challenge posed by the growing influence of evangelical sects is a concern to both progressives and conservatives within the church. In

February 1990, the spokesman for the archbishop's office, Monsignor Bismarck Carballo, denounced a media blitz undertaken by the Christian Broadcast Network as "trafficking with the hunger of the people."[37] Members of the base community movement seconded his objections. The $3-million campaign targeted Guatemala and El Salvador as well as Nicaragua and was expected to win more than 2 million converts. The continued growth of evangelical sects challenges the influence of the institutional church as a whole, but it may present opportunities for future collaboration between formerly antagonistic sectors of the church.

Conclusion

Faced with these new challenges, progressive clergy and religious will find it necessary to develop strategies which enable them to work within the official structures of the church. In recent years, their activities at the margin of the institutional church have made them an easy target for the bishops, who could accuse them of "parallel magisterium." It may be in the interests of the progressive church to repair its strained relations with some of the bishops, but this will be possible only within the context of national reconciliation. The emergence of a consensus whereby the country's principal political actors agree to work together in a project of national reconstruction would have a beneficial impact on the church's efforts toward internal reconciliation. A reduction in tensions within the church and in civil society in general may lead to a more tolerant attitude on the part of some of the bishops. In a less politically charged atmosphere, grassroots pastoral initiatives may not be seen as having such serious political implications. This, of course, would enable progressives to reestablish the ecclesial link between such initiatives and the institutional church.

As noted above, the prospects for such a national consensus emerging are mixed. Even if a consensus is forged in the near future, the possibilities of reconciliation within the church continue to be problematic in the archdiocese. Obando's unwillingness to tolerate diversity among his clergy is not likely to change. Although in the future he may view the progressive church as less of a political problem, it is almost certain that he will continue to regard it as an internal church problem. An indication of this was Obando's decision to deny the Dominicans' provincial superior a vote in the upcoming 1992 Church Council, purportedly because of an ongoing political feud with the Dominicans.[38] In other dioceses, which suffer from an acute personnel shortage and where internal divisions are nowhere near as severe, the prospects for internal reconciliation are much better. For example, on the Atlantic Coast the bishops have been more tolerant of different political positions and pastoral orientations. As a result, progressive clergy and religious are assured a greater degree of flexibility with which to implement grassroots pastoral strategies. It may be that the seeds of a revitalized progressive church will take root in isolated rural parishes. The challenge, however, will be to project such pastoral experiences on a national scale.

Despite the limitations on the progressive church in the wake of the opposition electoral victory, the changed political landscape may present new opportunities in the future. In the context of the Chamorro government, progressive clergy and religious may have an easier time defining their role within civil society. While the question of partisan identification with the FSLN and Sandinista-affiliated mass organizations will continue to serve as a source of some disagreement, opposition to UNO attempts to roll back programs that benefit poor Nicaraguans may provide a focus for unity. By defining its new role in terms of defending the social conquests of the past ten years, the progressive church may succeed in energizing that sector of the church committed to the empowerment of poor Nicaraguans. In short, the new political context may enable the progressive church to finally overcome the identity crisis which has limited its ability to influence civil society in recent years.

Notes

1. For an excellent discussion of the main features of the progressive church in Latin America, see Scott Mainwaring and Alexander Wilde, eds., *The Progressive Church in Latin America* (Notre Dame, Ind.: University of Notre Dame Press, 1989), pp. 4–34.

2. See Philip Williams, *The Catholic Church and Politics in Nicaragua and Costa Rica* (London: Macmillan, 1989), pp. 68–79.

3. Immediately after the triumph, two priests, Ernesto Cardenal and Miguel D'Escoto, became minister of culture and foreign minister respectively. Fernando Cardenal became director of the Sandinista Youth and then minister of education, and Edgar Parrales was appointed minister of social health, later to become Nicaragua's representative to the Organization of American States (OAS). A number of other priests and religious took up technical and advisory positions within various government ministries and institutions.

4. Fernando Cardenal was removed from the Jesuit order in December 1984, and Ernesto Cardenal and Miguel D'Escoto were sanctioned in January 1985. Edgar Parrales asked to leave the priesthood about the same time. Those priests sanctioned refrained from public priestly functions as long as they were in office.

5. Unlike other religious, who teach at universities, technical colleges, and schools (and who are not engaged in pastoral work), these priests are responsible to both their local bishops and their religious superiors.

6. Scott Mainwaring, "Grass-Roots Catholic Groups and Politics in Brazil," in Mainwaring and Wilde, *The Progressive Church*, p. 173.

7. *Amanecer*, no. 50 (June–July 1987), p. 22.

8. CDSs were organized at the urban block level and functioned as political decision-making bodies concerned with production, distribution, health, education, militia organization, and neighborhood security.

9. Interview with Rafael Aragón (provincial superior of the Dominicans in Central America), July 12, 1990.

10. *Amanecer*, nos. 7–8 (March–April 1982), p. 13.

11. Interview with Domingo Gatti, May 17–18, 1985, Juigalpa.

12. Daniel Levine, "Popular Religion and Political Change in Latin America," paper prepared for Latin American Studies Association International Congress, December 1989, pp. 9–10.

13. Mainwaring, "Grass-Roots Catholic Groups," pp. 154–158.

14. Rosa María Pochet and Abelino Martínez, *Nicaragua: Iglesia— Manipulación política o profecía?* (San Jose: Editorial DEI, 1987), p. 60.

15. In the El Jícaro parish (Nueva Segovia), for example, nine Delegates of the Word had been assassinated by the *contras* through 1984. Interview with Alfredo Gundrum (parish priest in El Jícaro), December 7, 1984, El Jícaro; for a collection of firsthand accounts of *contra* atrocities against Catholic lay leaders, see Teófilo Cabestrero, *Blood of the Innocent: Victims of the Contra War in Nicaragua* (Maryknoll, N.Y.: Orbis, 1985).

16. Interview with Bernard Wagner (parish priest in Wiwilí and Quilali), November 20, 1984, Managua; interview with Ramón Pardina (parish priest in San Juan del Sur), January 10, 1985, San Juan del Sur; interview with Enrique Coursol (parish priest in Totogalpa), December 2, 1984, Totogalpa.

17. Conferencia Episcopal de Nicaragua (CEN), "Carta del episcopado nicaragüense sobre la eucaristía, fuente de unidad y reconciliación," Managua, April 6, 1986.

18. *Nuevo Diario*, November 4, 1983.

19. *Amanecer*, no. 51 (June–July 1987), pp. 7–9.

20. Rubén López Ardón, "Instrucción diocesana 'eminente vocación' sobre los delegados de la palabra," Estelí, September 24, 1984. Although the bishop of Estelí is one of the more moderate bishops, as the only Nicaraguan among this group, he is under constant pressure from the hard-line bishops (most of whom are Nicaraguan) to adopt a tougher stance. Consequently, he has assumed a highly ambiguous position. On the one hand, he has sought to consolidate his authority within the diocese of Estelí; on the other, he was the only bishop to greet Miguel D'Escoto during the February 1986 "March for Peace."

21. *Envío*, November 1987, p. 32.

22. For more on this, see Williams, *The Catholic Church*, pp. 60–62.

23. Confidential interview.

24. *Envío*, March 1989, pp. 30–40.

25. *Envío*, December 1988, pp. 10–23.

26. Roger Lancaster, *Thanks to God and the Revolution* (New York: Columbia University Press, 1988), pp. 86–88.

27. During the strike, representatives from UNO and COSEP formed the National Salvation Committee, charging that Chamorro was incapable of dealing with the national emergency. The committee began organizing and distributing arms to paramilitary brigades, directly undermining the Chamorro government's political authority. See *Central America Report*, July 13 and 20, 1990.

28. For an excellent assessment of the postelection reconstruction period, see Laura Enríquez, et al., *Nicaragua: Reconciliation Awaiting Recovery* (Washington Office on Latin America, April 1991).

29. Interview with Comandante Luis Carrión, November 23, 1990, Managua.

30. See Williams, *The Catholic Church*, pp. 88–95, and Ana María Ezcurra, *Agresión Ideológica Contra la Revolución Sandinista* (Mexico City: Ediciones Nuevomar, 1983).

31. CEN, "Comunicado de la Conferencia Episcopal de Nicaragua" (Managua, June 4, 1990).

32. CEN, "Mensaje de la Conferencia Episcopal de Nicaragua" (Managua, August 15, 1990).

33. *Envío*, July 1990, p. 17.

34. *La Prensa Gráfica*, "La Iglesia Nicaraguënse Demanda Reducir Gasto Militar," November 25, 1991, p. 63.

35. Since the beginning of the war, the city's population has mushroomed from about 40,000 to slightly over 70,000.

36. Interview with Monsignor Benedicto Herrera, vicar general of Matagalpa, February 21, 1990, Matagalpa.

37. *Central America Report*, April 6, 1990, pp. 101–103.

38. The Dominicans were particularly outspoken in their support for the revolutionary process. At one point Obando tried to pressure the Dominican superiors to withdraw the entire order from Nicaragua. Interview with Rafael Aragón (provincial superior of the Dominicans in Central America), July 12, 1990, Managua.

IV

Protestantism and
Religious Pluralism

8

The Production of Christians: Catholics and Protestants in a Guatemalan Town

Sheldon Annis

In his classic work, The Protestant Ethic and the Spirit of Capitalism *(first published in Germany in 1904), the German sociologist Max Weber wrote that there is an "elective affinity," or self-serving relationship, between the rise of capitalist economic systems and the "ethics" embodied by Protestant religion, specifically the emphasis that Protestantism places on the value of the individual. Although Weber's paradigm is nearly a century old, it still serves as a basic pillar in the framework of analysis within the social sciences for Protestant movements. This is particularly true in Latin America, where the two earliest scientific studies of Protestantism in the region, Christian Lalive d'Epinay's* Haven of the Masses: A Study of the Pentecostal Movement in Chile *(1969) and Emilio Willem's* Followers of the New Faith: Culture, Change, and the Rise of Protestantism in Brazil and Chile *(1967), both measured Protestant growth in Chile during the 1960s from a Weberian perspective.*

In these essential works, both authors found that Protestant growth was most likely to occur among populations where the transition to market capitalism brought with it profound social disruption. Lalive thought that converts were most likely to be recent migrants to the city, former rural campesinos who lived on the margins of urban life without jobs or marketable skills. Willems, on the other hand, located most of his converts among the new petite bourgeoisie, the beneficiaries of "Protestant ethics" that enjoined believers to shun expensive vices such as drinking and gambling and encouraged the stewardship of marginal wealth.

From *God and Production in a Guatemalan Town* (Austin: University of Texas Press, 1987), 75–81, 85–87, 89–91, 93–95, 97–102, 104–6, 163–69 (photos omitted). © 1987 by Sheldon Annis. Reprinted by permission of the University of Texas Press and Sheldon Annis.

In this selection, Sheldon Annis offers a systematic study of economic differences between Catholics and Protestants in the Guatemalan town of San Antonio Aguascalientes, a predominantly Kak'chiquel Maya community located seven kilometers from the city of Antigua, a major tourist center. Although San Antonio, where many continue to wear native costume and speak the Kak'chiquel language, is an indigenous town, it is an atypical "traditional" community largely because of its close relationship with Antigua, which serves as an important market for San Antonio's major artisan industry, weaving, and thus guarantees a level of relative prosperity for San Antonio's residents. But in recent decades, additional forces have emerged to challenge San Antonio's indigenous identity: the violent earthquake of 1976, which killed many of the town's residents and brought Protestant missionaries in its wake; and the civil violence of the late 1970s and early 1980s, which introduced unprecedented social and political disequilibriums into the community. By the early 1980s, San Antonio was a town very much in transition, which, for Annis, made it an ideal testing ground for some of Weber's most important premises.

Sheldon Annis is a senior lecturer in geography and director of a distance learning Master's program for developing-country students in the field of international waters at the University of London, Royal Holloway College. He is the author and editor of four books, the most recent of which is Poverty, Natural Resources, and Public Policy in Central America *(1992).*

The cultural stability of the past four hundred years has been fractured during this century, on the one hand, by population pressure, growing landlessness, environmental deterioration, and military repression; and, on the other hand, by land windfalls, new technology, development programs, and expanding primary education. Both kinds of pressures have contributed to a surprisingly skewed distribution of wealth within the ostensibly homogeneous Indian community, and that growing maldistribution of wealth has, in turn, undermined the cultural rationale for production.

In a sense, two different types of productive systems have emerged—one an extension of the "*milpa* [cornfield]-promoting" forces, the other an extension of the "anti-*milpa*" forces. A key difference in these two systems lies in how campesino families choose to handle surplus product. In the first instance, they are willing to invest surplus product in symbolic acts that celebrate and reinforce communalism. Doing so provides an anchor in a dual sense: it *secures* in that it ties them into a stable and coherent cultural system, but it *restrains* in that production of local prestige precludes the purchase of significant power outside the village.

In the second instance, the families either have no surplus product to invest or choose to invest in expanding their economic opportunity. They reject the "cultural tax" and subordinate village-communal identification (and security) in exchange for a different set of rewards that can confer prestige, familial well-being, or spiritual gratification on a personal, nonvillage basis. In effect, they alienate themselves from the village-centricity that the *milpa* reinforces. Alternatively, their poverty may have already so marginalized them from full communal participation that the village alienates them. One way or another, their anchorage is lost and they must find new moorings.

In San Antonio, these distinct choices are manifested through and associated with religious affiliation. Very approximately: being Catholic is to be of the first system; being Protestant is to be of the second.

About 80 percent of the population in my survey called itself Catholic and about 20 percent Protestant. Yet seemingly clear-cut distinctions between who is Catholic and who is Protestant—and what a Catholic believes and does, versus what a Protestant believes and does—are obscured for two reasons. First, nominal church affiliation may not be a reliable indicator of how someone behaves. As elsewhere, a chasm often separates professed belief from action. In terms of behavior, San Antonio is filled with Catholic-like Protestants and Protestant-like Catholics.

Second and perhaps more important, there are many contemporary Guatemalan branches of both major religions, and though I have tried to concentrate here on what I consider the two trunks rather than the branches, the branches are not unimportant. In San Antonio and Santa Catarina alone, three distinct Protestant denominations are active.[1] Each has its own church, pastor, and separate affiliation to U.S., European, and Guatemalan umbrella groups. Similarly, as will be discussed, Catholicism in Guatemala today is by no means monolithic; indeed, its branches brush over upon the Protestant tree.

Bearing in mind these caveats, there still *are* deep differences between Protestant and Catholic, and I believe that these differences are more fundamental than intra-group variation. These differences extend far beyond religious practice. They carry over into such secular matters as farm production, handweaving designs, and political behavior.

Missionaries and the Growth of Protestantism in Guatemala

Although the term "Protestant" is used here—to distinguish it generically from "Catholic"—the term more commonly used in Guatemala and throughout Latin America is *evangélico* ("evangelical"). This usage is generally understood to exclude such groups as Jehovah's Witnesses, Mormons, and Adventists. It does include both the extreme and the moderate Pentecostal groups found in Guatemala.

The first Protestant missions to Guatemala—the Presbyterians, the Central American Mission, the Church of the Nazarene, and the Friends Mission—arrived within a twenty-year period beginning in 1882. They were encouraged, in part, by the liberal reformer, President Justo Rufino Barrios, who saw the missionaries as useful allies in piquing the Catholic Church and weakening its political power.[2] Under the liberal regime, most foreign Catholic clergy were expelled from the country, all Catholic Church property was expropriated, and the Church's power to act as a legally recognized entity was revoked.

By the first decade of the new century, Protestant missions were well established and actively proselytizing among the highland Indian population. As early as 1900, an evangelical and medical ministry was operating in Chichicastenango in the department of Quiché. Indeed, within a few years the four "pioneer missions" had ambitiously divided up the entire Indian territory by language and cultural group—in much the same manner as had the Spanish religious orders four hundred years earlier.[3]

In their first fifty or so years, the missionaries barely dented the entrenched Catholicity of Guatemala, despite the fact that severe restrictions on the Catholic Church begun by the liberals in 1871 marked probably the longest and most severe anticlericalism in all of Latin America. As late as 1967, Protestant sources estimated baptized membership to be no more than 1.6 percent of the total population.[4] Yet the missionaries were not easily discouraged. Bred and loyally supported by thousands of small-town churches in the North, they inched forward patiently. They expected, perhaps even welcomed, adversity. Through the decades of rejection, expulsion, and occasional violence they persisted—with a resoluteness that government workers, soldiers, Peace Corps volunteers, or development technicians seldom maintain. The missionaries thought in terms of lifetimes of work, not months. Supported by virtually inexhaustible funding and motivated by God rather than careerism, they came . . . and stayed.

Foreign colporteurs and itinerant preachers took on Indian assistants, and together they worked the periodic Indian ("solar") markets as shrewdly as did the ambulant vendors of Chichicastenango.[5] Wherever they went, they sought to "plant" a congregation—a group of believers meeting first in a home, soon in a rustic church. Each rescued soul was greeted as a miracle; and in a sense it was, for within each tale of personal salvation was the obligation to give public witness, and therein lay the seed for geometric membership expansion.[6]

The missionaries concentrated not just on salvation, but also on edification. That meant fortifying the new believers to the faith and keeping them spiritually renewed. Those edified souls were the key to success and the reward for patience, for they were to become witnesses to the Word and the real foot soldiers of the divine army. In short, the Protestant laity became an army of evangelists.

As the missionaries were replaced on the front lines by a second and third generation of national preachers, the foreigners began the more sophisticated work of institutionalizing support systems. First, they set up Bible-training institutes, then theological seminaries. They organized thousands of camp meetings, revivals, and retreats. Later they launched publishing houses, radio stations, and private-aircraft services. In a Sunday afternoon white elephant sale back in Akron, Ohio, a suburban Baptist congregation could raise enough money to build a country church in faraway Guatemala. And through mission headquarters in Guatemala City, the sister congregation could easily send down a retired farmer or electrical contractor to help out with the construction. Some of their everyday skills in Ohio (they could easily build a garage or remodel a rec room) were not necessarily everyday skills in Guatemala. It was not trivial to be able to rewire a generator, install a loudspeaker system, set a window frame, treat anthrax, or land a light plane on a country road.

Bible translation was a key to what became known as the Mayan Evangelical Ministry. Following William Cameron Townsend's rendering of the Bible into Cakchiquel, Wycliffe/Summer Institute of Linguistics (SIL) missionaries went on to translate the Bible into virtually every Indian language and major dialect.[7] [Guatemala's Academia de Lenguas Mayas has revised the spelling to the more phonetically accurate Kak'chiquel.] In 1931, the politically astute Townsend presented the first copy of his New Testament in an Indian language not to the Cakchiquel Indians, but to Jorge Ubico, the *caudillo*, who then asked Townsend to repeat the good work among the Kekchí.

When the Revolution of 1944 overthrew Ubico, that too boosted Protestantism because the new liberal government fostered a clear separation of religious and civil office. While the *cofrades* tended to fear and oppose the reformist Arévalo and Arbenz governments, Indian Protestants were active participants in the newly formed peasant leagues and agrarian committees.[8] By the late 1950s and early 1960s, the number of converts was still not large, but a foundation for future growth had been laid through a half-century of missionary work.

As the fact of a deep cultural change became evident, anthropologists started to document the process of conversion.[9] As the rate of conversion increased, they took up the more subtle questions of why and under what conditions Indian culture was receptive to the evangelists' message. Several categories of explanation have been discussed. These include: Protestant acceptance of individuals who are otherwise socially, economically, or psychologically maladjusted;[10] help in dealing with urban social isolation;[11] support in coping with alcoholism;[12] the spread of literacy;[13] the desire for economic gain;[14] the curing of disease;[15] and help in allaying the frustration of those who are experiencing "status incongruency."[16]

For whichever reasons—external promptings from the missionaries or internal changes within "modernizing" Maya culture—Protestant church growth did begin to take off. By 1976 Julian Lloret calculated that the overall evangelical population in Guatemala had risen to 4.5 percent, including 3.7 percent of the Indian population, and was growing by about 6 percent annually.[17]

In the late seventies and early eighties, three external events hastened the pace of conversion, as earlier linear growth began to expand toward its geometric potential. First, the earthquake of 1976 (which killed 20,000 and injured another 100,000 people) caused massive physical dislocation in the highlands. Some ninety villages were almost or completely leveled within a one-hundred-mile radius of Guatemala City. The physical fracturing of villages, the primary units of Indian cultural integration and economic activity, dramatically disoriented rural life and increased the number of "dispossessed peasants." At the same time, it provided the missionaries an opportunity to enter new communities, to preach on God's wrath, and to build new churches. Second, the war that brutally escalated during the Lucas García regime caused another kind of dislocation. Indians were the chief victims of the widening violence that for many became a maelstrom. The "hot" apocalyptic religion offered by the Protestants— a gospel of tears, shouting, and speaking in tongues—was sustaining and seemingly appropriate for the times. And third, during the tumultuous Ríos Montt regime, from March 1982 through August 1983, Protestantism was simply safer than Catholicism. Whether through prudence or religious revela-tion, the pace of conversion steadily quickened—until now, in the mid-1980s, probably a fifth or more of the Guatemalan population is Protestant.[18]

The Creed of the Village Protestant

How do people in San Antonio conceptualize and practice Protestantism? In the first place, many of the doctrinal distinctions that are familiar to U.S. Protestants are of no great consequence to Mayan Protestants. Whether, for example, the wafer is substantiated or transubstantiated is something I have never heard discussed in San Antonio.

When local people explain what being a Protestant means, they usually do so by contrasting Protestantism with Catholicism. They usually define in terms of a series of negatives. Generally, they make the following points, more or less in this order:

- Protestants do not drink, smoke, dance, or gamble. (Considerably more importance is attached to not drinking than to not smoking, dancing, or gambling.)
- Protestants do not venerate saints, and they flatly reject as idolatry all artifactual representations of saintly or demonic personages.
- They do not participate in any *cofradía*-related ritual.
- They reject *compadrazgo*, ritual godparenthood.
- They reject communal celebration of saints' days (*fiestas*), which involve the parading of religious images through the streets or the re-enactment of holy drama.

What do Protestants do? As elsewhere, Protestants in San Antonio focus on Christ the Savior. The key notion that Christ is a *personal* savior is ceaselessly repeated at meetings and in teachings. Salvation is through the personal Christ, who is the Son of God and who died and rose from the dead for the remission of sin. Protestant doctrine stresses that there is one God, creator of all things, and that everyone is created with direct responsibility to Him. The death and resurrection of Christ were the divine solution to sin and the purest expression of God's love. To sin is to reject that love, to betray—personally—God's gift.

Religious practice for the Mayan Protestant centers around personal testimony and personal prayer rather than group liturgy. To most, Satan is as real as a rock—but alive and slathering for souls, hunkering at the door of the home, the *cantina*, and the church. Lust is a badgering reminder that he is out there—waiting, tempting, reaching out to regain what he has lost. The stronger the temptations of the flesh, the greater the struggle. The stronger the resistance, the greater the ecstasy.

Probably half of all Guatemalan Protestants belong to Pentecostal sects.[19] Like the storefront Pentecostal church in Chicago, the Mayan church is filled with shouts of anguish and exclamations of praise. The rhythms of guitars, tambourines, and handclapping pick up the currents of emotion and spread the pain and joy.

As Robert Redfield pointed out, the response by Catholic natives to Protestantism may be conditioned by the extent to which the new religion resembles syncretic Catholicism in structure, belief, and values.[20] Certainly, the Protestant missionaries have understood this principle, and wherever possible, they have offered "functional substitutes"[21] to ease transitions. Church elders replace *cofrades*; camp days replace fiesta days;

singing replaces the Mass. Contemporary evangelical preachers discuss the nature of angels as "created spirits." But in this case, the spirits are subject to the will of one all-powerful God, as if the complex Mayan pantheon were not entirely depopulated but rather brought under the control of central authority.

The believer's transition from the old to the new religion is not easy. Even though conversion may be facilitated by apparently familiar functional analogs, the new meanings that invest old activities must still be placed upon emotional layering that is hundreds of years old and at the core of Mayan identity. I recall, for example, sitting in the home of a small congregation of evangelicals during the long fiesta days of Semana Santa (Holy Week). For San Antonio, the liturgical Easter drama is the most compelling and emotionally charged fiesta of the year.[22] Day by day, the community reenacts in the streets the story of the crucifixion and resurrection. From dawn, the *chirimía* and *tambor* have been playing their eerie, snake-charmer music on the steps of the Catholic church. Each Catholic family has constructed an *alfombra* (rug) of pine needles, colored sawdust, and flowers in front of its home (the children love the custom, like setting up a Christmas tree). Throughout the day, mournful processions kick through *alfombras*—destruction and renewal, destruction and renewal.

The small group of Protestants are far from immune to the high drama that is taking place within earshot. From their point of view, the streets are given over to Satan. The believers huddle together, their guitars and tambourines in hand, as if clutching to sides of a lifeboat. The approaching procession is at once innocent, yet as seductive as childhood memories. It is their common past and their own symbols that wind toward them, calling from the street.

So as the *anda* [platform] bearers—clouded in a somnolent haze of incense and sweating beneath their purple robes—approach the Protestant home, the believers inside are finely tuned. The monster outside is hypnotic, and they begin to break its spell with jubilant exclamations. By the time the procession reaches the Protestant house, it is met with heretical cacophony: on the street, the baleful sounds of trumpet, trombone, and bass drum; from the house, a rising chorus of hallelujahs and shouts of praise. As the procession passes, angry eyes glare from the purple robes outside; but inside the house there is noisy rejoicing. It has been, in a dual sense, a *rite of passage*.

The Holy Trek: *Del suelo al cielo*

The notion that there is an entrepreneurial "Protestant ethic" has, of course, advanced to conventional sociological wisdom since Max Weber's classic statement on the subject, *The Protestant Ethic and the Spirit of Capitalism*. From the foregoing section, it should be clear that conversion to Protestantism among Guatemalan Indians is considerably more complex than simply rationalizing economic gain. Yet on the other hand, there *is* a Protestant ethic; and the draw of the new creed at the village level is closely related to the fact that it encourages personal rather than collective use of wealth.

The fact or lack of surplus capital is particularly important for those two groups of producers who are at the margins of *milpa* stability: the "petty capitalists" and the "dispossessed peasants." This section will examine the theological dimension of economic activity in greater detail; and the final section of this chapter will show some empirical differences between Protestant and Catholic economic behavior.

By all accounts, it is "cheaper" to be a Protestant than a Catholic. San Antonio Protestants do not hesitate in explaining the practical advantages of a religion that venerates a god who is inexpensive to serve. Expanding upon this theme, missionaries have unabashedly promoted the material benefits of surrender to Christ. This is so much the case that the accusation "He just did it for the money" is frequently leveled by both Protestants and Catholics at converts of dubious spiritual sincerity.

William Cameron Townsend, the founder of Wycliffe Bible Translators/Summer Institute of Linguistics and the first missionary in San Antonio, was the son of a poor tenant farmer. He grew up in Orange County, California, where citrus-grove owners provided a helping hand to the Townsends in the form of a minister's scholarship to the poor but worthy youth. Townsend was deeply affected by his father's struggle with indebtedness and the family's escape from poverty.[23] Possibly because of this family history, debt deeply offended Townsend. From his point of view, the ritual extravagance of the Maya paved the way to their economic, spiritual, and biological enslavement; and Townsend worked against it with all the passion, instinct, and ego of a liberator.[24] He excoriated the "Romish church," which he invariably linked rhetorically to "the saloon keeper and witch doctor," for perpetuating the bondage of Indians through promotion of alcohol-related debt.

In his prolific writings for missionary publications, Townsend frequently recounted conversion stories of individual Indians. The path to salvation typically was linked to explicit economic motivation.[25] One such story is "A Rich Chief's Family Getting 'Saved,' " which Townsend published in 1926:

> Don Jacinto was the wealthiest chief in San Antonio, and in keeping with the position he had occupied during his lifetime, his funeral was

the longest celebrated and with the most rum. The drink feast lasted for over a month and, indeed, his sons did not let up except for brief breathing spells until they had finished the fortune their father had left them. At different times they would try to brace up and call a halt. Upon these occasions they would often come to the mission station and ask for some medicine to cure them. Time and again we would explain them the Gospel and assure them that that was the only sure remedy. They were fearful, however. Their old father had instilled into them something of his own hatred of the Gospel. On the other hand was the desire to reform in time to save a little of their inheritance from being lost. This very financial interest seemed to make it necessary for the Lord to let them come to the end of their rope. And the eldest son, don Teodoro, quickly arrived there. Poverty stricken and alone, a virtual tramp away on the hot lowlands, he breathed his last. . . . A short time after his death his oldest son accepted Christ and is now a faithful and prosperous member of the San Antonio congregation. Then a daughter of the old chief, a bright young woman, one of the few in her tribe who can run a sewing machine, accepted the Lord.

Don Apolinario was the favorite of his father. He was given every opportunity to get an education and came to be a school teacher. Several times he was principal of the government school in San Antonio. For two years he ran a school of his own, which the children of the principal families of the town attended. But his terrible enemy, drink, was continually after him until he finally lost his home, his lands, and the respect of all. Barefoot, and with ragged clothes, the once proud son of the rich old chief had barely been able to eke out a living for his family with his hoe. His nephew and half sister kept pointing him to Jesus until finally at a special service he made a profession of faith. A different look came into his eyes. He testifies that since then he has had no desire for liquor. The townspeople soon saw the change. The Mayor went to him and asked him if it were so that he had been converted. When don Apolinario replied that it was, the Mayor offered him the position of the public school. Pray for him.[26]

This notion that economic advancement is a sign of spiritual grace is an endlessly reiterated theme in Protestant evangelism. "*Del suelo al cielo,*" said Florentina Carmona reflectively. A now-prosperous textile merchant, she recalled her family's fifteen-year rise from dirt poverty to relative wealth. She uses the phrase as a double (triple) entendre.[27] The sense of it is, "from dirt floor to the sky; from rags to riches; from earth to Heaven."

During the course of fieldwork, I collected about half a dozen "*suelo al cielo*" stories from successful Protestants. The stories inevitably resemble the one from the Carmona family. The accounts begin with the teller in ignorance or in a fallen spiritual state. There has been some loss, usually through profligate behavior that the narrator later will come to recognize as sin. Typically, the family fortune has been squandered, frequently through a practice associated with traditional folk Catholicism. The crucial moment comes when the reprobate finally recognizes as vice what he or she previously regarded as virtue—or if not virtue, at least as innocuous. This moment of recognition is described as an emotional, divinely guided, revelatory experience.

Frequently such accounts involve sexual profligacy or alcoholism. The bonds of the family are stretched to the breaking point. Often there is a crisis, such as an illness, that brings events to a head. The sufferer has been to a local curer, possibly to the *ajitz'* (shaman) in Santa Catarina, the shrine of Maximón in San Andrés Itzapa, or the image of Don Diego in San Miguel Dueñas. He or she is disillusioned, depressed; the doors of life seem to be closing.

At this point, a guide appears—a tract, a radio sermon, an evangelist, or counsel from a converted relative. The sinner hears and understands what was previously shrugged off; goes to church, where God is revealed; and, in a bolt of understanding that will later be acknowledged as the most profound experience of life, repents, makes a decision for Christ, and is saved.

This spiritual struggle parallels an economic struggle. Economic gain is both the path and the reward. Investment in economically unproductive social institutions is not only a waste; it is a sin. Typically, the ensuing economic-spiritual struggle stretches through years of trial, temptation, backsliding, and rededication. Many informants describe an anorexic-like compulsion to save, i.e., "We got up at four every morning, dressed in rags, only ate beans and corn for a year until we could buy the truck."

In its basic elements, this story has probably changed little in this century. Writing more than sixty years ago, Townsend recounted the story of his first convert in San Antonio, Silverio López:

> One day, Silverio's little daughter took sick, or rather it came on to her gradually. Her little stomach swelled up all out of proportion while the rest of her body became thin and she lost all desire to work or play. The age-long custom of his people dictated that he consult a witch doctor. The sage instructed him to buy candles and burn them before certain images at different Romish shrines. For two weeks he labored, spending 200 pesos, the sum total of his capital. In spite of all the father's efforts and the medicine man's best enchantments, the child died. One hundred pesos was required for her burial. These he borrowed from the witch and later paid them back by 18 days of hard labor. He was a disgusted Indian, but later when another child took sick in the same way, he went again to consult a witch doctor, only this time he sought out a different one (to no avail and at further expense). . . .
>
> Silverio then went to a saloon keeper who rubbed the child's stomach with oil (also to no avail). . . . so he returned to the first shaman who advised that he buy more candles. On the road to Antigua to buy the candles, he discovered a scrap of scripture with the words, "My house shall be called the house of prayer, but ye have made it a den of

thieves (Matt. 21:13)." . . . Surely it referred to the witch doctors and
their co-conspirators, the priests. They certainly had robbed him and he
was only one of the multitudes of victims. . . . He would look elsewhere
for help.[28]

One contemporary "*suelo al cielo*" family now operates a heavy-duty,
four-ton, Mack diesel truck on the Pacific coast and a three-quarter-ton
Ford pickup in the region. Since 1958, the family has variously owned
four trucks, two buses, and an automobile. Their path, which began with
conversion and two small inherited plots of land in the mid-1950s, has
not been smooth. The elderly head-of-household experienced one devastating loss after another with his vehicles—a twenty-year roller-coaster
ride with alcohol, accidents, temptations of the flesh, bus route licensing
difficulties, thrown rods and blown gasket heads, the loss of faith and
family, and seemingly endless confrontations with police and motor vehicle bureaucracies.

Watching his grown sons unload his *second* vegetable crop of the
year (his was the first mechanical irrigation system in San Antonio) from
the bed of his truck, he told me about his first vehicle. For three years he
had risen to work in the fields before dawn and saved every penny, denying himself and his family all but the most meager diet. Finally, with the
income from two successive, successful carrot harvests and the sale of
half his land, he was able to make a down payment on a truck—only to be
wiped out a few short weeks later in "about twenty minutes" when he
failed to understand the seriousness of an oil leak. He smiles ruefully at
the memory. But he reminds himself, ever the optimist and Christian philo-
sopher, "It is through rectification of our ignorance that we are redeemed."

A Catholic Cultural Tax

The extravagant and nearly obligatory nature of ritual-related drinking
has lessened considerably since the time when Don Jacinto's mourning
sons consumed their inheritance. As it has throughout Mesoamerica, the
financial burden of formal *cofradía* participation has decreased substan-
tially in recent generations;[29] and what I refer to as "Catholic" in these
pages should not be taken too narrowly as meaning "*cofradía*-related
ritual"—much less should it be assumed that this element describes the
large and complex contemporary Catholic Church in Guatemala.

To set the context of Catholicism in San Antonio, it may be helpful to
distinguish at least four variants that have not taken strong root in the
town.

1. The revolutionary Catholic Church. Particularly since the Second
Vatican Council (1962–1965) and the Bishops' Conference in Medellín,

Colombia, in 1968, the theology of liberation has of course evolved into a major force. In Guatemala and throughout Latin America, religious workers have become increasingly involved in political struggle.[30] In light of Guatemala's history of violence and repression, philosophical questions such as "Is investment in celebration as worthy as investment in land?" may have become trivial, or at least do not describe the cutting edge of Church thinking. Yet in San Antonio, liberationist issues have not fired the local imagination. As far as I know, in the immediate San Antonio area there has been almost no significant Church-led political activity in recent years. (One notable exception was the death of Father Hermogenes, a priest in the nearby Quinizilapa town of San Miguel Dueñas, who was killed about 1978 for his involvement in a land-water dispute.)

2. *Costumbrista* sects. Elsewhere in Guatemala, communities have sometimes been bitterly divided between Mayan traditionalists (where there are strong *cofradías*) and apostolic groups who are more in line with central Church authority. In Aguacatán, the struggle of various religious sects (including Protestant as well as Catholic factions) is brilliantly described in Douglas Brintnall's *Revolt against the Dead*. In well-educated, already "modernized" San Antonio, however, the traditionalists are not strong, influential, or well organized. When people cannot cure illness by a visit to the pharmacy or health clinic, they occasionally seek out a shaman in Santa Catarina or nearby towns, but shamanism as an institution is not as deeply entrenched as it is in, say, the Quiché area.[31]

3. Charismatic sects. Several years before my fieldwork, a priest who briefly promoted a sect of *carismáticos* worked in the town. That experience involved much handclapping and singing and probably was intended to compete directly with the robust evangelical cults. Although there is still a small group of Catholics who call themselves *carismáticos*, the sect is much reduced (the proponent priest having been driven out) and is not a serious rival of either the mainstream Catholic or the evangelical churches.

4. Catholic Action. About twenty-five years ago, a new apostolic sect known as Acción Católica (Catholic Action) began missionizing within the Church itself. This movement now represents "modern Catholicism" in most parts of rural Guatemala and elsewhere in Latin America. Catholic Action incorporates features of Protestantism and inverts many traditional Catholic values. In an important sense, just as Protestantism borrows from Catholicism and incorporates "functional substitutes" to ease transitions, so too Catholic Action borrows from and incorporates Protestantism. For example, Catholic Action recasts the traditional notion of spiritually purifying poverty into an opposition between the sacred and the material, with economic advancement being good and both *ladino* domination *and* the wealth-dissipating *cofradía* being exploitative.[32]

Although Catholic Action exists in San Antonio, primarily through the effort of several activists, it is nevertheless not a major force in the town as it is in other Guatemalan communities.[33]

The Catholic Church in San Antonio might be described as the "garden variety"—that is, the community is tended by a diocesan priest who lives in the parochial seat of San Miguel Dueñas and visits the town regularly to celebrate Mass and fiestas. Without a resident pastor, religious practice is dominated by *catequistas* whom the priest instructs and organizes, and by heads-of-household. Most prayer and religious practice takes place within the home.

Three *cofradías* are active in San Antonio today, but they are no longer controlling institutions. They are viewed primarily as fiesta-organizing committees and have little actual authority beyond that specific responsibility.[34] On the other hand, although formal *cofradía*-directed expenses have declined, active participation in Catholic ceremonial life still requires substantial investment of resources. The magnitude of this investment is suggested by Table 1, which lists the ceremonial expenses of a family of two adults and five children over the course of one year.

As it happens, this young, exceptionally poor family owns neither land nor any other substantial material assets. The household *sitio* on which the family lives and the twelve *cuerdas* that the husband works are borrowed from his father. Total family wealth is equivalent to only $297, placing the family in the seventh percentile among the seventy-four families in the sample. Their income (as opposed to their assets) is derived entirely from what the family grows on the borrowed land, the husband's day labor, the occasional sales of textiles, and the wife's irregular weaving lessons for foreigners.

Although the husband theoretically has twelve *cuerdas* at his disposal, he is unable to farm the entire amount. He plants only three *cuerdas* in corn and one *cuerda* in beans (his family's nutritive subsistence base)[35] and three *cuerdas* of carrots and one *cuerda* of *camote* (his two cash crops). He does not plant his other four *cuerdas* or farm more intensively because he can neither afford hired labor nor rely on his wife (who cares for a seven-year-old, a five-year-old, a three-year-old, a two-year-old, and a six-month-old baby) to help him in the fields. Lacking funds to buy sufficient fertilizer or pesticides, he cannot afford to grow potentially more profitable vegetable crops, much less afford the nutritive risk to his family if these crops should fail. Furthermore, in exchange for usufruct, the harvest from a portion of "his" land is pledged to his father, and he must also work for several days without pay on his father's land. So despite the evident need to grow either more food or more cash crops, he would be hard-pressed to handle more than the eight *cuerdas* that he presently plants.

Because he lacks the capital to purchase the inputs that would justify the investment of time, he uses his "spare time" (i.e., intervals between his own peak demands of labor) to work as a *mozo* [hired hand] on his neighbor's land. Sometimes he can find work as an unskilled helper for a local mason. All in all, he works about eighty days per year as a wage laborer.

Taking into account his financial situation, the $159.50 per year in ceremonial expenses shown in Table 1 represents a significant investment—indeed, nearly a quarter of the family's total income. Moreover, this is probably a conservative calculation. First, this budget assumes no major crisis or family passage, e.g., a death and burial (about $100–250), a birth and baptism ($20–30), or a marriage (roughly $200–400). Second, it includes no ritual-related curing for illnesses that go beyond the pharmacy, health post, or a physician in Antigua. Such items might include prayers, consultations with curers, the purchase of candles, food, and *guaro* (a local, clandestine alcoholic beverage) for offerings, or supplicatory visits to religious shrines. Considering that this is a family with five undernourished children under eight years of age, health problems are a regular and predictable expense. Third, the budget includes the fulfillment of no special religious obligations, participation in minor fiestas, or visits to fiestas in neighboring towns. San Antonio families are well aware of fiesta days in a dozen or so nearby towns and religious shrines; when money is available, they enjoy traveling to venerate special saints or religious patrons. (This family has not been able to afford the major pilgrimage to the shrine of the Black Christ of Esquipulas, near the Honduran border).[36] Fourth, it includes no *cofradía* expense. Though this male head-of-household has not served in the *cofradía* and expresses no interest in doing so, he estimates that prodded participation would cost about $40 for himself and his wife. Finally, but perhaps most important for judging the veracity of the budget, this estimate includes a ceremonial alcoholic consumption expense of only $18. Knowing the family well, having drunk with them, I am quite certain that this is a genteel understatement,[37] though I have not taken the liberty of adjusting the data to match my suspicions.

In short, the $159.50 estimate, which amounts to about 24 percent of this family's total income, is probably not unrealistic.[38] Is a quarter of their income, particularly in the face of grinding poverty, a bad investment? Though the family is financially poor, it certainly is not without resources or hope. Apart from the spiritual rewards and psychological security derived from firm beliefs, the family also knows that the system will eventually work to improve their fortune. The father someday will inherit the tiny household plot and the twelve *cuerdas* presently borrowed from his father. At about the same time, the sons will be old enough to help work the land; and the wife, with three adolescent daughters to assist

Table 1. Fiesta Expenses for One Catholic Family

January: Fiesta de Dulce Nombre de Jesús	
Husband's participation in Baile de los Moros (Dance of the Moors)	
Rents horse for procession	$5.00
Rents saddle	1.50
Buys mask for dance	2.00
Buys material for costume	5.00
Contributes to fiesta committee	3.00
Buys sword	2.00
Subtotal	*18.50*
Family's expenses	
Food, special meals, entertaining relatives	10.00
Liquor	5.00
New clothes for five children[a]	20.00
Contribution to fiesta committee	2.50
Firecrackers and skyrockets	5.00
Flowers	2.00
Candles and church offerings	2.00
Subtotal	*46.50*
April: Semana Santa (Holy Week)	
Offering in church	3.00
Special meals (bread, honey, vegetables, etc.)	25.00
Liquor	5.00
Flowers (including *alfombras*)	5.00
Candles	2.00
Subtotal	*40.00*
June: Fiesta de San Antonio (titular fiesta)	
Offering in church	3.00
Offering in canton chapel	2.00
Special meals	15.00
New clothing for two adults[a]	20.00
Liquor	8.00
Flowers	3.00
Candles	2.00
Bullfights and entertainment	1.50
Palos de monte (Easter palms)	3.50
Toys, gifts for children, treats at the street fair	5.00
Subtotal	*63.00*
August: Asunción (Assumption)	5.00
September: Virgin of Dolores and National Independence Day	5.00
November: Día de los Santos (All Saints' Day)	4.00
December: Pascuas (Christmas season)	17.50
Total	**199.50**
[a]Minus adjustment for purchase of clothing	−40.00
Adjusted total	**159.50**

her, can look forward to expanded weaving production and sales. In the meantime, life has a sense of orderliness—the family can accept the present and feel a certain assurance about the future. No shame or social stigma is attached to their poverty. It would not occur to this family that their privation is caused by sloth or moral turpitude or that they are not good people. Positioned within a society that does not measure life by material standards, their lives ebb and flow within an orbit larger than ambition. In fiestas, they celebrate the subsumption of self-identity within community identity. Just as they accept the Catholic paradox of the Trinity—that there can be more than one in One—so too, in celebration, individuals are one and more than one. Celebration punctuates daily life: it orders the random flow of events into cycles, but more important, it renders the trivial significant.

Whether such punctuation is a sufficient return on economic activity is an existential question to which I have no answer. But from the Protestant point of view, that question is easy to answer: no. The $159.50-a-year ritual expenditure by this family is not only "waste"; it is "sin." Because village Catholicism supposedly encourages such vice, the Protestants view the priest and the Church to be flatly guilty of theft. The sum of $159.50, a Protestant would likely point out, is adequate to buy a fairly good *cuerda* of *milpa* land. By changing priorities, a family such as the one described above could theoretically "advance" from its present poverty, landlessness, and "dispossessed-peasant" status to nutritive self-sufficiency and the ownership of five *cuerdas* in about five years. The husband could hire one or two seasonal helpers and boost his carrot output . . . and then reinvest that return on an even more profitable mix of crops the following year. Or, with nutritive self-sufficiency guaranteed in five years (and no rental obligation), he could begin investing ceremonial savings in a household business—for example, in a sewing machine to boost the productivity of his wife's nascent textile operation.[39] Or if after several successful harvests the family sold its accumulated land, it would be able to make a down payment (about 30 to 40 percent is required) on a small, used four-cylinder pickup truck. Whether or not they are successful in achieving such goals, this is more or less how Protestants think and try to act; and it is certainly how they like to pejoratively describe Catholics as *not* thinking and *not* acting.

Comparing the Economic Performance of Protestants and Catholics[40]

I do not wish to imply that all Catholics are happily and innocently impoverished and that all Protestants are compulsive savers who become financial super-achievers. That isn't the case. And even from an economic point of view, the marginally greater amount of money that Catholics invest in communalism is not necessarily a "bad investment." The $159.50 that the family described above invests in celebration might be fairly described as a "cultural tax," but it is not necessarily nonutilitarian. In light of Guatemala's overarching class barriers, reinforced by ethnicity and enforced by political oppression, investment in community rather than personal gain, as Waldemar Smith argues, does not seem unreasonable.[41]

Yet the larger confluence of "anti-*milpa* forces" that are undercutting traditional communal stability also works to make personal gain both more attractive and more necessary. As argued elsewhere, ideological rationalization of personal gain is not the only—and probably not even the most important—incentive to conversion; yet, by and large, Protestants do seem better geared and far more motivated than Catholics to pursue lifestyles that will either lift them out of poverty or protect hard-won financial gain.

The most fundamental dissimilarity between the Protestant and Catholic economic positions is suggested by Table 2, a correlation matrix for three variables: land, wealth, and income.

Table 2. Correlation among Wealth, Income, and Land, by Religion

		Total Wealth		Income
Income	(C)	.50***		
	(P)	.12		
Value of land	(C)	.92***	(C)	.47***
	(P)	.71**	(P)	.13

C: Catholic (61 households)
P: Protestant (13 households)
*p .05
**p .01
***p .001

As would be expected, there is high intercorrelation among the variables. Among Catholics, all three variables are highly and significantly correlated with each other at the .001 significance level. For Catholics, it is almost literally true that land *is* wealth ($r = .92$). "Income and land" and "income and wealth" are both highly positive, about .5. The implication, simply, is that the economic performance of Catholics, measured by either total income or total wealth, is highly associated with how much land they have.

For Protestants, land and wealth are still highly correlated, though less so and at a lower level of statistical significance. More interesting, however, income is *not* significantly associated with land value, nor is it significantly associated with wealth. The implication is that Protestants, unlike Catholics, create livelihood strategies that are not necessarily dependent on land. Probably this is because most Protestant converts come from the ranks of "dispossessed peasants." Most are from families pushed to the point at which rent exceeds their consumption-maintenance costs, that is, families driven to a state of landlessness. Those whose spiritual-economic paths follow the *"suelo al cielo"* route tend to pick up land on the way *or* find potentially more lucrative means of investment that are not necessarily land-based.

This lessened Protestant dependence on land as a source of wealth and income is further illustrated by comparing the elements of household wealth among Protestants and Catholics (Table 3). Here, family wealth is broken down into five elements, ranked according to the descending order of the ratio of Catholic to Protestant values. The average Catholic family owns 1.23 times as much land as the average Protestant. However, for every other element the value of Protestant holdings exceeds that of Catholics. Overall, the total average Catholic wealth is only .81 of the average Protestant wealth, despite the apparent Catholic advantage in the critical land variable.

Table 3. A Comparison of Elements of Household Wealth, by Religion[a]

	(A) Average Catholic Wealth from This Source ($)[b]		(B) Average Protestant Wealth from This Source ($)[c]		(C) Catholic/ Protestant Ratio
(1) Land	2,245	(61)	1,825	(40)	1.23
(2) Household plot	858	(23)	987	(22)	.87
(3) Textiles	428	(12)	673	(15)	.64
(4) Animals	44	(1)	205	(4)	.21
(5) Machinery, tools, vehicles, business inventory	119	(3)	866	(19)	.14
Total	**3,694**	(100)	**4,556**	(100)	.81[d]

[a]Data from survey of 74 households: 61 Catholic, 13 Protestant.
[b]Figures in parentheses are percentages of the Catholic total.
[c]Figures in parentheses are percentages of the Protestant total.
[d]The ratio of the Catholic and Protestant totals.

The most striking discrepancy between the two groups is in machinery, tools, vehicles, and business inventory. Catholic wealth in this category equals only .14 of Protestant wealth. The presence of one bus-owning household (that of Florentina Carmona) among the thirteen Protestant families greatly inflates the average values in this category; nevertheless, despite the statistical distortion, it is certain that many Protestants have turned toward transportation as an alternative to traditional farming. In a separate survey of vehicle ownership in San Antonio and San Andrés, I identified forty-three vehicles belonging to thirty-five different house-holds. Of these, 49 percent of the families, who owned 51 percent of the vehicles, were Protestant, while only about 18 percent of the general popu-lation is Protestant.

The propensity of Protestants to develop nonfarm sources of income is reflected in Table 4. This table shows, first, the mean values for Catho-lic and Protestant subincomes for each of the nine major elements of total household income, as well as the percentage of total income for either group that each of the nine represents. Second, it compares the Catholic and Protestant values and ranks the elements in descending order of the ratio of values.

Table 4. A Comparison of Elements of Household Income, by Religion[a]

	(A) Average Catholic Income from This Source ($)[b]		(B) Average Protestant Income from This Source ($)[c]		(C) Catholic/ Protestant Ratio
(1) Small-scale vegetable marketing	61	(5)	3	(<1)	20.33
(2) *Petate*-making	17	(1)	1	(<1)	17.00
(3) Children's wages outside household	14	(1)	1	(<1)	14.00
(4) Male wages outside household	486	(40)	424	(29)	1.15
(5) Total agricultural income	311	(26)	353	(24)	.88
(6) Textile sales	64	(5)	111	(8)	.58
(7) Female wages outside household	42	(3)	90	(6)	.47
(8) Business income	205	(17)	445	(30)	.46
(9) Animal production	11	(1)	43	(3)	.26
Total	**1,211**	(100)	**1,471**	(100)	.82[d]

[a]Data from survey of 74 households: 61 Catholic, 13 Protestant
[b]Figures in parentheses are percentages of the Catholic total, here rounded.
[c]Figures in parentheses are percentages of the Protestant total.
[d]The ratio of the Catholic and Protestant totals.

As in Table 3, the elements are ranked from "most Catholic" to "most Protestant." Several points concerning Table 4 require explanation. First, almost no Protestants engage in small-scale vegetable marketing or *petate* [woven reed mat] making. These two activities are largely extensions of the production logic of the "*milpa* technologist"; and, not surprisingly, as economic alternatives they are not particularly attractive, even to poor Protestants. Second, although there is almost no reported wage income for children among Protestants, and children's wages account for only 1 percent of total income among Catholics, it should not be inferred that children do not work. Rather, most families find their children to be more productive as workers within the household, not as wage earners.[42] Children are ideal *milpa* laborers: they weed, they harvest small quantities of crops for domestic consumption, they carry messages and meals to and from the fields. Protestant children, however, are less likely to assume these roles because, first, their parents' lives are less likely to be organized around *milpa* production and, second, their parents are more likely to emphasize education. Third, Catholic males earn more from wages outside the household than do Protestant males, both absolutely and as a proportion of total income. However, the broad category "wage labor outside the household" tends to obscure the more significant difference, that is, *how* this income is earned. For Catholics, wage labor is most often *mozo* labor. It supplements *milpa* income as land per family declines and more land must be rented to bring total planting up to subsistence size. Protestant wage laborers, on the other hand, tend to seek higher-paid, upwardly mobile occupations that lead to small businesses. The items in Rows 6, 8, and 9 of Table 4—textile sales, business income, and animal production—all reflect the greater Protestant disposition toward business activity. In each case, the business-related income is both absolutely and relatively more important for Protestant than for Catholic families.

A typical maximizing Protestant "*suelo al cielo*" family optimizes resources within the "newer" sectors of the San Antonio economy, but carries over the logic and ingenuity of *milpa* management. For example, one of my neighbors was fortunate to have acquired land during the agrarian reform of the late 1950s. Instead of buying more land, he branched into new ventures, utilizing family members as managers and operators. For instance, one adult son, who maintains a separate household, operates the family truck. The father continues to work the land, principally with hired *mozo* labor; the son makes regular runs to the southern coast to sell produce, purchasing additional vegetables from his neighbors or charging a fee for transport to the higher-paying, distant market. While on the coast, he buys or transports loads of mangos, papayas, and melons; and he also picks up fodder for his two cows from a small piece of land that his neighbor rents from a *finquero*. When the oldest son returns, the father and his youngest son (a twelve-year-old whose primary obligation is school) drive a load of cow manure to the family's nearest vegetable plot. Meanwhile, the daughter-in-law has set up a small butcher shop. She sells fresh meat, without refrigeration, over the counter two or three times a week from the front room of her house. When a cow is slaughtered, part is retailed in the family shop, and the rest is wholesaled in Antigua. The son also uses his frequent trips to and from Antigua and the coast to buy additional fresh meat. Keeping an eye on the tiny *tienda* and caring for her own small child, the daughter-in-law is assisted by one of the older children (her niece). Meanwhile, her mother-in-law operates a tourist *tienda* on the road leading into town. With the family truck at her disposal, she occasionally makes selling trips to Guatemala City. Although she is an expert weaver and *petate* maker herself, she buys or commissions all her stock from her neighbors.

Given the Catholic land advantage (Table 3) and the Protestant emphasis on nonfarm activity, it is not surprising that Catholics earn a relatively higher proportion of their total family income from agriculture than do Protestants. However, *despite the fact that Protestants own less land*, Protestant agricultural income actually *exceeds* Catholic farm earnings (a Catholic/Protestant ratio of .88). Table 5 takes a closer look at performance in agriculture. The several variables relating to agriculture are again listed in descending order of the Catholic-to-Protestant ratio.

Table 5. A Comparison of Agricultural Performance, by Religion[a]

	(A) Catholic Average	(B) Protestant Average	(C) Catholic/ Protestant Ratio
(1) Number of *cuerdas* rented	3.5	1.7	2.06
(2) Total *cuerdas* (owned + rented)	16.5	10.9	1.51
(3) Number of *cuerdas* owned	13.0	9.2	1.41
(4) Production of corn (lbs./person/day)	1.9	1.5	1.27
(5) Value of land owned ($)	2,245	1,825	1.23
(6) Number of *cuerdas* planted	11.5	10.4	1.11
(7) Income from *milpa* ($)	114	104	1.10
(8) Total agricultural income ($)	311	353	.88
(9) Average value of each *cuerda* owned ($)	172	198	.87
(10) Income from cash crops ($)	173	219	.79
(11) % of land planted	70	96	.73
(12) Value of output per *cuerda* ($)	24	38	.63

[a]Data from survey of 74 households: 61 Catholic, 13 Protestant.

The fact that Protestants have higher agricultural incomes than Catholics is all the more surprising given that Catholics own 1.41 times as much land and rent more than twice as much land. When owned and rented land are combined, Catholics have a total of one-and-one-half times as much land as Protestants. Nevertheless, Catholics do less well than Protestants in virtually every measure of agricultural productivity. Catholic agricultural income is only .88 and Catholic income from cash crops is only .79 that of the Protestants, underscoring the fact that when Protestants do farm, they are more likely to plant high-yielding commodities rather than corn and its typical *milpa* intercrops. Protestants also farm more intensively: they plant 96 percent of their land, compared to 70 percent for Catholics. As a result, the effective land gap is narrowed so that, overall, Catholics plant only an average of 11.5 *cuerdas* compared to an average 10.4 *cuerdas* planted by the Protestants. Protestants also seem to obtain the better land. As a result of frequent buying and reselling of plots, they own a disproportionate share of the higher-yielding vegetable and coffee bottomland from the former lake. This is reflected in Row 9, which shows that an average *cuerda* of Protestant land is worth $198, versus $172 for that of Catholics. Finally, because they own better land, plant more intensively, and plant a higher proportion of cash crops, Protestants achieve an overall output per *cuerda* of $38, versus $24 per *cuerda* for Catholics. The only agricultural variable in which Catholics outperform Protestants is corn production, which no doubt reflects the greater Catholic reliance on the *milpa*.[43]

Conclusion

I have tried to show how not only the economy but also, to some extent, the ideology of the town is a product of colonial relations. Separate but unequal spheres were established that allowed economic subsumption to be offset by a limited cultural autonomy. What we now think of as Indianness is less a relic of a more glorious, pre-Hispanic Mayan past than a cultural package that solidified Hispanic control.

Despite their frequent right-wing political identification today, in at least one sense the early Protestant missionaries were grassroots revolutionaries. They viewed Indians as being spiritually, biologically, and economically enslaved. In their eyes, the Church, alcohol, and debt were the instruments of that enslavement—and they, the missionaries, were the liberators. Unlike the contemporary liberationist Catholic Church—which considers Indians to be *politically*, and from there, economically enslaved—the missionaries did not attack or even necessarily question the organized structure of oppression. They did not challenge the *finca* owners or the government; rather, they attacked the culture.

The missionaries saved and edified relatively few Indian souls during their first half-century of proselytizing. But they preached a strong message, oriented themselves upon the prevailing winds of cultural change, and laid the organizational groundwork for future mass conversions. In that "witness" and public testimony were key aspects of Protestantism, every convert had the potential to start a chain reaction. In the late 1970s and early 1980s, the process accelerated: an earthquake fractured the physical grounds of cultural unity, a counterinsurgency war created a nightmare of psychological insecurity, and a Protestant president gave the evangelistic message an official stamp of approval.

The evangelical chain-letter is in the mail. Today, well over 30 percent of Guatemalans are Protestant.[44] Yet, as this chapter shows, conversion may be nurtured but is not caused by foreign missionaries. Certainly the missionaries have toiled to liberate the Maya from their culture—and certainly they have been aided by earthquakes, war, and a zealot president —but the fact that the message has been heard in the village reflects a deeper, gradual erosion of the economy and ideology of colonial relations. In a sense, the forces that have undercut the replicability of the "*milpa* technologists' " world—the same forces that have replaced them with "dispossessed peasants" and "petty capitalists"—have prepared the ground for the conversion process. And then, the relatively better economic performance of Protestants, whether at the rich or poor end of the economic scale, has reinforced their spiritual choices with a material rationale.

Notes

1. A 1978 field survey of Protestant church membership in Guatemala found 40 large denominations and 160 smaller sects. See Instituto Internacional de Evangelización a Fondo (IINDEF) and Servicio Evangelizador para America Latina (SEPAL), *Directorio de iglesias, organizaciones y ministerios del movimiento protestante: Guatemala* (San Francisco de Dos Ríos, Costa Rica: IINDEF, 1981), 15.

2. The missionary view of the often-recounted story of Barrios inviting in the Presbyterian Mission is told in Paul Burgess, *Justo Rufino Barrios: A Biography*, 2d ed. (Quezaltenango, Guatemala: El Noticiero Evangélico, 1957).

3. Julian Lloret, "The Mayan Evangelical Church in Guatemala" (Doctor of Theology diss., Dallas Theological Seminary, 1976), 65–84; Paul Burgess, ed., *Historia de la obra evangélica presbiteriana en Guatemala* (Quezaltenango: Tipografia "El Noticiero," 1957),

4. William Read, Victor Monterroso, and Harmon Johnson, *Latin American Church Growth* (Grand Rapids: William B. Eerdmans, 1969), 157. They do not provide sources or explain their methodology. Lloret, who studied church growth in the late 1970s, doubts this 1.6 percent estimate and believes their estimated

9 percent rate of annual growth is unrealistically high (Lloret, "Mayan Evangelical Church," 246).

5. William Cameron Townsend, like a whole generation of evangelists before him, astutely worked the market routes as a traveling Bible salesman fully twenty years before anthropologists such as Robert Redfield "discovered" the organizational importance of Indian markets. See Robert Redfield, "Primitive Merchants of Guatemala," *Quarterly Journal of Inter-American Relations* I, no. 4 (1939): 42–46.

6. In reviewing church growth over the last decades, a church researcher recently wrote, "When the Gospel first reaches someone in a previously unchurched family, village or small community it can frequently spread rapidly. Each new church is a seed planted with the potential to grow 30 fold, 60 fold or 100 fold" (James Montgomery, "The Case for Research: Part 4, Factors of Growth," *Global Church Growth* 20 [July–August 1983]: 265).

7. See Ethel Wallis and Mary Bennett, *Two Thousand Tongues to Go* (London: Hodder & Stoughton, 1966); and Wycliffe Bible Translators and Summer Institute of Linguistics, *Who Brought the Word* (Santa Ana, CA: Wycliffe, 1963). Less friendly views of Wycliffe-SIL activity in Latin America are David Stoll, *Fishers of Men or Founders of Empire? The Wycliffe Bible Translators in Latin America* (Cambridge, MA: Cultural Survival, 1982); Peter Åaby and Soren Hvalkøf, *Is God an American? An Anthropological Perspective on the Missionary Work of the Summer Institute of Linguistics* (Copenhagen: Survival International, 1981) and Pedro Alisedo et al., *El Instituto Lingüístico de Verano* (Mexico City: Proceso, 1981).

Despite ample SIL/Wycliffe publicity that Townsend's was the first Bible in an Indian language, a British and Foreign Bible Society had translated one Gospel into Cakchiquel at least fifteen years earlier. Townsend must have known about it since the Central American Mission distributed it (David Stoll, personal communication). By the early 1930s, Townsend had shifted away from his missionary work in San Antonio and Patzún and refocused his energies on linguistics. He dropped out of the Central American Mission and largely relegated San Antonio to his less effective brother, Paul.

8. Ricardo Falla, "Evolución político-religiosa del indígena rural en Guatemala, 1945–65," *Estudios Sociales Centroamericanos* 1 (January–April 1972): 27–41; Robert Wasserstrom, "Revolution in Guatemala: Peasants and Politics under the Arbenz Government," *Comparative Studies in Society and History* 17, no. 4 (October 1975): 443–78.

9. For a report on the conversion of nearly a third of San Pedro la Laguna's population to five competing Protestant sects, see Benjamin Paul and Lois Paul, "Changing Marriage Patterns in a Highland Guatemala Community," *Southwest Journal of Anthropology* 19 (1963): 131–48. See also June Nash, "Protestantism in an Indian Village in the Western Highlands of Guatemala," *Alpha Kappa Deltan* 30 (Special Issue, 1960): 49–58; and Benson Saler, "Religious Conversion and Self-Aggrandizement: A Guatemalan Case," *Practical Anthropology* 12 (1965): 107–49.

10. J. Nash, "Protestantism"; Saler, "Religious Conversion"; E. A. Nida, "The Relationship of Social Structure to the Problem of Evangelism in Latin America," *Practical Anthropology* 5 (1958): 101–23.

11. W. E. Carter, "Innovation and Marginality: Two South American Case Studies," *América Indígena* 30 (1965): 383–92, 436; Bryan Roberts, "Protestant Groups

and Coping with Urban Life in Guatemala City," *American Journal of Sociology* 73 (1967): 753–67.

12. James D. Sexton and Clyde Woods, "Development and Modernization among Highland Maya: A Comparative Analysis of Ten Guatemalan Towns," *Human Organization* 36 (1977): 156–72.

13. H. Siverts, "Political Organization in a Tzeltal Community in Chiapas, Mexico," *Alpha Kappa Deltan* 30 (Special Issue, 1960): 14–28.

14. Saler, "Religious Conversion"; Sol Tax and Robert Hinshaw, "The Maya of the Midwestern Highlands," in *Handbook of Middle American Indians*, vol. 7, *Ethnology, Part One*, ed. Robert Wauchope and Evon Z. Vogt, pp. 69–100 (Guatemala City: Ciencía y tecnología para Guatemala, Cuaderno #4, 1985); and Ricardo Falla, *Quiché rebelde: Estudio de un movimiento de conversión religiosa rebelde a las creencias tradicionales, en San Antonio Ilotenango, Quiché, 1948–70* (Guatemala City: Universidad de San Carlos Press, 1979), 185–87.

15. Robert Harmon and William Kurtz, "Missionary Influence on Maya Medical Behavior: Results of a Factor Analysis" (Paper presented to the 33rd Annual Meeting of the Society for Applied Anthropology, Tucson, 1973).

16. Ruben Reina and Norman Schwartz, "The Structural Context of Religious Conversion in Petén, Guatemala: Status, Community, and Multi-community," *American Ethnologist* I (1974): 157–92.

17. Lloret, "Mayan Evangelical Church," 246. For an analysis and critical interpretation of Protestant church growth in Guatemala, see also Jesús García-Ruiz, *Las sectas fundamentalistas en Guatemala* (Austin: University of Texas Press, 1964).

18. By 1981, the total active, baptized twelve-years-or-older membership of *all* Protestant groups, not just evangelicals, was enumerated as 334,453. Accepting the four-to-one ratio of nonactive members/children to active members used in this study, the "Protestant community" stood at about 1.3 million, or just over 18 percent of the total population (IINDEF and SEPAL, *Directorio*, 61). A more conservative estimate put the Protestant portion of the population at 15 percent (Julian Lloret, "Forces Shaping the Church in Central America," *CAM Bulletin* [Summer 1982]: 3). In 1982, unidentified Protestant groups were reported as claiming 22 percent of the population, with some sects boasting of annual growth rates of 15 percent (Marlise Simons, "Latin America's New Gospel," *New York Times Magazine*, November 7, 1982, p. 45). A claim of "20 percent or more" for 1983 is made by James Montgomery, "The Case for Research: Part 3, The Factors of Growth," *Global Church Growth* 20 (March–April 1983): 250. On the basis of recent growth patterns, he further projects that Guatemala will be fully 50 percent Protestant by 1990 ("The Case for Research: Part 6, Projections for Growth," *Global Church Growth* 20 [September–October 1983]: 303).

19. Following a pattern similar to that in other parts of Latin America, Pentecostal churches in Guatemala have grown much faster than the original "pioneer" missions, such as the Presbyterians. According to Montgomery, "By 1950, Pentecostals comprised 13 percent of the evangelical community. This increased to 20 percent in 1960, to 31 percent in 1967 and all the way up to 54 percent in 1980." At present, Pentecostal and non-Pentecostal churches are of roughly equal size. See "The Case for Research: Part 3."

20. Robert Redfield, *The Village That Chose Progress: Chan Kom Revisited* (Chicago: University of Chicago Press, 1962).

21. Julian Lloret, for many years field director of the Central American Mission (CAM), pointedly used this phrase, "functional substitute," in his dissertation while describing "strategies for future expansion." Of Bible conferences, for example, he says: "In a real sense these conferences are a functional substitute for the traditional religious festivals and provide opportunity for everyone to contribute to corporate religious activity just as they did before" ("Mayan Evangelical Church," p. 269). Ironically, but perhaps with a certain poetic justice, this is the same pattern that occurred during the Catholic evangelization of the Indians in sixteenth-century Mexico and Guatemala. Robert Ricard, in *The Spiritual Conquest of Mexico* (Berkeley: University of California Press, 1974), discusses the friars' attempts to relate particular cults to particular prehistoric gods. To do that, they placed churches or shrines on the sites of pre-Hispanic temples to gods with attributes similar to those of the Christian saints to whom the post-Conquest shrines were dedicated.

22. G. Alexander Moore, in *Life Cycles in Atchalán: The Diverse Careers of Certain Guatemalans* (New York: Teachers College Press, 1973), provides a particularly effective description and interpretation of Semana Santa ritual in the town of Alotenango, a few kilometers southwest of San Antonio.

23. James and Marti Hefley, *Uncle Cam* (Waco, TX: Word Books, 1974); Stoll, *Fishers of Men*, 28–29.

24. Despite his liberationist attitude at the grassroots, Townsend appeared to make no political judgments against the larger system of debt peonage. He did not attack *finca* owners or *contratistas*. In fact, in his novel, *Tolo, the Volcano's Son*, he portrays God as a kindly *finquero*.

25. In an analysis of eight San Antonio-Santa Catarina conversion stories published by Townsend between 1919 and 1929, Stoll found that seven contained explicit economic motivation. The stories describe people who were severely taxed, indebted, and even bankrupted by costly ritual obligation. Their present or future prosperity was tied to freedom from this obligation (David Stoll, "The Founder in Guatemala," unpublished draft of *Fishers of Men*).

26. William Cameron Townsend, "A Rich Chief's Family Getting 'Saved,' " *Central American Bulletin* 15 (September 1926).

27. From alcoholic profligacy, the family has risen to be the wealthiest household among my seventy-four-household survey sample. Florentina and her daughters operate one of the largest tourist *tiendas*. Her husband and son-in-law farm considerable land and operate a bus between San Antonio and Antigua.

28. William Cameron Townsend, *One of Guatemala's Indians: His Witch Doctor and a Torn Tract* (missionary brochure). Silverio López, like Don Apolinario, then began his climb. With the revelatory scrap of paper in hand, he sought out the evangelical pastor in Antigua, who saved Silverio on the spot and cured the daughter with simple medication for parasites. By 1926, Silverio was working with Townsend as the pastor of five small congregations. This follow-up account of the Silverio story is reported in W. F. Jordan, *Central American Indians and the Bible* (New York: Fleming H. Revell, 1926), 15–16. However, according to Stoll, who followed up the story in the field, "Fifty years later the man's son could not recall Townsend's story of swindle and woe. He did describe his father's drinking problem, which together with his weakness for women forced him to leave the Protestant church" (Stoll, *Fishers of Men*, p. 33).

29. By way of contrast, as late as the early 1960s in Zinacantán (whose ceremonial organization was intensively studied during the years of the Harvard

Chiapas Project), an adult male was described as having to spend from $4 to $1,100 in order to discharge one of fifty-five yearly ceremonial posts (Frank Cancian, *Economics and Prestige in a Maya Community* [Stanford: Stanford University Press, 1965]). Eric Wolf says, "Evidence from Middle America indicates that a man may have to expend at least the equivalent of one year's local wages to act as sponsor in a community ceremonial. Expenditures of from two to twenty times this amount are noted for particular communities" (*Peasants*, Englewood Cliffs, NJ: Prentice-Hall, 1966, p. 7). Paul Diener reports ritual expenditures of about 25 percent of income ("The Tears of St. Anthony: Ritual and Revolution in Eastern Guatemala," *Latin American Perspectives* 5 [1978]: 92–116).

30. Among the many discussions on this subject, see several pertinent chapters in Daniel H. Levine, *Churches and Politics in Latin America* (Beverly Hills, CA: Sage, 1980); also, Margaret E. Crahan, "International Aspects of the Role of the Catholic Church in Central America," in *Central America: International Dimensions of the Crisis*, ed. Richard E. Feinberg, pp. 213–235 (New York: Holmes and Meier, 1982); and more generally, Penny Lernoux, *Cry of the People* (London: Penguin Books, 1980). In reference to Guatemala, see Luisa Frank and Philip Wheaton, *Indian Guatemala: Path to Liberation* (Washington, DC: EPICA Task Force, 1984); Thomas R. Melville, "The Catholic Church in Guatemala, 1944–1982," *Cultural Survival Quarterly* 7 (Spring 1983): 23–27; and Philip Berryman, *The Religious Roots of Rebellion: Christians in Central American Revolutions* (Maryknoll: Orbis, 1984). For a historical view of the Church's prerevolutionary period, see B. J. Calder, *Crecimiento y cambio de la iglesia católica guatemalteca, 1944–1966* (Guatemala City: Editorial José Pineda Ibarra, 1970).

31. For a detailed description of contemporary Mayan religion in Momostenango, Quiché, see Barbara Tedlock, *Time and the Highland Maya* (Albuquerque: University of New Mexico Press, 1982).

32. Kay B. Warren's analysis of the subject is particularly helpful. See *The Symbolism of Subordination: Indian Identity in a Guatemalan Town* (Austin: University of Texas Press, 1978).

33. The struggle between Catholic Action and traditionalist sects in San Antonio Ilotenango, Quiché, is described in Falla, *Quiché rebelde*.

34. San Antonio *cofradías* are of the "faded" type, to use the classificatory system in Billie de Walt, "Changes in the Cargo Systems of Mesoamerica," *Anthropological Quarterly* 48 (April 1975): 87–105.

35. This is slim fare for a family of seven. All but the oldest children appear to be mildly malnourished. The two- and three-year-old children have been treated in a clinical malnutrition project at the Instituto para Nutrición para Centroamérica y Panamá (INCAP) in Guatemala City.

36. Several hundred thousand pilgrims visit the Black Christ at Esquipulas throughout the year. It is one of Central America's most important pilgrimage centers. The major celebration and peak migration is during January. To the best of my knowledge, no one from San Antonio still makes the trip by foot—much less on their knees, as many did in the past. Each year, at least one or two buses are chartered in the town (ironically, from a Protestant family in 1978, the year that I joined a local group for the pilgrimage). To reduce expenses, most food for the two- to three-day trip is packed picnic-basket style. About ten people jammed into our tiny, two-twin-bed hotel room. All in all, a family's total cost for the trip is roughly $30. Keep in mind, however, that a $30 "vacation expense" on an an-

nual income of $650 is equivalent to $1,100 out of a $24,000-a-year income, without taking into account the greater elasticity of the latter.

37. The difficult question arises as to whether or not *all* alcoholic consumption should be viewed as a Catholic ceremonial expense. Certainly, the Catholic Church does not openly condone drinking; in fact, priests inveigh against drunkenness, and most parishes sponsor vigorous abstinence programs, including active support for Alcoholics Anonymous chapters in towns such as San Antonio. Nevertheless, while Catholics condemn *drunkenness*, Protestants condemn *alcohol*—and in this regard all Protestant sects are unbending. The critical difference, then, is that Protestants believe it is sinful to drink (whether or not they do), and Catholics do not. Indeed, Catholic ritual is associated with drinking; the Church advocates moderation but sends ambiguous signals by looking the other way during fiestas. Among Protestants, on the other hand, abstinence has been elevated to a tenet of faith.

38. See Diener, "Tears of St. Anthony," 92, for comparable figures in eastern Guatemala. He reports: "While it is impossible to estimate exactly the amount of 'ritual waste' resulting from ritual practices, on the basis of nearly 200 very detailed household economic surveys gathered over two years, I would suggest that traditional Indians may spend as much as 25 percent of their income in this fashion."

39. Parenthetically, if the heads of this family were inclined to pursue such logic—which they are not—they would be quite capable of carrying it out. Both husband and wife are frequent newspaper readers, and they are adept with numbers. The husband frequently borrowed books that happened to be around my house: *A Hundred Years of Solitude* by Gabriel García Marquez, *The Wonderful Clouds* by Françoise Sagan; a Spanish translation of the *SPSS Manual*. When and if he returned them, he was prepared to discuss them.

40. Since Weber, there have been a plethora of Catholic-Protestant comparative economic studies. As N. D. Glen and R. Hyland noted in 1967, "the relationship of religion to economic and occupational success is the most viable topic of debate in the sociology of religion in the United States" ("Religious Preference and Worldly Success: Some Evidence from National Surveys," *American Sociological Review* 32, no. 1 [1967]: 73). For a fairly good review of the literature on Catholic-Protestant economic performance in Latin America and a case study of the central Mexican town of Nealticán, see David Clawson, "Religious Allegiance and Economic Development in Rural Latin America," *Journal of Interamerican Studies and World Affairs* 26, no. 4 (November 1984): 499–524.

41. Waldemar R. Smith, in *The Fiesta System and Economic Change* (New York: Columbia University Press), develops the argument that "it is barriers of social class which entrap and isolate peasants, and that ceremonial giving is a result rather than a cause of their constrained position."

42. Boys begin accompanying their fathers to the fields at the age of six or seven. When they are even smaller, both boys and girls begin running errands and taking care of their even-younger siblings. In a separate survey of household chores by twenty-one children, I found that parents generally view an eight-year-old as capable of providing about two hours of productive work per day, rising to nearly a full day's work by an out-of-school fifteen-year-old.

43. A second reason is specific to this particular sample. The largest landholder in the seventy-four-family sample is a Catholic who received land during the 1950s land reform. He claimed to have planted 150 *cuerdas* of corn during

the year in which this survey was carried out. This exceptionally large amount was sufficient to significantly raise the overall Catholic average.

44. See notes 18 and 19 above for estimates and projections of the number of Guatemalan Protestants.

9

Born Again in Brazil: Spiritual Ecstasy and Mutual Aid

R. Andrew Chesnut

The following selection is a discussion of Pentecostalism in a predominantly female congregation in a baixada *(urban slum) of Belém, in the Amazonian region of Brazil. Pentecostalism is a type of Christianity that emphasizes the "signs and wonders" described in the Book of Acts of the New Testament. Initiation into Pentecostalism is through "baptism in the Holy Spirit," made manifest through such physical signs as glossolalia (speaking in tongues), miraculous healing, and ecstatic movement or dance. Pentecostalism is by far the fastest-growing faith in Latin America today, accounting for nearly 80 percent of Protestant affiliation across the region. It is particularly important in Brazil, which is home to more Protestants than any other nation in Latin America.*

Although most of the interview subjects in Andrew Chesnut's article belong to the Assembly of God, which was founded by foreign missionaries, many Brazilians belong to one of the two fast-growing mega-churches known as the Igreja Universal do Reino de Deus (Igreja Universal) and Brasil para Cristo, both of which were established and continue to be run by powerful charismatic leaders within the country. Both Brasil para Cristo and Igreja Universal control churches numbering thousands of members, and they recently have begun sending out missionaries to other parts of Latin America and to the United States.*

From "Assembly of the Anointed: Pentecostalism and the Pathogens of Poverty in an Amazonian City of Brazil, 1962–1993" (Ph.D. diss., University of California, Los Angeles, 1995), 176–206. Reprinted by permission of R. Andrew Chesnut.
*See Cecília Loreto Mariz, *Coping with Poverty: Pentecostals and Christian Base Communities in Brazil* (Philadelphia: Temple University Press, 1994).

R. Andrew Chesnut is assistant professor of history at the University of Houston. He is the author of Born Again in Brazil: The Pentecostal Boom and the Pathogens of Poverty *(1997).*

> Being Pentecostal means being a person filled with power, a different kind of person, a person who lives in communion with God. Because in order to have power, we have to live in communion with God. So a Pentecostal is a person full of power, a person of real power. When a *crente* (believer) really prays hard for a person possessed by demons, the demons leave right away; and when we pray for a sick person, the illness goes away.
>
> —Sandra Andrade (interview with author)

Speaking on what it means to be a Pentecostal, Sandra, a twenty-five-year-old member of the Assembly of God and high-school student, identifies the essence of her evangelical faith: power. Whether emanating from the secular or sacred, power instills in its possessors a sense of the possible. The fact that Portuguese and Spanish, as Romance languages, employ the same word for the noun "power" (*poder*) and the verb "to be able" (*poder*), reveals much about the essence of power. To possess power is to be able to exercise some degree of control over one's environment —the greater the power, the larger the environment that one is able to influence. Of course, spiritual and temporal power are not perfectly inter-changeable, but, as evidenced by the Pentecostals of Latin America, spiritual strength can be harnessed for secular purposes.

More specifically, it is the experience of divine power in their every-day lives that defines Latin American Pentecostals. From glossolalia to their personal relationship with Jesus, *crentes* live and express their faith in terms of *poder divino*. For example, baptism in the Holy Spirit, the experiential and doctrinal core of the Pentecostal religion, is first and foremost an act of explosive power. If the cathartic eruption of spiritual baptism were contained within the walls of the temple, as some scholars argue, *crença* (belief) would have nothing to offer the common people in their daily struggle to survive. But the walls separating the sanctuary from the street cannot contain the spiritual blast within. Believers carry the force of the Holy Spirit with them, out of the church and into the house and street. There, in their everyday lives, the poor, from the *baixadas* of Belém to the *ciudades perdidas* (shantytowns) of Tijuana, employ the power of the Spirit to cure the afflictions of poverty and immunize them-selves against future infection. This chapter examines how, after the ini-tial cure through conversion, converts are able to access sacred power through both the Holy Spirit and the community of believers and exert it to repair the damage inflicted by the violence of material deprivation. Put differently, what did Sandra mean when she told me that "being Pentecos-tal means being a person filled with power"?

Baptism in the Holy Spirit

Crentes, like Umbandistas, popular [folk] Catholics, and all practitioners of popular religion in Brazil, elevate the experiential component of their faith over the doctrinal. In response to my question about illiteracy being a barrier to leadership positions in the Assembly of God (Assembléia de Deus, or AD), Neuza Sá, a widowed *crente*, stressed the dominance of the spirit over the letter: "If a person has faith in God, nothing is difficult. I have seen many people who don't know how to read or preach really well. But there are many who know how to read but can't preach because they want to preach by the letter. The true Gospel is the one preached through practice and biblical stories, not by the letter."

Ecstasy is one of the principal ways in which Pentecostals receive the power of the Spirit. In contrast to cerebral historic Protestantism, which engages only the mind in worship, the Pentecostal *culto* aims at the body and the soul. The Pentecostal God is not a remote figure to be contemplated in silence but a dynamic force to be experienced by the entire being. Pentecostalism provides its followers with several means of achieving spiritual rapture, but none is as potent as baptism by the Holy Spirit.

Although not as universally experienced as faith healing, baptism by the Holy Spirit is such a fundamental part of Pentecostal identity in Brazil that those who have not received it feel less than spiritually whole and often express doubts about the vitality of their faith. The Pentecostal belief in baptism by the Holy Spirit derives from biblical references in the Gospels and the Book of Acts. John the Baptist, immersing believers in the River Jordan, preached, "I baptize you with water; but he who is mightier than I is coming, the thong of whose sandals I am not worthy to untie; he will baptize you with the Holy Spirit and with fire" (Luke 3:16). Indeed, Pentecostals take their name from the first instance of the spiritual baptism of the Disciples on the day of Pentecost (literally, fifty days after Passover):

> When the day of Pentecost had come, they were all together in one place. And suddenly a sound came from Heaven like the rush of a mighty wind, and it filled all the house where they were sitting. And there appeared to them tongues as of fire, distributed and resting on each one of them. And they were all filled with the Holy Spirit and began to speak in other tongues, as the Spirit gave them utterance. (Acts 2:1–4)

In opposition to traditional Protestants and Catholics who regard spiritual baptism as a significant but purely historical event, Pentecostals affirm that the same power bestowed almost two millennia ago is available to today's believers.

Spiritual baptism, along with conversion, emerges as one of the defining moments in my Pentecostal informants' life histories. Some Belenenses (residents of Belem) could not recall the number of children they had but remembered the precise moment of their baptism and described it with detail and emotion as if it had occurred just hours before our interview. Almost four-fifths (79.4 percent) of my interviewees had been baptized by the Holy Spirit, usually several months after becoming members but sometimes many years later.

Spiritual baptism provides a phenomenological bridge for poor Brazilians familiar with spirit possession in African-Brazilian religion. Like the Umbandista "horse" or medium "ridden" by its spirit, the *crente* is taken by and filled with the power of the Holy Spirit. Although the term "possession" in Brazilian Pentecostal discourse denotes demonic invasion of an individual, Pentecostals receiving spiritual baptism are clearly "possessed" by the power of the Holy Spirit. In psychological terminology, the baptized lapse into a disassociated state of consciousness, marked by ecstatic utterances, clonic spasms, and explosive bodily energy. Perhaps the phrase "spiritual orgasm" best captures the climactic ecstasy of the event.

The great power that *crentes* experience during spiritual baptism is often expressed in language borrowed from two other sources of ecstasy and altered states of consciousness—drugs and sex. AD Evangelist Antonio Amolina related his baptism by the Holy Spirit in terms of the injections administered in the ubiquitous Brazilian pharmacies for everything from the common cold to "nerves":

> Look, I felt the power like a force that descends over you, like when you feel bad and someone comes and gives a strong injection and then you feel energized. You want to say "Alleluia" and "praise God," shaking from His power. It is a very special force that overcomes you, a power that people say cannot be put into words. It's something that happens only once in a lifetime. (Interview with author)

While the evangelist employed medical metaphors to convey the power he felt, Ovidio Pinheiro, the seventy-seven-year-old retired night watchman and doorman at a small AD church in the suburb of Terra Firme, described his baptism in terms of the sedating effect of alcohol, one of the most common sources of altered states of consciousness on the urban periphery:

> I felt anesthetized, like when you're plastered (*porre*). I felt so full of power when the Holy Spirit worked in me. I was in a chair when the light struck me and I blanked out and fell to the ground. But I didn't feel anything; I felt anesthetized, filled with power and speaking tongues. Later, when it was over, we got up and ended the service. A brother

said, "Look, you're covered with blood." And when I went back to church the next day, I was healed. (Interview with author)

Metaphors of drug-induced ecstasy also permeate Pentecostal women's accounts of baptism, but more salient is a subtext of eroticism largely absent from male narratives. In Latin American Pentecostalism as well as in most branches of Christianity throughout the world, the Holy Spirit is a decidedly masculine being; it penetrates the believer, injecting her with seminal power. Although male sexual identity in Brazil is not as rigidly constructed as in other parts of Ibero-America, the erotic imagery expressed in female baptismal narratives would take on, due to the Holy Spirit's masculine identity, homoerotic subtones in the male narrative. The image of the Holy Spirit as a supernatural and super lover also complements the popular female conception of Jesus as the consummate husband, the loyal spouse who never abandons his wife, and, despite great hardship, always provides for his family.

The men in the life of Rosilea Garcia, a member of the Igreja Universal do Reino de Deus (IURD), particularly her alcoholic father, lacked the potency of the Holy Spirit, which baptized her during a prayer service:

Look, I felt a very intense light, you know? I felt hands. I felt like praying but not the same way other people were, and I began to talk to God, and it seemed like I was trying to touch, to encounter, to embrace God, you know? It seemed like He wanted to speak only with me, you understand? It was like He wanted to be only with me that night. It was a very, very beautiful thing, a new experience for me. I confess to you that when I went to sleep that night, I had a beautiful dream of God. (Interview with author)

Forty-three-year-old civil servant and *Assembleiana* (AD member) Julite Pantoja, wearing only a towel, received a more eruptive Holy Spirit in the intimacy of her bedroom:

I was so lost in heavenly prayer that I didn't even realize that I had finished my bath. I entered my bedroom and knelt, wearing just a towel. But when I began to pray again, something happened: all my words came out in the tongues of angels, in foreign tongues. It was really an explosion of the Holy Spirit in my life. I couldn't control myself, and from so much tongue-speaking, the sisters began to come to my room and saw that I was being baptized by the Holy Spirit. It was complete joy (*gozo*).[1] During the rest of the day, I couldn't even look at the sky or feel my own breathing because I felt God in everything. When I looked up at the sky, there were foreign tongues. I would look at a tree and there were foreign tongues. I felt an intense fire inside me. It really was a marvelous day for me, an unforgettable experience. Now I no longer have any doubts about baptism by the Holy Spirit. (Interview with author)

Thus, baptism by the Holy Spirit infuses *crentes* with a tremendous sense of power through *ekstasis*, or the sensation of being taken out of place. The disassociated state of consciousness induced by spiritual baptism allows believers to transcend their oppressive social locus. Like the hypnotic effects of psychotropic drugs and sex, spiritual baptism suspends ordinary time and place, allowing the believer to float in an extraordinary sacred space devoid of the demons of everyday poverty. In analyzing possession trance, anthropologist I. M. Lewis identifies the oppressive social reality that engenders the need for escape and release: "The circumstances which encourage the ecstatic response are precisely those where men feel themselves constantly threatened by exacting pressures which they do not know how to combat or control, except through those heroic flights of ecstasy by which they seek to demonstrate that they are the equals of the gods."[2] But the ecstatic power of the trance is not merely an opiate-like flight from reality. Rather, spiritual baptism also fills believers with the strength to face a harsh reality and to persevere.

The power transmitted by the Holy Spirit also serves as divine protection from both natural and supernatural evil. Reflecting the clientalism that continues to characterize Brazilian social, political, and religious relationships, the Holy Spirit operates as a sort of divine patron offering protection in exchange for service and loyalty. In addition to its role as the ideal lover and spouse, the Holy Spirit is the perfect *patrão* who demands unswerving fealty from his clients in return for the security of sustenance. With little defense against rising crime, unemployment, and prices, poor Brazilians' perception of their need for supernatural protection from societal evil has increased sharply.

The testimonial pages of the *Estandarte Evangélico* record this growing demand for a supernatural protector. It was not until the early 1980s that stories of divine protection appear regularly, though still overshadowed by myriad accounts of faith healing. Much of the testimony relating to protection involves incidents of home burglary. Under the front-page caption, "Thief Puts Down Stolen Object upon Seeing Bible," one *Assembleiano* testified that a thief who had broken into his home left promptly upon seeing an open Bible on the kitchen table but not before penning a note admonishing the family to keep the back door locked.

Psalm 91 is the quintessential statement of divine protection for Brazilian Pentecostals. Workers at the Igreja do Evangelho Quadrangular (IEQ) mother church in Belém have distributed printed copies of the cherished verses with the heading, "Psalm 91 Divine Protection." Worshippers were told, "A thousand shall fall at your side, and ten thousand at your right hand; but it shall not come near you. Only with your eyes shall you behold and see the recompense of the wicked" (Psalm 91:7–8).

Gifts of the Spirit

Although the Pentecostal faithful experience spiritual baptism only once in a lifetime, they have continuous access to spiritual power through the gifts of the Holy Spirit. As Bishop Edir Macedo of the IURD writes, charismata, or the *dons do espírito* (gifts of the spirit) are yet further proof of the power of God.[3] Prior to being possessed by the Holy Spirit, the majority of *crentes* adhered to the faith through the supreme gift of faith healing, which heads the category of gifts that Bishop Macedo has aptly named *dons de poder* (gifts of power). This category also includes the spiritual presents of miracles and faith. Due to their unspecified and rather general nature, the latter two are not as salient as others. Tongue-speaking or glossolalia is indubitably the apex of the second category of inspirational gifts. While Brazilian Pentecostals, especially members of the AD and God Is Love, regard the gift of prophecy with awe, a much greater proportion speak the "tongues of angels" than prophesy. Those who can simultaneously interpret the messages of tongue-speakers into Portuguese possess the third type of inspirational charismata: interpretation of tongues. In contrast to the abundant gift of tongues, glossolalic interpretation is distributed sparsely. Less prominent are the three gifts of revelation: knowledge, wisdom, and the discernment of spirits. My Belenense informants tended to conflate the three under the general rubric of revelation.

Charismatic power among Brazilian Pentecostals is distributed according to the variables of sex, denomination (here, the AD, IURD, and IEQ), and ecclesiastical rank. At the time of our interviews, almost three-quarters of my interviewees claimed to be endowed with at least one spiritual gift. Glossolalia emerged as the most common one for both sexes and for all three denominations; indeed, 41.8 percent of all informants declared themselves to be active speakers of tongues. Revelation and faith healing ranked a distant second and third, distributed respectively among only 15.2 percent and 11.4 percent of all believers. The remaining gifts, with the exception of prophecy among women, were statistically insignificant.

The greatest determinant of spiritual gifts among Belenense *crentes* is denominational affiliation. While 83.3 percent of all *Assembleianos* surveyed spoke in tongues or possessed some other form of charismata, only a slight majority (54.2 percent) of *Quadrangulares* (IEQ members) and members of the IURD were spiritually gifted. Those endowed with gifts followed the pattern of their AD brethren in claiming glossolalia more than any other. Likewise, revelation and faith healing ranked as the second and third most practiced gifts.

The greater distribution of charismata among *Assembleianos* is at first glance a bit perplexing. One would expect, according to sociological theory, the spirit to be weakest where the institutionalization process has developed to the fullest. As one of the nation's two oldest Pentecostal denominations, the Assembly of God stands as the epitome of the Pentecostal institution, with a salaried pastorate, seminaries, and a publishing house. Moreover, many of my older AD informants asserted that the Holy Spirit had been more active in the past. But it is not only institutionalization per se that dampens the spirit; of equal significance is the organizational model of the church. The AD's organizational design, though centralized, has left the churches of the *baixadas* with sufficient autonomy to maintain the priesthood of all believers. Services in the small temples can last for up to three hours, as members of the congregation ascend to the pulpit to sign a hymn, read a Bible passage or the weekly calendar, and give testimony. I, myself, was a frequent participant in AD *cultos*.

The relatively democratic and participatory liturgy of AD churches in the *baixadas* gives way to the more autocratic and centralized practice of many postmodern and some modern churches. IURD liturgy, in particular, reintegrates elements of traditional Catholic hierarchy. Responding to my observation that common members never step into the pulpit to sing a hymn or deliver a biblical message, Rosilea Garcia explained:

> Look, that's not done in the [Igreja] Universal because the pulpit is something very sacred in the IURD. If someone who has sinned approaches the pulpit, a malign spirit can strike him down. So that's why no one goes to the pulpit to preach or pray. The only time a person can step into the pulpit is when the pastor calls him to give testimony. (Interview with author)

Pastors of the IURD—and the IEQ, to a lesser extent—mediate ecstatic power in a manner that is only seen in the larger churches of the AD, especially the central temples. Postmodern Pentecostals are not so much the practitioners of spiritual gifts as they are the recipients. Exorcism and faith healing in the IURD are gifts possessed and practiced by pastors on ordinary believers. Most members have been healed or exorcised, but very rarely have they themselves been used by God to cure another person. Hence, the power of the "priests" accounts for much of the denominational difference in the distribution of spiritual gifts. Postmodern Pentecostal pastors have appropriated much of the power of the Holy Spirit for themselves, thus leaving the laity as objects of charismata but not practitioners.

The distribution of charismata also depends on the variable of sex. In every denomination, women are more endowed with spiritual gifts than men. Of my total group of informants, 80 percent of the women were spiritually gifted, compared to 62.5 percent of the men. Factoring in denominational differences, AD women manifested charismata twice as often as men of the IURD and IEQ. My female interviewees spoke in tongues and received revelations from God and the Holy Spirit twice as often as did men. Swiss sociologist Christian Lalive d'Epinay also found Pentecostal women in Chile to be more charismatic, especially glossolalic, than their male counterparts.[4]

The unequal allocation of spiritual gifts between the sexes is a function of power and culture. It is the socially weakest who, in compensation for their temporal impotence, most seek spiritual power. And in twentieth-century Brazil, slum dwellers and rural women, particularly *negras* (blacks) and *mulatas* (mixed black and white), stand the furthest from the center of power. Not only victims of classism and racism, poor Brazilian women also suffer material and psychic stress owing to their subordinate role in a patriarchal society. Without husbands or *amigos* to bring home a meager paycheck, they frequently live in abject poverty. Adding to the need for spiritual release from mundane suffering is cultural conditioning, which endows women with greater sensitivity to perceive and feel the Holy Spirit. The majority of Spiritist mediums, Umbandista parents-of-the-saints, and Catholic healers are women since the spiritual realm in Latin America is predominantly feminine. Men may direct the *ecclesia*, but women have greater access to the *spiritus*.

Although faith healing is the most common spiritual gift received by Brazilian Pentecostals, glossolalia is the most practiced form of charismata by ordinary members. In its first form, tongue-speaking serves as a seal or proof that a believer has been baptized by the Holy Spirit. If a *crente* does not manifest angelic utterance during or shortly after spiritual baptism, then the baptism is rejected as illegitimate and perhaps the work of lesser spirits than the Holy Spirit itself. The second type of ecstatic speech usually erupts spontaneously during prayer.[5] A few of my informants even broke into glossolalia during our interviews.

In the temples of Belém and the rest of Brazil, glossolalic speech sounds remotely similar to Hebrew. I suspect that tongue-speakers unconsciously transmogrify biblical words of Hebraic and Aramaic origin into ecstatic utterance. A common speech pattern shared by most Brazilian *crentes* suggests that glossolalia, as researcher Marion Aubree argues, is learned behavior.[6] Pentecostals, however, believe glossolalia to be a divine tool by which the Holy Spirit uses the faithful as media to broadcast its message. Lacking the gift of interpretation, most *crentes* must have an interpreter translate the speech into Portuguese.

It is not surprising that those whose social voice is muted by the *poderosos* (powerful) should speak so loudly and fluently in the language of the Holy Spirit. This spiritual language allows the poor to speak like saints and not like *populares*, whose Portuguese is denigrated and ridiculed by the elite guardians of culture. Glossolalia, then, is not "the language for people without language," as some have posited.[7] Deviating from the correct language of official society, popular Portuguese possesses a wealth of colorful idioms and slang that is no less language than the polished speech of the college educated. Rather than "language for people without language," glossolalia is speech for those whose tongue is tied by official society, particularly for poor women of color. When an entire congregation bursts into charismatic utterances, it is the amplified female voices that send the researcher scrambling for his earplugs.

Besides tongues and faith healing, what *Assembleianos* collectively refer to as "revelation" is the only other spiritual gift of any practical significance. Prophecy, while technically an inspirational gift, tends to get lumped under the rather ambiguous rubric of revelation. An essentially female phenomenon, revelation transforms believers who are deprived of official means of communication, such as regular postal and telephone service, into divine messengers, God's spokeswomen. Dreams and visions are powerful media through which God reveals Himself to *crente* women of the *baixadas*.

Bishop Macedo's accurate perception of prophecy as a tool of female subversion applies equally to the dreams and visions of revelation. What is often revealed to women are the sins and transgressions of men, more particularly their husbands. A vision allowed forty-two-year-old homemaker and *Assembleiana* Noemi Pessoa to perceive her husband's philandering:

> Before my husband took up with that woman, I had a vision of an enormous ball floating over the church. It was a day when I was praying in church, and that ball was very black and went by making a lot of noise. When I finished praying, I spoke with a sister, and she told me that I was going to pass through some type of tribulation. I prayed and prayed for the Lord to reveal the meaning of that vision to me. A lot of time passed and my husband was already with that woman, but I still hadn't found out. It was years later that I found out about his lover, at the end of their relationship. It was better that way because my suffering was less. When they told me about his lover, it was then that I came to understand the meaning of that black ball that I had seen years ago. (Interview with author)

The dreams and visions associated with the gift of revelation grant *crente* women the moral authority to challenge the sinful behavior of both Pentecostal and non-Pentecostal men. Sometimes the fear of divine retribution provoked by prophecy is enough to cause a man to turn away from his errant ways. Armed with the moral authority of revelation, Pentecostal women discover a powerful new weapon for confronting a cheating husband or wayward pastor. Like his prominent colleague Bishop Macedo,

Pastor-President Firmino Gouveia felt so threatened by uncontrolled revelation and prophecy that in a weekly administrative meeting in late 1971 he admonished members not "to frequent the homes of certain sisters and brothers with the intention of finding out the will of God about certain matters. Such behavior must be banished from the church."

Less subversive is the only other significant spiritual gift in terms of praxis: faith healing. In addition to its central role in the conversion process, faith healing continues to be the primary form of charismata experienced by the mature believer. Although the *crente* has recovered much of his physical, psychological, or spiritual health through conversion, the world of material deprivation continues to spawn pathogens from which permanent access to *cura divina* provides considerable protection. The afflicted adherent has access to the healing hands of the pastor and the curative prayers of an entire congregation of believers.

One of the great paradoxes of Brazilian Pentecostalism's prize gift of the Holy Spirit is that it is received much more than actively practiced. In other words, the great majority of my informants had been healed through faith, but only a small minority (11.4 percent) had been "used" themselves by the Holy Spirit as healing agents in the cure of another person. The gift of faith healing appears to be limited to pastors and exceptionally devout believers, usually female. With the exception of John Page, who argued that pastors monopolized all forms of charismata, no other research on Latin American Pentecostalism has addressed the question of the distribution of spiritual gifts.[8]

Lacunae in the research notwithstanding, the institutional need to control charismatic power explains the unequal distribution of the practice of faith healing. In a religion that thrives because of faith healing, the power of the pastor depends greatly on his talent as a healer. He claims that he himself does not cure; the Holy Spirit merely uses him as a vessel. But the Pentecostal preacher known for effecting powerful cures will attract standing-room-only crowds. In contrast, the preacher lacking curative charismata might find himself shepherding a reduced flock. In summary, while great power is experienced as a recipient of Pentecostalism's most valued gift, the greatest power is reserved for the privileged few who administer the gift.

Hymns of Healing

Although technically not a spiritual gift, Pentecostal music merits consideration as a potent source of ecstatic release, particularly for women. In my interviews, I asked my informants what things gave them the most pleasure in life. In third place, after only church and family, women most frequently cited sacred music as their greatest joy. Men also responded to rousing hymns but generally did not attach as much significance to music. So fundamental is music to Pentecostal liturgy in Brazil that it typically composes two-thirds of the *culto*. Background mood music soothes the soul when worshipers are not singing such hymns as "Cristo Cura, Sim!" (Christ Heals, Indeed!) and "Jesus Me Tirou da Lama" (Jesus Pulled Me Out of the Mud).

Pentecostal churches in Brazil and throughout the world have been extraordinarily adept at incorporating local folk and popular music into the worship service. The sensual rhythm of *carimbó* suffuses many of the hymns sung at the small AD temples in the *baixadas* of Belém.[9] In churches where youth groups actively participate in the music, hymns are often popular tunes heard on the radio and in soap operas that have been set to evangelical lyrics by Protestant recording artists. No church has perfected this process as much as has the IURD. Songs by Leandro and Leonardo (the kings of *sertanejo* [backlander] pop) and Roberto Carlos, and the lively theme from the Xuxa television show aid members of the Igreja to achieve spiritual ecstasy. One *Assembleiana*, Maria Santos, a forty-two-year-old homemaker, was even cured through a hymn:

> Now, my voice isn't one of those finely tuned voices, but it's the voice that God gave me to sing. In fact, the Lord cured me through hymns. When I lived in the interior, I was sick and depressed with terrible headaches. One day I had a really bad headache so I lay down and began singing a hymn, and when I was in the middle of it, I began to get happy, and the Lord began to speak to me. He said He was going to make me happy, that He was with me, that He was taking care of me, and that I should feel His presence. And then Jesus did the job right away. Jesus always works miracles with me through hymns. (Interview with author)

The Congregation as Mutual Aid Society

If charismata and baptism by the Holy Spirit inject *crentes* with a spiritual force that allows them to cope more effectively with the everyday crises of poverty, then the church community functions as a mutual aid association, providing material and psychological assistance to members in need. The congregation, however, does not supplant the family as the primary network of mutual aid among poor Brazilians. Rather, the church community serves as an additional network that members can access if and when kin relationships fail. Sociologist Bryan Roberts's discovery in the late 1960s that evangelical churches were one of the few types of voluntary associations functioning on the urban periphery of Guatemala, applies to the slums and shantytowns of Brazil.[10] Left to fend for themselves by an indifferent, if not antagonistic, state, the urban poor must create their own mutual aid associations. In late twentieth-century Brazil, Pentecostalism stands out as one of the principal poor peoples' organizations.[11]

The Templo Central of the AD in Belém has sporadically practiced institutional charity through its food drives and medical and legal clinics. Yet it is not primarily as a religious institution but as a community of believers that the church offers mutual aid. Of the 73.9 percent of my informants who had accepted some type of material aid through the church, the vast majority had received it as an offering from fellow members rather than as a direct donation from the Templo Central. At most of the services I attended in the *baixadas*, the pastor would ask the congregation to make a special offering for a *crente* family in crisis, usually one of health or employment. Many worshipers probably knew which brother or sister in faith would benefit from the donation, but the pastor, out of respect for the family members' dignity, maintained their anonymity. Maria Santos was saved from ignominious suffering by her fellow believers:

> So I had to have an operation, and two weeks later my husband fell ill with a lung problem and couldn't work. The brothers and sisters couldn't believe how skinny he got. But I believe that this was all so God could act in our lives. So at that time there was a very good-hearted pastor, and when my husband got sick, the pastor gathered the church together and told them that we needed help from the church and that they shouldn't deny us aid. And, thank God, it was a blessing, wasn't it? We never lacked anything at home. God even used people who weren't *crentes* to help us. One sister made sure that we always had some meat at home. Her husband worked with meat, and she would bring meat home for us. Another sister would bring a liter of milk each day. So I thank God that everything is the fulfillment of His Word. After a couple of weeks, he [her husband] recuperated and began to work again for Jesus as well as for us. (Interview with author)

Poor Pentecostals also aid each other without pastoral mediation. A liter of milk might appear at the home of an unemployed *crente* before the pastor is even aware of the situation. Although Brazilian Pentecostalism does not abolish ecclesiastical hierarchy, its rejection of the Catholic *compadrio*, or godparent relationship, in favor of a community of "brothers and sisters in faith" allows a member to experience the smaller congregation as an extended family. Roseline Nascimento, a twenty-seven-year-old *Assembleiana* and high-school student, contrasted the anonymity of her old faith with the fraternity of her new one: "It's different because in our church we are a family, everybody knows each other. Not like the Catholic church where everybody leaves right after Mass and no one knows each other."

Not all congregations are like Roseline's in the poor neighborhood of Guamá where believers, as rural migrants from the interior of the state, share the bonds of culture and social class. Outside the relatively homogeneous AD congregations of the *baixadas*, the larger, more differentiated churches, such as the Templo Central and the *sede*, or seat, of the IURD (strategically located across the street from Belém's long-distance bus terminal), do not permit the same degree of mutual aid. Here the congregation as family rarely exists. Instead of congregating in small groups outside the temple to socialize after the *culto* had ended, worshipers at the large churches scampered to catch the bus home. At the conclusion of services at the IURD *sede*, people were in such a hurry to get home that I had to dart about frantically to arrange two or three interviews. In marked contrast, *crentes* at churches in the slums were so eager to be interviewed that I could only meet with a small fraction of those who wanted to tell me their life histories.

Another less common but notable function of the Pentecostal network of mutual aid is as a job bank. Some 16.3 percent of my interviewees, mainly men, had found work through church contacts. Several of the women worked as domestic servants for middle-class *crente* families, and a few of the men earned minimum wage as security guards and janitors at the Templo Central. Despite some employers who complain that Pentecostal workers have their eyes fixed on Heaven instead of on the task at hand, *crentes* have earned a reputation in Brazil for honesty, sobriety, and peacefulness—traits that privileged Brazilians usually do not attribute to the *povão*, or rabble. The wife of a well-known sociologist, overhearing my conversation with her husband on Pentecostalism, explained that she hired only evangelical *dómesticas* because they do not steal and drink nothing stronger than *guaraná* (the national soft drink). Corruption scandals involving prominent Pentecostal pastors and politicians may have tarnished the *crente* reputation for honesty, but in the early 1990s pastors continue to serve as employment agents, recommending certain church members to employers.

Possibly even more consequential than the material benefits derived from church membership is the psychological and spiritual support provided by the community of believers. Joined by the common diseases of poverty, believers experience healing power not only in hymns and prayers but also in embraces and visits from their spiritual brothers and sisters. Even in the poorest churches, where some people worship barefoot, the passionate hymns and moving testimonies exude a sense of solidarity that proclaims, "Yes, we are the downtrodden of the earth, but with the Holy Spirit and each other, we are spiritual victors."[12]

The congregation as a spiritual and psychological network of solidarity is especially important to *crente* women. Prayer circles and women's groups often resemble the psychological support groups for abused and battered women that have proliferated in the United States during the last decade. Temporarily removed from the stress of their impoverished homes, women, gathered in prayer, carve out an alternative space where they comfort each other and vent their frustrations. As Darcy Neves, a twenty-nine-year-old member of the IURD and nurse's assistant, explained, much of the discussion in women's groups centers on marital and domestic strife. Responding to my question regarding the predominance of women in her church, Darcy said:

> Look, the majority of women who attend church have problems with their husbands. These are the problems that most afflict them. For example, sometimes the husband suddenly gets another woman out there. So at church we have prayer groups, and, through prayer, God removes the other woman from her path. Also the majority of women at church are young women, and most young women have emotional problems. A wife often has problems with her husband when he drinks too much, and they fight constantly. And so here at church we get together to pray. Through prayer, God blesses the couple. (Interview with author)

Thus, crentes are further able to reclaim and preserve their health through the spiritual and ecclesiastical tools of charismata and mutual aid. Pentecostals, in achieving spiritual ecstasy through baptism by the Holy Spirit, the gifts of the Spirit and music, temporarily transcend the state of their oppressive reality. Believers, imbued with spiritual force, no longer regard the demons of want as so formidable; filled with the Holy Spirit, they pass intrepidly through the many roadblocks raised by hostile forces on the back streets of the urban periphery. Pentecostalism also infuses its followers with the power to surmount the countless obstacles of grinding poverty as members of the community of believers. As active constituents of congregations in the *baixadas*, the faithful create mutual aid societies that complement the primary network of kin relationships. For the slum dweller struggling to stay afloat in the maelstrom of material deprivation, the church as community provides the material, spiritual, and psychological succor that can make the difference between health and illness.

Notes

1. *Gozo* in both Portuguese and Spanish can also connote sexual pleasure.

2. Jeannette H. Henney, "Function of Shakerism," in Felicitas D. Goodman, Jeannette H. Henney, and Esther Pressel, *Trance, Healing, and Hallucinations* (New York: John Wiley & Sons, 1974), 101.

3. Edir Macedo, *O Espiritu Santo* (Rio de Janeiro: Gráfica Universal, 1993), 101.

4. Christian Lalive d'Epinay, *Haven of the Masses: A Study of the Pentecostal Movement in Chile* (London: Lutterworth Press, 1969), 203.

5. Pentecostals assert that glossolalia only occurs spontaneously, but it soon became evident to me that while ecstatic utterance, particularly the kind manifested during preaching, if not rehearsed, it is often quite formulaic.

6. Marion Aubree, "O transe: A resposta do xangô e do pentecostalismo," *Ciencia e Cultura* 37 (July 1985): 1074.

7. Lalive d'Epinay, *Haven of the Masses*, 199.

8. John Page, " 'Brazil para Cristo': The Cultural Construction of Pentecostal Networks in Brazil" (Ph.D. diss., New York University, 1984), 227.

9. Carimbó is the most popular of the regional rhythms in the state of Pará. *Belenenses* dance to the African-influenced music in pairs, hunched over and spinning hypnotically.

10. Bryan R. Roberts, "Protestant Groups and Coping with Urban Life in Guatemala City," *American Journal of Sociology* 73 (1968): 754.

11. Diana Brown asserts that in the mid-1980s, Umbanda was also developing into a mutual aid society on the urban margins. See Diana Brown, *Umbanda: Religion and Politics in Brazil* (Ann Arbor: UMI Research Press, 1986), 100.

12. This phrase is taken from an IEQ pamphlet entitled "Proclamation of Victory."

Suggested Readings

The readings cited here by no means represent the comprehensive body of literature on religion in Latin America. The corpus of work on this particular topic encompasses an unusually wide range of disciplines, interests, and methodologies. Some material is clearly confessional, and some polemic; certain studies are written by openly partisan priests and missionaries, others by scholars who attempt to suspend their beliefs (or lack of them) in intellectual "objectivity." The studies of religion in Latin America range from older historical narrative and descriptive ethnography to more recent data quantification, deconstructive textual analyses, and evaluations of religious behavior in terms of gender, politics, and ethnicity. I have tried to provide a listing of some–but only some–of the best and most representative works on the topics that appear in this volume with the hope that this list will serve as a starting point for the reader to develop a more thorough bibliography appropriate to his or her regional or thematic interests.

The Institutional Church and Emerging State
in the Nineteenth Century

The best general history of the Catholic Church in Latin America, though dated, continues to be J. Lloyd Mecham's *Church and State in Latin America* (Chapel Hill, NC, 1966), although this book does not cover any material later than the mid-1960s and does not touch at all on Liberation Theology. A much more current study is Enrique Dussel, ed., *The Church in Latin America, 1492–1992* (Maryknoll, NY, 1992). Otherwise, general histories break down by country. Some of the older but still useful national church histories include: Isidoro Alonso et al., *La Iglesia en Peru y Bolivia* (Madrid, 1962); Enrique Amato, *La Iglesia en Argentina* (Buenos Aires, 1965); and Mary P. Holleran, *Church and State in Guatemala* (New York, 1949). Two excellent national studies include Daniel Levine, *Religion and Politics in Latin America: The Catholic Church in Venezuela and Colombia* (Princeton, 1981), and Brian Smith, *The Church and Politics in Chile: Challenges to Modern Catholicism* (Princeton, 1982), both of which grapple with the issues posed by Liberation Theology and military governments and the emergence of competitive religious groups such as Protestants and Mormons.

The literature on the conflict between Church and state in the nineteenth century is fairly extensive, but a disproportionate amount is limited to the case of Mexico. Again, Mecham's work continues to be the classic text on this topic, but several monographs update and expand on his efforts significantly. A good overview of the philosophical roots of anticlericalism is José Sanchez, *Anticlericalism: A Brief History* (Notre Dame, IN, 1972). Two exemplary studies that offer precise descriptions of the divestment of Church funds under Liberal governments in Mexico include Michael Costeloe, *Church Wealth in Mexico, 1800–1856* (New York, 1967), and Jan Bazant, *Alienation of Church Wealth in Mexico: Social and Economic Aspects of the Liberal Revolution, 1856–1875* (New York, 1971). Another valuable work that addresses Church wealth from the Reforma through the Porfiriato is Robert Knowlton, *Church Property and the Mexican Reform, 1856–1910* (DeKalb, IL, 1976).

For other countries, the expropriation of Church wealth is best described within the context of the broader Liberal-Conservative conflict. Beyond the national histories listed above, such works as Herbert J. Miller's *Iglesia y estado en el tiempo de Justo Rufino Barrios* (Guatemala City, 1976) and "Conservative and Liberal Concordats in Nineteenth-Century Guatemala: Who Won?" *Journal of Church and State* 33 (1991):115–30 provide useful descriptions of the incremental impact of Liberal reform on the institutional structure of the Catholic Church. A sophisticated new study of the impact of Conservative government on Church structures and leadership in Central America is Douglass Creed Sullivan-Gonzales, *Piety, Power, and Politics: The Role of Religion in the Formation of the Guatemalan Nation-State, 1821–1871* (Pittsburgh, 1998).

Judaism

The literature on Judaism in Latin America is relatively sparse, and much of it tends to deal more with issues of Jewish cultural identity than with actual religious beliefs and practices. Judith Larkin Elkin has produced several strong historical studies of Latin American Judaism; her *Jews of Latin America* (Chapel Hill, NC, 1980) is a basic text, followed by a well-conceived thematic volume coedited with Gilbert Merxx entitled *The Jewish Presence in Latin America* (Reading, MA, 1987). Other useful studies include Seymour Liebman's *New World Jewry, 1492–1825: Requiem for the Forgotten* (New York, 1982), which focuses primarily on the Inquisition in the New World. Of the cultural studies, which tend to look at issues such as Jewish writers in the Americas, a good work of more general interest is Irving Louis Horowitz, *Jewish Ethnicity and Latin American Nationalism* (New Brunswick, NJ, 1976).

Millenarianism

The grassroots religious responses to the political struggles of the nineteenth century are fairly well documented. The groundbreaking study on millenarianism is Anthony Wallace, "Revitalization Movements," *American Anthropologist* 38 (1956): 264–81, part of the theoretical foundation for Victoria Bricker's classic study, *The Indian Christ, the Indian King: The Historical Substrate of Maya Myth and Ritual* (Austin, TX, 1981), which examines several Maya religious episodes, particularly the Talking Cross of Yucatán, in terms of ethnic revitalization. The essential text for this topic is Norman Cohn, *The Pursuit of the Millennium: Revolutionary Millenarians and Mystical Anarchists of the Middle Ages* (New York, 1961), which is not only about millenarianism in Europe during the Middle Ages but also lays out the theoretical groundwork on which most of the more recent region-specific literature continues to be based. Bryan Wilson, *Magic and Millennium* (London, 1973), is another important contribution to the theoretical understanding of millenarian movements, as is Sylvia Thrupp, ed., *Millennial Dreams in Action* (New York, 1970), a useful collection, now unfortunately out of print, in which noted scholars contribute articles that place several Latin American millenarian movements in the context of Cohn's typologies.

There are several monographs that deal directly with millenarianism in Latin America. Kevin Gosner's *Soldiers of the Virgin: The Moral Economy of a Colonial Maya Rebellion* (Tucson, AZ, 1992) is an excellent ethnohistorical study of a millenarian episode that occurred in the same region as the one described by Jan Rus (this volume) but at a somewhat earlier period. Two other essential studies that touch on how power issues are mediated through religious venues in colonial Mesoamerica include Nancy M. Farriss, *Maya Society under Colonial Rule: The Collective Enterprise of Survival* (Princeton, 1984); and Serge Gruzinski, *Man-Gods in the Mexican Highlands: Indian Power and Colonial Society, 1520–1800* (Stanford, CA, 1989).

Because Brazil has historically been a fertile environment for millenarianism, it is also the object of a number of valuable monographs on such movements. Some of the best theoretical work has been done by Maria Isaura Pereira de Queiroz, *O messianismo no Brasil e no mundo* (São Paulo, 1965), who attributes millenarianism's popularity in Brazil not only to social and economic causes but also to metaphysical factors such as anomie, or moral meaninglessness. One of the country's most famous writers, Euclides da Cunha, in his best-known book, *Rebellion in the Backlands* (*Os sertoes*) (Chicago, 1944), chronicles the defeat of the followers of Antônio Conselheiro, the leader of a doomed utopian community in the late nineteenth century, which was later described in Mario Vargas Llosa's historical novel, *War of the End of the World* (*La guerra del fin del mundo*) (Mexico City, 1985). Two good monographs, Aldenor Benevides, *Padre Cícero and Juazeiro* (São Paulo, 1969), and Manoel Caboclo e Silva, *Jesus, São Pedro e o ferreiro: Rei dos jagadores* (São Paulo, 1978), focus on the prophet and mystic Padre Cícero, who healed and preached in Brazil's northeast in the last years of the nineteenth century. Todd Diacon's well-researched *Millenarian Vision, Capitalist Reality: Brazil's Contestado Rebellion, 1912–1916* (Durham, NC, 1991) examines a religious-based rebellion against the expansion of market capitalism in the early twentieth century.

Indigenous Religion and Beliefs

The literature on indigenous popular religion, or "folk Catholicism," is substantial, and most of the studies are grounded in ethnography. Mesoamerica alone has generated an extensive body of anthropological work, much of it the product of the Harvard Chiapas Project, which sent its most promising students and faculty into the Tzotzil Maya community of Zinacantán in the 1960s and 1970s. Many of the ethnographies of Mesoamerica are concerned with the *cofradías* (religious brotherhoods) and the economic process that accompanied the traditional "cargo" system in Maya areas, using the theoretical framework established by Eric Wolf some forty years ago in his still-influential article, "Closed Corporate Communities in Mesoamerica and Central Java," *Southwestern Journal of Anthropology* 13 (1957): 1–18. Some of the best in this canon include Frank Cancian, *Economics and Prestige in a Maya Community: The Religious Cargo System in Zinacantán* (Stanford, CA, 1965), which is updated by Cancian, *The Decline of Community in Zinacantán: Economy, Public Life, and Social Stratification, 1960–1987* (Stanford, CA, 1992); Evon Vogt, *Zinacantán: A Maya Community in the Highlands of Chiapas* (Cambridge, MA, 1969); and Vogt, *Tortillas for the Gods: A Symbolic Analysis of the Zinacantán Rituals* (Cambridge, MA, 1976). A richly textured study that addresses millenarianism, syncretism, and folk relations with the state is Serge Gruzinski, *Man-Gods in the Mexican Highlands*, cited above.

In his multilayered study *Revolt Against the Dead: The Modernization of a Maya Community in the Highlands of Guatemala* (Newark, NJ, 1979), Douglas Brintnall explores how traditional community and religious traditions and power relations are challenged when capitalism is introduced into peasant economies, a theme that also is applied to Oaxaca, Mexico, in James B. Greenberg, *Santiago's Sword: Chatino Peasant Religion and Economics* (Los Angeles, 1981). Other important studies that measure traditional religious venues against the decline of the traditional community include: Ruben Reina, *The Law of the Saints: A Pokomam Pueblo and Its Community Culture* (New York, 1966); Jan Rus and Robert Wasserstrom, "Civil-religious Hierarchies in Central Chiapas: A Critical Perspective," *American Ethnologist* 7 (1980): 466–78; Flavio Rojas Limas, *La cofradía: Reducto cultural indígena* (Guatemala City, 1988); R. A. M. Van Zantwijk, *Servitude of the Saints: The Social and Cultural Identity of a Tarascan Community in Mexico* (Amsterdam, Netherlands, 1967); and Robert Wasserstrom, "The Exchange of Saints in Zinacantán: The Socioeconomic Bases of Religious Change in Southern Mexico," *Ethnology* 17 (1978): 197–210.

Four outstanding works that provide a critical analysis of religious change and economic (as well as political) transition, all in Guatemala, are Ricardo Falla, *Quiché rebelde: Estudio de un movimiento do conversión religiosa, rebelde a las creencias tradicionales en San Antonio Ilotenango, Quiché, 1948–1970* (Guatemala City, 1979), and Falla, "Evolución politico-religiosa del indígena rural en Guatemala, 1945–1965," *Estudios Sociales Centroamericanos* 1 (San José, 1970); Kay Warren, *The Symbolism of Subordination: Indian Identity in a Guatemalan Town* (Austin, TX, 1978); and John Watanabe, *Maya Saints and Souls in a Changing World* (Austin, TX, 1992). An excellent study that measures religious obligations from an economic determinist perspective is Michael Taussig, *The Devil and Commodity Fetishism in South America* (Chapel Hill, NC, 1980).

Other studies view religious activities in Mesoamerica from a structuralist perspective, offering both useful analyses and rich descriptions of religious practices and beliefs in the communities under examination. These studies are grounded in the theoretical construct provided by Clifford Geertz's momentously influential work, *The Interpretation of Cultures* (New York, 1973), in which he describes religion as an internally logical motivating system of symbols. See, for example, Luis Batz, *Las cofradías de San Pedro la Laguna, Sololá* (Guatemala City, 1991); Benjamin Colby and Lore M. Colby, *The Daykeeper: The Life and Discourse of an Ixil Diviner* (Cambridge, MA, 1981); James Dow, *Santos y supervivendias: Funciones de la religión en una comunidad otomí, México* (Mexico City, 1974); Calixta Guiteras-Holmes, *Perils of the Soul: The World View of a Tzotzil Indian* (New York, 1961); and John A. Ingram, *Mary, Michael, and Lucifer: Folk Catholicism in Central Mexico* (Austin, TX, 1986). One of the best single-volume collections in this area is Gary Gossen, ed.,

Symbol and Meaning Beyond the Closed Community: Essays in Meso-american Ideas (Albany NY, 1986), which offers theoretically rich essays by several noted scholars on various aspects of Mesoamerican religiosity, using Geertz and others as a basis for symbolic analysis.

Other studies look at indigenous peoples in terms of religious syn-cretism, or the blending of two or more faiths. The earliest of these are descriptive enthographies that are now useful as historical resources, such as Oliver LaFarge, *The Year-Bearer's People* (New Orleans, 1931), and Maude Oakes, *The Two Crosses of Todos Santos: Survivals of Mayan Re-ligious Ritual* (New York, 1951). The theoretical base for the study of syncretism in Latin America appears in Donald Thompson, *Maya Pagan-ism and Christianity: A History of the Fusion of Two Religions* (New Orleans, 1954), and is further supported by William Madsen, *Cristo-Paganism: A Study of Mexican Religious Syncretism* (New Orleans, 1960), and Madsen, "Religious Syncretism," in *Handbook of Middle American Indians* (Austin, TX, 1976), 369–492, as well as Munro S. Edmundson, *Nativism, Syncretism, and Anthropological Science* (New Orleans, 1960).

More recently, some critics have rejected the idea of syncretism. To support this view, scholars have produced studies that examine ancient traditions of ritual and shamanism, often with an emphasis on gender, by noting that women's roles in formal religious forums are often subverted even outside the Western tradition. See, for example, Barbara Ehrenreich and Deirdre English, *Witches, Midwives, and Nurses: A History of Women Healers* (New York, 1973); and Irene Silverblatt, *Moon, Sun, and Witches: Gender Ideologies and Class in Inca and Colonial Peru* (Princeton, 1987). Although it covers an earlier period, no bibliography on religion in Latin America would be complete without mention of Sabine MacCormack, *Religion in the Andes: Vision and Imagination in Early Colonial Peru* (Princeton, 1991), which introduces a context for understanding the merger of Andean religious motifs with classical European philosophy.

The topic of pilgrimage has not attracted as much scholarship as the *cofradía*, but what does exist is illuminating. A good explanation of the role of pilgrimage in medieval Spain appears in William Christian, *Local Religion in Sixteenth-Century Spain* (Princeton, 1981). Michael Sallnow, *Pilgrims of the Andes: Regional Cults in Cuzco* (Washington, DC, 1987) provides a study that is rich in historical and ethnographical detail, as does his later book, *Contesting the Sacred: The Anthropology of Chris-tian Pilgrimage* (New York, 1990). Finally, the multi-author volume by Ross Crumrine and Alan Morinis, eds., *Pilgrimage in Latin America* (Westport, CT, 1991), offers an expansive, multidisciplinary assessment of pilgrimage and is especially good for the Andean region.

Religions of the African Diaspora

The religions of the African diaspora in the Americas have attracted considerable attention, but the works on this topic are very uneven, perhaps owing to the unmerited sensationalism that popular culture attributes to these religions. The exception is the literature on Brazil, which tends to be serious and analytically sound. Ruth Landes's 1947 study of Candomblé in Salvador, Bahia, *The City of Women*, remains a classic and was recently reissued by the University of New Mexico Press (Albuquerque, 1994). One of the most solid theoretical studies continues to be Roger Bastide, *The African Religions of Brazil: Towards a Sociology of the Interpenetration of Civilizations* (Baltimore, 1978). An insightful work on Candomblé is Seth and Ruth Leacock, *Spirits of the Deep: A Study of an Afro-Brazilian Cult* (Garden City, NY, 1975), while a good comparative study is Vagner Goncalves da Silva, *Candomblé e umbanda: Caminhos da devocao brasileira* (São Paulo, 1994). Two excellent monographs (though still unavailable in English) are Regina Novaes, *Os escolhidos de Deus* (Rio de Janeiro, 1985) and Carlos Rodrigues Brandão, *Os Deuses do Povo: Um estudo sobre religião popular* (São Paulo, 1980). Both describe the dynamic role that African-based religions continue to play among Brazil's rural, and particularly urban, poor. Diana Brown, *Umbanda: Religion and Politics in Brazil* (Ann Arbor, 1986), discusses the increased popularity of Umbanda and its potential as a source of political and ethnic identity, an issue that is also touched on in Rowen Ireland, *Kingdoms Come: Religion and Politics in Brazil* (Pittsburgh, 1991).

Haitian voodoo may show up regularly in horror movies and thrillers, but it appears all too infrequently in serious scholarship on New World African religions. Maya Deren, *Divine Horsemen: The Voodoo Gods* (New York, 1953), though dated, continues to be an essential study. Wade Davis, *The Serpent and the Rainbow* (New York, 1987), provides real insight into the function of voudan's secret societies in ritual punishment through zombification, and it is undoubtedly the only book in this bibliography to have been made into a B-movie. Luc de Heusch, "Kongo in Haiti: A New Approach to Religious Syncretism," *Man* 24 (2) (1989): 290–303, delivers a comparative approach to Haitian and Congolese belief structures. Offering a more Eurocentric but equally valuable view is George Mac-Donald Mulrain, *Theology in Folk Culture: The Theological Significance of Haitian Folk Religion* (New York, 1984).

Cuban Santería and the other Afrocentric religions of the Spanish-speaking Caribbean have not garnered much scholarly attention either, although several books, including Brian Gates, ed., *Afro-Caribbean*

Religions (London, 1980); George Simpson Eaton, *Religious Cults of the Caribbean: Trinidad, Jamaica, and Haiti* (Rio Piedras, PR, 1980); and Mercedes Cros Sandoval, *La religión afrocubana* (Madrid, 1975), provide some useful overviews. The single best book on Santería is Joseph M. Murphy's *Santería: African Spirits in America* (Boston, 1988), which offers solid contextualizing analysis against a background of ethnographic description. Of related interest is James T. Houk, *Spirits, Blood, and Drums: The Orisha Religion in Trinidad* (Philadelphia, 1995).

There are a number of studies that deal with the religions of Jamaica, which are not based in African and slave practices but which do invoke an African cultural reference. Perhaps because of its impact on popular culture, Rastafarianism is the subject of several monographs. The best of these include: Ivor Morriah, *Obeah, Christ, and Rastaman: Jamaica and Its Religion* (Cambridge, Eng., 1982); Joseph Owens, *Dread: The Rastafarians of Jamaica* (Kingston, Jamaica, 1976); Roger Ringenberg, *Rastafariansim: An Expanding Jamaican Cult* (Kingston, 1978); Michael G. Smith et al., *The Rastafarian Movement in Jamaica* (Kingston, 1960); and Anita Waters, *Race, Class, and Political Symbols: Rastafarianism and Reggae in Jamaican Politics* (New Brunswick, NJ, 1975). The particular manifestation of possession practiced in Jamaica by a group called the Spiritual Baptists is chronicled in Angelica Pollak-Eltz, "The Shango Cult and Other African Rituals in Trinidad, Grenada, and Carriacou and the Possible Influence on the Spiritual Baptist Faith," *Caribbean Quarterly* 39 3/4 (1993): 12–26. Other studies of ecstatic Jamaican Protestantism include Ashley Smith, *Real Roots and Potted Plants: Reflections on the Caribbean Church* (Kingston, 1984), and Smith, *Pentecostalism in Jamaica* (Kingston, 1975).

Liberation Theology

By way of contrast, there is probably no aspect of contemporary religiosity in Latin America that has attracted so much scholarly output as Liberation Theology. Because the body of literature is so large, the books here are organized by theme and country. For an understanding of the actual theology behind the process, see Gustavo Gutiérrez, *A Theology of Liberation: History, Politics, and Salvation* (Maryknoll, NY, 1973), the work that gave name to the movement; and Gutiérrez, *The Power of the Poor in History* (Maryknoll, NY, 1983). In his highly influential essay, *Pedagogy of the Oppressed* (New York, 1970), Paulo Freire lays the groundwork for compassionate praxis. Ernesto Cardenal, *The Gospel in Solentiname* (Maryknoll, NY, 1976), is a case study of the process of *concientización* in a small Nicaraguan Christian base community, while

José Míguez Bonino, *Doing Theology in a Revolutionary Situation* (Philadelphia, 1975), advances the theological discussion of applied praxis.

Important studies that examine the historic Jesus in the context of Liberation Theology are Juan Luis Segundo, *The Liberation of Theology* (Maryknoll, NY, 1976); Jon Sobrino, *Christology at the Crossroads: A Latin American Approach* (Maryknoll, NY, 1978); and Sobrino, *Jesus in Latin America* (Maryknoll, NY, 1986). A more fully evolved study of Christology within a liberationist context is Leonardo Boff, *Passion of Christ, Passion of the World: The Facts, Interpretations, and Their Meaning Yesterday and Today* (Maryknoll, NY, 1987), a work that provoked the Vatican to punish the author with a year-long censure of silence. Lesser-known works that provide useful ecumenical views of Liberation Theology from the vantage point of Protestant theology are Guillermo Cook, *The Expectation of the Poor: Latin American Basic Ecclesial Communities in Protestant Perspective* (Maryknoll, NY, 1985); Jeffrey Hadden and Anson Shupe, eds., *Prophetic Religion and Politics* (New York, 1986); and José Míquez Bonino, *Christians and Marxists: The Mutual Challenge to Revolution* (Grand Rapids, MI, 1976).

Outside of the studies listed above, all of which are written by clergymen and theologians, there are several works that attempt to assess the praxis of Liberation Theology across Latin America in a sympathetic and fairly comprehensive fashion, but from a lay perspective. First among these is Penny Lernoux, *Cry of the People* (London, 1980), a passionate and accessible study by the late correspondent for the *National Catholic Reporter* who introduced Liberation Theology to a wide lay audience in the United States. Two essential volumes edited by Daniel Levine, *Churches and Politics in Latin America* (Beverly Hills, CA, 1980), and *Religion and Political Conflict in Latin America* (Chapel Hill, NC, 1986), offer early scholarly assessments across the region. David Batstone, *From Conquest to Struggle: Jesus of Nazareth in Latin America* (Albany, NY, 1991) is an overview that is useful in assessing Liberation Theology after the assassination of Archbishop Oscar Romero, as is Philip Berryman, *Stubborn Hope: Religion, Politics, and Revolution in Central America* (New York, 1994), which updates his earlier and encyclopedic *The Religious Roots of Rebellion: Christians in Central American Revolutions* (Maryknoll, NY, 1984). Scott Mainwaring and Alexander Wilde, eds., *The Progressive Church in Latin America* (Notre Dame, IN, 1989), provide a definitive collection of articles that evaluate Liberation Theology in Central and South America at midpoint, prior to the assassination of the six Jesuits in El Salvador, supported by Edward L. Cleary's *Born of the Poor: The Latin American Church since Medellín* (Notre Dame, IN, 1990). Two intriguing studies of Liberation Theology in the wake of the Cold War are

Edward L. Cleary and Hannah Stewart-Gambino, *Conflict and Competition: The Latin American Church in a Changing Environment* (Boulder, CO, 1992); and Paul E. Sigmund, *Liberation Theology at the Crossroads: Democracy or Revolution?* (New York, 1990). A comprehensive survey of the Medellín to Santo Domingo period in the Catholic Church in Latin America appears in Enrique Dussel, ed., *Resistencia y esperanza: Historia del pueblo cristiano en América Latina y el Caribe* (San José, Costa Rica, 1995).

In terms of national studies of Liberation Theology, Brazil has been the object of considerable scholarly attention, primarily because Liberation Theology set down deep roots there so early. Some of the best studies of liberationist Catholicism in Brazil include: Thomas Bruneau, *The Political Transformation of the Brazilian Catholic Church* (New York, 1974), one of the best early analyses in English on the Brazilian Church, which is updated by Bruneau, *The Church in Brazil: The Politics of Religion* (Austin, TX, 1982); Madeleine Adriance, *Opting for the Poor: Brazilian Catholicism in Transition* (Kansas City, 1986); Rolando Azzi, *O Catolicismo popular no Brasil: Aspectos históricos* (Petrópolis, Brazil, 1978); and Emmanuel De Kadt, *Catholic Radicals in Brazil* (New York, 1970). L. B. A. Fernandes, "The Contribution of Basic Ecclesial Communities to an Education for Social Transformation in Brazil" (Ph.D. dissertation, Harvard Graduate School of Education, 1985), looks at the particulars of how liberationist analysis impacts the larger social project of education. Scott Mainwaring, *The Catholic Church and Politics in Brazil, 1916–1985* (Stanford, CA, 1985), is a complex and richly textured historical study of the Brazilian Church in a critical period of its development.

Recently published works on the Catholic Church in Brazil tend to look not only at Liberation Theology but also at how other types of socioreligious movements impact the poor. See, for example, John Burdick's excellent *Looking for God in Brazil: The Progressive Catholic Church in Urban Brazil's Religious Arena* (Stanford, 1992); and Rowen Ireland's definitive *Kingdoms Come*, cited above. Other essential works that are unavailable in English are Scott Mainwaring and P. Krischke, eds., *A igreja nas bases em tempo de transição* (Porto Alegre, 1986); P. Ribere de Oliveira, *Religião e dominacão de classe: Génese, estructura e fundacão do catolicismo romanizado na Brasil* (Petrópolis, 1985); and Regina Novaes, *Os escolhidos de Deus* (Rio de Janeiro, 1985). The last two are elegant theoretical texts that measure Liberation Theology's movement through the *favelas* of the urban poor. Rubem Alves, *Protestantism and Repression: A Brazilian Case Study* (Maryknoll, NY, 1979), provides an analytically sophisticated study of how the praxis of Liberation Theology articulates with the expansion of Protestantism.

Because of the role that Catholic activists played in the insurrection against Anastasio Somoza and for the high profile that Catholic clergy cast in the early days of the Sandinista government, Nicaragua has been the focus of several excellent monographs. The best of these include Michael Dodson and Laura Nuzzi O'Shaughnessy, *Nicaragua's Other Revolution* (Chapel Hill, NC, 1991), which also deals with the efforts of liberal Protestants in the revolution; and Roger Lancaster, *Thanks to God and the Revolution: Popular Religion and Class Consciousness in the New Nicaragua* (New York, 1988). See also Margaret Randall, *Christians in the Nicaraguan Revolution* (Vancouver, 1983). Although it was influential as a political and social force elsewhere in Central America during the same period, there are surprisingly few books that specifically examine Liberation Theology in El Salvador and Guatemala, perhaps because of the implicit dangers of working on that topic in those countries. Without question, Berryman's two volumes (see above) offer the most exhaustive studies of the region as a whole. For Guatemala, see Bruce Calder, *Crecimiento y cambio de la Iglesia Católica en Guatemala, 1944–1966* (Guatemala City, 1970), a revised version of "Growth and Change in the Guatemalan Catholic Church, 1944–1966" (Master's thesis, Department of History, University of Texas, 1968). A powerful account of the conflict between the prophetic Church and the Salvadoran state in the last years of the civil war is Teresa Whitfield, *Paying the Price: Ignacio Ellacuría and the Murdered Jesuits of El Salvador* (Philadelphia, 1994).

There are several good national studies of Liberation Theology in Spanish South America, particularly in Colombia. These include Daniel Levine's *Religion and Politics in Latin America*, cited earlier; and Kenneth Medhurst, *The Church and Labour in Colombia* (Manchester, England, 1984). For Peru, the homeland of Gustavo Gutiérrez, one of Liberation Theology's premier theologians (see above), see Rodrigo Sanchez-Arjona Halcon, *La religiosidad popular católica en el Peru* (Lima, 1981); Manuel Marzal, *La transformación religiosa peruana* (Lima, 1983); and Luis Pásara, *Radicalización y conflicto en la iglesia peruana* (Lima, 1986). The literature on Chile and Argentina is scant but is quite good: José Comblin, *The Church and the National Security State* (Maryknoll, NY, 1979), is a brave and insightful study of the Church during the Dirty War in Argentina and elsewhere, now supplemented by Michael Burdick, *For God and the Fatherland* (Ithaca, NY, 1995), which critically examines the program of "National Catholicism" in Argentina. Brian Smith's *The Church and Politics in Chile*, cited earlier, is an exemplary study of the Church under the Pinochet dictatorship.

Two countries in some ways lie beyond the pale of Liberation Theology: Cuba and Mexico, thus accounting in part for why the literature about modern Church-state relations in both of them is so thin. Be that as it may, Michael Tangleman's *Mexico at the Crossroads: Politics, the Church, and the Poor* (Maryknoll, NY, 1995) is an excellent recent monograph about the Church in Mexico and its cautious relationship with the PRI. More current still is Roderic Ai Camp's definitive *Crossing Swords: Politics and Religion in Mexico* (New York, 1997). For Cuba, John Kirk, *Between God and the Party: Religion and Politics in Revolutionary Cuba* (Gainesville, FL, 1989), is an enormously useful study about this anomalous case. For a domestic view of Christians in Cuba, see John Clark, *Religious Repression in Cuba* (Miami, 1985). And finally, for an analysis of Liberation Theology in the postrevolutionary era, see David Batstone, Eduardo Mendieta, Lois Ann Lorentzen, and Dwight N. Hopkins, eds., *Liberation Theologies, Postmodernity, and the Americas* (New York, 1997).

Protestantism and Mormonism

The meteoric growth of Protestantism in Latin America in recent decades has provoked a deluge of scholarly output of varying degrees of utility and sophistication. For the region, two pioneering studies of Protestantism are Christian Lalive d'Epinay, *Haven of the Masses: A Study of the Pentecostal Movement in Chile* (London, 1969), and Emilio Willems, *Followers of the New Faith: Culture, Change, and the Rise of Protestantism in Brazil and Chile* (Nashville, TN, 1967), which place the study of Latin American Protestantism within the theoretical framework laid out by Max Weber, thus tying Protestantism to the growth of entrepreneurship and capitalism. A work that clearly quantifies the relationship between growing commercial capitalism and Protestant affiliation is Sheldon Annis, *God and Production in a Guatemalan Town* (Austin, TX, 1987). Two panoramic general studies take to task these conventional economic interpretations. David Stoll, *Is Latin America Turning Protestant? The Politics of Evangelical Growth* (Berkeley, CA, 1990) offers an innovative analysis of Protestant growth measured against contemporary political considerations, a case that he further develops in *Between Two Armies in the Ixil Towns of Guatemala* (New York, 1993). David Martin, *Tongues of Fire: The Explosion of Protestantism in Latin America* (Oxford, Eng., 1990), takes a more sociocultural view of Protestantism as the "Latinization of American religion," giving particular consideration to Pentecostalism, the most important variety of Protestantism in the region.

The missionary movement that brought U.S. Protestants to Latin America beginning in the latter half of the nineteenth century has attracted the attention of a number of historians, who have examined the consequences from both North American and Latin American perspectives. The

Swiss historian Jean-Pierre Bastian has provided much of the overall theoretical understanding for this topic in several volumes that deal with Latin America in general terms and with Mexico in particular. These include: Jean-Pierre Bastian, *Breve historia del protestantismo en América Latina* (Mexico City, 1986); Bastian, *Le protestantisme en Amérique Latine: Une approche socio-historique* (Geneva, 1994); Bastian, *Los disidentes, sociedades protestantes y revolución en México* (Mexico City, 1989); Bastian, ed., *Protestantes, liberales y francmasones: Sociedades de ideas y modernidad en América Latina, siglo XIX* (Mexico City, 1990); and Bastian, *Protestantismo y sociedad en Mexico* (Mexico City, 1983). In *Protestants and the Mexican Revolution: Missionaries, Ministers, and Social Change* (Champaign, IL, 1990), Deborah Baldwin gives us a thoroughly documented study of missionaries in northern Mexico on the eve of the Revolution. For Guatemala, see Virginia Garrard-Burnett, *Protestantism in Guatemala: Living in the New Jerusalem* (Austin, TX, 1998). For histories of the missionary movements in specific countries in South America, see Calvin Redekop, *Strangers Become Neighbors: Mennonite and Indigenous Relations in the Paraguayan Chaco* (Scottsdale, AZ, 1980); and Ignacio Verara, *El protestantismo en Chile* (Santiago, 1962). Peter Wagner, *The Protestant Movement in Bolivia* (Pasadena, CA, 1970) is written by a North American missionary who later became one of Pentecostalism's international advocates.

Many of the studies of missions in Latin America in the late nineteenth and early twentieth centuries are cast in terms of dependency and cultural imperialism. General works along these lines include Prudencio Damoriena, *El protestantismo en América Latina*, 2 vols. (Friburg, 1962), the first serious study of Protestantism in the region; and Orlando Costas, *El protestantismo en América Latina hoy: Ensayos del camino* (San Jose, Costa Rica, 1975). Peter Wagner, *Latin American Theology: Radical or Evangelical?* (Grand Rapids, MI, 1980), offers a conservative North American counterpoint to this view. For specific country studies that subscribe to the dependency model, see Emilio Pantojas García, *La iglesia protestante y la americanización de Puerto Rico, 1898–1917* (Bayamón, PR, 1976); Daniel Rodriguez Díaz, *Ideológicas protestantes y misiones: El caso de Puerto Rico, 1898–1930* (Mexico City, 1979); and Ernest Sweeney, *Foreign Missionaries in Argentina, 1838–1962: A Study of Dependence* (Cuernavaca, Mexico, 1970).

The increased polarization of politics in the 1970s and 1980s, dovetailing as it did with the rapid expansion of Protestantism, precipitated an increased body of literature that equated Protestantism in Latin America with the expansion of U.S. cultural and political hegemony in the region. Waldo César, *Protestantismo o imperialismo na América Latina*

(Petrópolis, Brazil, 1968) is one of the earliest of this genre, while one of the best-known studies is Peter Åaby and Soren Hvalkøf, *Is God an American? An Anthropological Perspective on the Missionary Work of the Summer Institute of Linguistics* (Copenhagen, 1981). David Stoll, *Fishers of Men or Founders of Empire? The Wycliffe Bible Translators in Latin America* (Cambridge, MA, 1982), examines the controversial work of the Summer Institute of Linguistics in Latin America, while Hugo Assman, *A igreja electrónico e seu impacto na América Latina* (Petrópolis, 1986), also available in Spanish as *La iglesia electrónica* (San José, Costa Rica, 1986), assesses the impact of televangelists on the middle class. Along the same lines are two studies that examine the work of the Mormon Church in light of that group's strong cultural and financial ties to the United States. These include: John Heinerman and Anson Shupe, *The Mormon Corporate Empire* (Boston, 1985); and Mark Allbrecht and Paul Rogers, *Hidden in Plain Sight: Uncovering Mormon Mission and Evangelism Strategies* (Seattle, 1987). A more recent study that uses market theory to examine the global expansion of fundamentalism is Steve Brouwer, Paul Gifford, and Susan D. Rose, *Exporting the American Gospel: Global Christian Fundamentalism* (New York, 1996). Susanne Hoeber Rudolf and James Piscatori, eds., *Transnational Religion, Fading States* (Boulder, CO, 1997), present a series of essays that suggest ways in which religion plays into emerging patterns of transnational sovereignty and conflict. Amy L. Sherman's *The Soul of Development* (New York, 1997) discusses development in Guatemala in terms of religious worldviews.

Over the past few years, a number of scholars have begun to assess Protestantism in Latin America as an internal as opposed to an external dynamic, measuring by turn the forces that move people to convert and the comparative advantage that they find within the process of conversion. Among the best of these diverse works are: Carlos Garma Navarro, *Protestantismo en una comunidad totonaca de Pueblo* (Mexico City, 1987); R. Andrew Chesnut, *Born Again in Brazil: The Pentecostal Boom and the Pathogens of Poverty* (New Brunswick, NJ, 1997); again, Rowen Ireland, *Kingdoms Come*; Cecília Loreto Mariz, *Coping with Poverty: Pentecostals and Christian Base Communities in Brazil* (Philadelphia, 1994); and Mariz, "Pentecostalism y alcoholismo entre los pobres del Brasil," *Cristianismo y Sociedad* 105 (1990): 39–40. Since women make up the majority of converts, Elizabeth Brusco, *Evangelical Religion and the Reformation of Machismo in Colombia* (Austin, TX, 1996), measures conversion as a means of gaining gender parity.

Virginia Garrard-Burnett and David Stoll, eds., *Rethinking Protestantism in Latin America* (Philadelphia, 1993) is a multiauthored volume that assesses Protestantism from the grass roots up, as a mechanism of reconstructing community and individual identity in postmodern Latin America. Several other studies examine the impact that religious pluralism introduces into community dynamics. See, for example, John Watanabe, *Maya Saints and Souls in a Changing World*, cited earlier, which discusses not only Protestant conversion but also the decline of traditionalist beliefs. Two monographs that develop similar themes in South America include Karl W. Westmeier, *Reconciling Heaven and Earth: The Transcendental Enthusiasm and Growth of an Urban Protestant Community, Bogotá, Colombia* (New York, 1986); and Norman E. Whitten, Jr., *Cultural Transformations and Ethnicity in Modern Ecuador* (Champaign, IL, 1981). A sophisticated study on these issues is Anne Hallum, *Beyond Missionaries: Toward an Understanding of the Protestant Movement in Central America* (Lanham, MD, 1996). An intriguing examination of Protestantism as a maturing phenomenon is Daniel R. Miller, ed., *Coming of Age: Protestantism in Contemporary Latin America* (Lanham, MD, 1994).

Finally, as the fastest growing sector within Latin American Protestantism, Pentecostalism has attracted a singular amount of scholarly energy. One of the first important studies that dealt with Pentecostalism in the region as an independent phenomenon is Stephen Glazier, ed., *Perspectives on Pentecostalism: Case Studies from the Caribbean and Latin America* (Lanham, MD, 1980). Glazier's anthology describes specific cases that in many ways fit the model found in the earlier theoretical work of Ioan Lewis, *Ecstatic Religion* (New York, 1971). David Martin's *Tongues of Fire* (see above) clarifies many of the theoretical issues raised by Pentecostalism's attractiveness in Latin America while drawing heavily from the research that appeared in earlier country-specific studies. These include Jean-Baptiste August Kessler, *A Study of the Older Pentecostal Missions and Churches in Peru and Chile* (Goes, Netherlands, 1964); Norbert Johnson, *The History, Dynamic, and Problems of the Pentecostal Movement in Chile* (New York, 1970); Cornelia Flora, *Pentecostalism in Colombia: Baptism by Fire and Spirit* (Cranbury, NJ, 1976); J. C. Hoffnagel, "The Believers: Pentecostalism in a Brazilian City" (Ph.D. dissertation, Indiana University, 1978); Francisco Cartaxo Rolim, *Pentecostais no Brasil: Uma interpretação socio-religiosa* (Petrópolis, 1985); and Ashley Smith's already cited *Pentecostalism in Jamaica*. More recent is Alejandro Frigerio, ed., *El pentecostalismo en la Argentina* (Buenos Aires, 1994), a slim but provocative volume, and Harvey Cox, *Fire from Heaven: The Rise of Pentecostal Spirituality and the Reshaping of Religion in the Twenty-First Century* (Reading, MA, 1995), which devotes only one chapter to Latin America but offers a solid theoretical construct for understanding Pentecostalism in general. Two studies that examine Pentecostalism in a variety of cultural contexts are Edward L. Cleary and

Hannah Stewart-Gambino's edited volume, *Power, Politics, and Pente-costals in Latin America* (Boulder, CO, 1997), and Benjamín F. Gutiérrez, ed., *En la fuerza del espiritu: Los Pentecostales en América Latina: Un desafío de las iglesias historicas* (Guatemala City, 1995).

Suggested Films

There are a number of video documentaries that focus on the variety of religious expression in Latin America. Though burdened by the arch tone of its narrator, the best overview is *South America Journey: A Continent Crucified* (BBC and Washington, DC, Public Broadcasting System, 1987), which ranges in one hour from colonial Catholicism to Umbanda and the Mormons. *The Americas* series produced an excellent video on Liberation Theology in Nicaragua titled *Miracles Are Not Enough* (WGBH, Boston, The Americas Series, Annenberg Corporation for Public Broadcasting Collection, 1993, 60 minutes). *Romero*, a feature-length film starring Raúl Julia, offers an impassioned view of the life and times of San Salvador's martyred archbishop. A good, if dated, film that documents the celebration of traditional public ritual in the Maya town of Chamula, Chiapas, Mexico, is *Appeals to Santiago*, available in 16mm and now in video (Contemporary Films/McGraw Hill, 1968, 27 minutes, produced for the University of California, School of Social Studies). The documentary *Voodoo and the Church in Haiti* takes an insightful look at African religion in the New World (Nine Morning Productions, produced by Andrea E. Leland and Bob Richard, University of California, Berkeley, UC Extension Media Center, 1988, 40 minutes). Finally, Bill Moyers applies his particular wisdom to the question of religious conflict, decisionmaking, and politics in Latin America in three programs in his series, *God and Politics* (WNET, New York, 1987, produced by Elena Mames, Gail Pelett, Greg Pratt, and Jan Falstad): "The Kingdom Divided" (58 minutes); "The Battle for the Bible" (50 minutes); and "On Earth as It Is in Heaven" (59 minutes).